Assessing Young Children

Delmar Publishers' Online Services
To access Delmar on the World Wide Web, point your browser to:
http://www.delmar.com/delmar.html
To access through Gopher: gopher://gopher.delmar.com
(Delmar Online is part of "thomson.com", an Internet site with information on more
than 30 publishers of the International Thomson Publishing organization.)
For information on our products and services:
email: info@delmar.com
or call 800-347-7707

Assessing Young Children

Gayle Mindes, Ed.D.
Professor of Education
De Paul University
Chicago

Harold Ireton, Ph.D.
Associate Professor
University of Minnesota
Department of Family Practice and Community Health
Health Sciences Center
Minneapolis

Carol Mardell-Czudnowski, Ph.D.
Professor of Special Education, Emeritus
Northern Illinois University, DeKalb

Delmar Publishers

I⟨T⟩P™ An International Thomson Publishing Company

Albany • Bonn • Boston • Cincinnati • Detroit • London • Madrid • Melbourne
Mexico City • New York • Pacific Grove • Paris • San Francisco • Singapore • Tokyo
Toronto • Washington

NOTICE TO THE READER

Cover Design: Timothy J. Conners

Delmar Staff

Publisher:	Diane McOscar
Acquisitions Editor:	Jay Whitney
Associate Editor:	Erin J. O'Connor
Production Editor:	Marah Bellegarde
Art and Design Coordinator:	Timothy J. Conners
Editorial Assistant:	Glenna Stanfield

COPYRIGHT © 1996
By Delmar Publishers
a division of International Thomson Publishing Inc.

The ITP logo is a trademark under license.

Printed in the United States of America

For more information, contact:

Delmar Publishers
3 Columbia Circle, Box 15015
Albany, New York 12212-5015

Nelson Canada
1120 Birchmont Road
Scarborough, Ontario
Canada, M1K 5G4

International Thomson Publishing
  Asia
221 Henderson Road
#05-10 Henderson Building
Singapore 0315

International Thomson Publishing
  Europe
Berkshire House 168-173
High Holborn
London, WC1V 7AA England

International Thomson Editores
Campos Eliseos 385, Piso 7
Col Polanco
11560 Mexico D F Mexico

International Thomson Publishing—
  Japan
Hirakawacho Kyowa Building, 3F
2-2-1 Hirakawacho
Chiyoda-ku, Tokyo 102 Japan

Thomas Nelson Australia
102 Dodds Street
South Melbourne, 3205
Victoria, Australia

International Thomson Publishing
  GmbH
Konigswinterer Strasse 418
53227 Bonn, Germany

1 2 3 4 5 6 7 8 9 10 XXX 01 00 99 98 97 96 95

Library of Congress Cataloging-in Publication Data

Mindes, Gayle.
   Assessing young children / Gayle Mindes, Harold Ireton, Carol Mardell-Czudnowski.
     p.   cm.
     Includes index.
     ISBN 0-8273-6211-0
     1. Child development—United States—Testing. 2. Early childhood education—United States—Evaluation. 3. Educational tests and measurements—United States. I. Ireton, Harry. II. Mardell-Czudnowski, Carol. III. Title.
LB1131.M6146 1995
371.2'6—dc20

95-24098
CIP

To the women in my life: my mother—Juanita, Marcia, Carla, Dean Henny, the book club, Dean Barbara, Marie and the many others who have supported, encouraged and been there.

gayle

To the parents and teachers of our children—the everyday heroes who hold the future in their hands.

Harold Ireton

To my six grandchildren—Amir, Daphy, Sam, Dror, Josiah, and Ilana—who have renewed my feelings about the awesomeness of child development.

Carol

Contents

Preface

We live in a challenging time for American education. Accountability, management of scarce resources, Goals 2000, multicultural curriculum, and inclusion are some of the important issues facing educators today. For early childhood educators, the first formal teachers in the lives of young children, the challenges are enormous. Parent partnership, respect for cultural diversity, appropriate early intervention assessment, and linking curriculum and assessment practices appropriately are a few of the demands. The crafting of an assessment system is one of the most important roles for early childhood educators. All of the major challenges impact this role. Therefore, early childhood teachers must be mindful of the responsibilities they assume as they assess and participate in teaching, evaluation, and placement of the young children and families they serve. Thorough knowledge of child development, knowledge of formal and informal assessment measures, variables in consultation with parents, and portfolio and authentic assessment are required competencies for the professional early childhood educator. Early childhood assessment decisions impact infants, young children, and their families for life. This book addresses theory and provides illustrations of appropriate practice for prospective teachers, as well as a discussion of current trends for experienced teachers.

We wish to thank the thousands of children, parents, undergraduate and graduate students, and colleagues who have influenced our thinking and practices over the years. In particular, we appreciate the care and hard work of Lynn Van Stee, Loyola University, who compiled and wrote the reviews of early childhood tests. We wish to thank our colleagues at DePaul University, Roosevelt University, Northern Illinois University, and the University of Minnesota for their assistance and support. We are especially indebted to our colleague Marie Donovan of Harvard University for her supportive critiques and editorial suggestions.

We appreciate the support and encouragement from Jay Whitney, Erin O'Connor, Tim Conners, Marah Bellegarde, Glenna Stanfield, and others behind the scenes at Delmar.

Our appreciation is extended to the reviewers enlisted through Delmar for their constructive criticism and helpful suggestions. They include:

Leah Adams, Ph.D.
Eastern Michigan University
Ypsilanti, MI

Angela Buchanan, Ph.D.
DeAnza College
Cupertino, CA

Cindy M. Campbell
Lamar University
Port Arthur, TX

Jeffrey I. Gelfer, Ph.D.
University of Nevada
Las Vegas, NV

Jerri J. Kropp, Ph.D.
Georgia Southern University
Statesboro, GA

Kathleen Stegmaier
Butler University
Indianapolis, IN

Finally, we thank our families for their continuous patience and encouragement of all our endeavors.

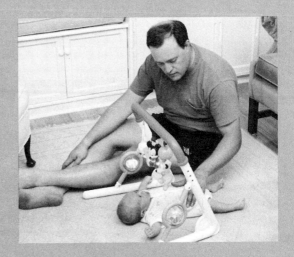

CHAPTER 1

A Comprehensive Assessment System for Birth through Age Eight

Terms to Know
- stakeholders
- assessment
- techniques
- accountability

CHAPTER OVERVIEW Assessment is an integral part of the total picture of child care and education. Information gathered through informed observation and other ways guides the countless decisions at the heart of solid and appropriate instruction and intervention. Some of these decisions can be made easily and as a matter of course. Should the program move on to the next theme in the curriculum? Are children growing in their abilities to follow directions and to share cooperatively? Other decisions, by their nature, require more systematic and intensive assessment information collection due to the life consequences that may result. Does this child need to be enrolled in a special program? What opportunities will result? What, if any, stigma may be attached to such placement?

By definition, best practice dictates that all decisions be based upon assessment information gleaned from multiple sources. Too, all the stakeholders in the care and education for the child—parent, teachers, and other related service personnel—must be included in the process. Since the techniques for gathering information and the steps involved in intervention

and educational decision making are varied, the task of assessing young children is a tremendous responsibility. The aim of this book is to help you begin to learn the rudiments of assessment; the why, the how, and the what to do with assessment information gathered. Toward this end, this initial chapter focuses on exploring the early childhood assessment system.

Topics Discussed
- The age span of early childhood
- Matching assessment methods to early childhood settings
- Defining and creating a comprehensive assessment system
- Current issues in the assessment of young children

The age span of early childhood

Birth through age eight . . . wow . . . think of the differences: Cute and helpless babies depending on the adults in their lives—for care, nurtu-

rance, and development; energetic and determined toddlers moving away from the adults to stake out and explore their world through play, helping themselves to feed and dress; fanciful and creative preschoolers launching into friendships and dramatic play; earnest and curious young school agers attacking the challenges of reading, writing, mathematics, and technology. In these eight intervening years, children change more than during any other life period.

Beginning with the reflexes of the newborn, through the first smile, word, and step, the infancy years fly. Toddlers establish autonomy, self-help skills, and sophistication in language and movement. Preschoolers cooperate with each other, develop themes in their play, and learn elaborate cognitive and gross- and fine-motor skills. At school age, young children engage their curiosity for the purpose of learning, become even more self-sufficient in their own care, and play games with rules in their leisure. These developmental changes and milestones, and others, occur in a social/cultural context that influences the acquisition and elaboration of this growth. (cf Berk, L. E. 1994)

Parents, caregivers, teachers, and others who impact the lives of young children must not only be familiar with the broad aspects of development in this period—the usual and typical growth patterns—but must also be sensitive to variations within typical development that affect temperament, learning style, fine- and gross-motor skills, and language acquisition. These significant adults must remember that developmental processes in young children occur in a social context shaped by diverse familial, cultural, geographic, social, and economic factors influencing developmental progress. In a big way, the age span of early childhood contributes to the complexity for developing a comprehensive assessment system. Intricately intertwined with the issue of the age span is the difference in types of settings where infants, toddlers, and young children are served. Along with diverse purposes for the implementation of care, education, and intervention, the complexity of the assessment task is staggering. Before looking at types of assessment, you must consider the places where care and education of young children occurs.

Matching assessment methods to early childhood settings

The care and education of infants and toddlers occurs at home, in home child care, and in group child-care settings. Those with special needs are found in early intervention settings. Among other things, caregivers in these settings need to know,

- what the crying baby wants.
- when to feed, diaper, and soothe babies.
- when to talk with and stimulate with toys.
- when to allow "me do it."
- when something is "off" with the baby and whether the problem is serious.

In each of these situations, caregivers assess the needs of the baby by observation. They compare their knowledge of the individual baby to past experience with the baby, to their experiences with babies in general, and to their knowledge of infant/toddler development. After reflecting on their observations, caregivers change the intervention, routine, or educational plan. When caregivers believe that their capacity to care appropriately and responsively for a particular infant/toddler is limited, the next assessment step is parent involvement. This conversation evolves from the regular and routine conversations that have set the tone for parent partnerships and collaboration as discussed in *Chapter Two*. Thus, the discussion of concern can proceed more naturally when a basic rapport is already established between caregiver and parent. So, by comparing caregiver knowledge with parent knowledge regarding a troubling problem, the difficulty can be resolved or referred for specialist evaluation. Details of this process are discussed in *Chapter Nine*.

Preschoolers can be found in all of the locations described above (home, home-based child care, and child-care centers). In addition, young children are located in compensatory educational programs for "at risk"; special programs for those with disabilities; and increasingly, in inclusive environments. Among other things, caregivers and teachers in these settings need to know

- when to move the story time to closure.
- when to change the curricular theme.
- when to intervene in child/child conflict.
- when to provide enrichment activities for a precocious reader.
- when to ask the speech therapist or other related service person to come in and look at a particular child.

Many of the decisions of preschool caregivers and teachers in these and other situations involve a consideration of the group of children and the group's best interests. These are teaching decisions that teachers and

caregivers make based on the overall plan for the center or program and the pacing decisions that teachers make based on the needs of the group for the particular day. Assessment methods for these situations can be accomplished through the use of observation. Informed observation consists of knowledge of child development, curricular goals, and expected learning outcomes. An integral part of the use of informed observation is the choice of a record-keeping system. All of these matters are discussed in *Chapter Three*.

For those decisions that involve a question or concern about developmental progress or process, the first step is conversation and collaboration with the child's parents discussed in *Chapter Two*. If parents and caregivers or teachers have serious concerns, a referral for specialists' assessment may be in order. The use of tests for these occasions is discussed in *Chapter Five*. Special issues of preschool age children and the current events influencing philosophy and program practice are discussed in *Chapter Ten*.

Young school age children are located in all of the settings (at home, in home child care, and center-based child care) and in public and private settings where they begin "school" with all the privileges and responsibilities associated with formal education. Teachers of primary age children and their caregivers need to know

- when to use cooperative group activities for the curricular goal.
- how to incorporate whole language activities in the teaching theme.
- how to prepare children for the accountability tests in their school.
- what kind of "homework" will meet the needs of the children, the after-school setting, and the parents.
- how to mainstream, or include, the young child with special needs in the group.

Assessment decisions in these situations appropriately rely, first, on teacher observation, *Chapter Three*. Tests are a feature of the primary years, discussed in *Chapter Five*. Special assessment techniques for including and referring children with special needs are discussed in *Chapter Six*. The special issues of the primary years, including accountability, are discussed in *Chapter Eleven*.

In each early childhood setting, the need for information about infant/toddler/child progress varies. Collecting information, choosing appropriate methods, thinking about the information gathered, and planning the next step based on the assessment is approached and handled in different ways by each of the young child's "important people." The primary "important people," or **stakeholders,** in the "need to know" loop or assessment system are each child's parents and caregivers/teachers. These, however, are not the only stakeholders in the process; others include related service personnel, program funders and administrators, legislators, and the public at large. Each of these stakeholders seeks different pieces of information.

Parents want to know how their children are developing and learning. They are interested not only in their own opinions, but informed opinions shared by caregivers and teachers in informal and formal conversations, conferences, and reports. These strategies are discussed in *Chapter Seven*. Because paraprofessionals want to meet the needs of the child in the particular setting they will want to be able to make decisions about particular children and groups based on the guidelines developed by the teachers they collaborate with. Teachers and specialists need information to keep programs running well for the groups of children and for particular children with special needs. Administrators, policy boards, and legislators are accountable for the progress of groups of children. They need to know that programs are working.

Each stakeholder comes with varying degrees of knowledge about the unfolding of development during the early childhood age span. Parents, paraprofessionals, policy boards, and legislators have practical

TABLE 1.1 Method of assessment and frequency of use

Stakeholder	Observation	Special alternative method	Test and performance assessment
Parent	daily and routinely	rarely	never
Paraprofessional caregiver	daily and routinely	rarely	under supervision
Infant teacher	daily and routinely	rarely	screening, regularly
Infant specialist	daily and routinely	often	diagnostic
Paraprofessional preschool caregiver	daily and routinely	rarely	under supervision
Preschool teacher	daily and routinely	sometimes	screening and performance tasks
Preschool specialist	daily and routinely	often	diagnostic
Primary paraprofessional caregiver	daily and routinely	never	under supervision
Primary teacher	daily and routinely	sometimes	screening, diagnostic, performance tasks, accountability
Primary specialist	daily and routinely	often	diagnostic
Administrators	rarely	never	review results for accountability
Policy boards	rarely	never	review results for accountability
Legislators	rarely	never	review results for accountability

knowledge, diverse experiential knowledge, and various pieces of contextual information. Most do not have professional information. The professionals—caregivers/teachers, administrators, and related service personnel—have diverse training experiences that shape their notion of best ways to gather assessment information. All stakeholders have the best interests of young children in mind. The definition and criteria for the demonstration of the progress of development and education vary with the stakeholders. Thus, defining a comprehensive assessment system for young children is extremely complicated.

⊞ Defining and creating a comprehensive assessment system

In view of the myriad and differing needs of stakeholders outlined above, creating and implementing a truly comprehensive assessment system is an enormous task. It is not an insurmountable one, however, as you will learn by reading this book. Keep in mind that as a teacher, you will be one of the important stakeholders in the lives of young children. You will plan to gather information to assist you in guiding learning for the children you serve. In addition, you will need to document child progress and communicate regularly with the other stakeholders—the child, his parents, administrators, boards, and ultimately, legislative bodies. The procedures for gathering information discussed in this book are drawn from the following beliefs:

- Children learn best when their physical needs are met and they feel psychologically safe and secure.
- Children construct knowledge.
- Children learn through social interaction with adults and other children.
- Children's learning reflects a recurring cycle that begins in awareness and moves to exploration, to inquiry, and finally to utilization.
- Children learn through play.
- Children's interests and "need to know" motivate learning.
- Human development and learning are characterized by individual variation.
(Bredekamp & Rosegrant, 1992, pp. 14–17)

With these beliefs in mind, you will pick from the assessment techniques discussed, the ones suited to the needs of your program. Your decisions will be based on knowledge of the needs of the particular age span you serve and the setting for your program. An illustration of the Building Blocks in the assessment process follows. Each of the blocks is multidimensional and interactive with the other blocks.

Definition of assessment

Before considering the design of an assessment system, it is important to define what is meant by assessment. The definitions are many. Common elements of the definitions, include the ideas that assessment

- is a process.
- is a decision-making tool.
- can apply to an individual or a group.
- generates products.

In this book, **assessment is a process for gathering information to make decisions about young children. The process is appropriate when it is systematic, multidisciplinary, and based on the everyday tasks of childhood. The best assessment system is comprehensive in nature. That is, the assessment yields information about all the developmental areas: motoric, temperament, linguistic, cognitive, and social/emotional.**

A comprehensive assessment system must consider the following factors:

- the child as an individual and as a group member
- the other stakeholders—parents, teachers, administrators, policy board members, and legislators—as participants in the process as well as consumers of the products
- the program philosophy and the curriculum or intervention strategy of the program
- the purpose for evaluating, measuring, or documenting progress
- available methods and the accuracy, usability, and meaning of the results

The settings for the age span contribute to an immense task for the development of a comprehensive assessment system, because the meaning of assessment varies with each of the factors.

Assessment information may be gathered in a variety of formal and informal ways. **Techniques** employed for gathering information must be nondiscriminatory and continuous and must result in meaningful documentation of child progress. Too, the technique must yield information that can be used easily and accurately by stakeholders.

Techniques for assessment decisions must be matched to purpose. Why is the information needed? What will happen when the information is gathered? Will changes in care or education follow? Will stakeholders document existing knowledge? The answers to each of these questions will influence the choice of technique for information gathering. An analogy to consider—suppose you are cooking a dinner. If the dinner is a picnic, you may choose to fry a chicken at home or buy a bucket on the way to the park. You make this choice based on the weather—hot; food safety—no refrigeration; ease of serving; your skill as a cook; etc. If the dinner is a celebration for a friend who is retiring after 40 years of teaching, you will use your best recipe for chicken that may take several hours to prepare (or cater from the best). You make this choice based on the occasion—celebration, your skill as a cook, and the time you have available for preparation. If the dinner is for 200 at the local community center, you grab a friend or two and choose a baked chicken recipe that can be made easily by several cooks. You make the decision based on equipment available, food interests of the group, ease of preparation and serving.

In each of these situations, you considered the purpose of the dinner, the social context, the expectations of the participants, the techniques available in your repertoire, and the skill that you have in using them. No matter how casually you gathered information for this dinner decision, you matched the purpose of the dinner to the techniques employed. So it is with assessment. You must choose the techniques to suit the purpose. If you choose a test to gather information, you must know the important technical qualities of the test. You must consider factors of efficiency, accuracy, usability, appropriateness for the children you wish to examine, limits of the test, and others. All of these factors are discussed in *Chapters Four* and *Five.*

All assessment activities must be conducted for a particular purpose at a particular point in the lives of young children.

Decisions

Why are you gathering information on the children in your program? Because it is time to decide what to teach or how to modify your instruction or intervention; it is time to report progress to parents; there is a concern about developmental progress on the part of parents or others; it is required to determine eligibility for service for special needs; or it is time to be accountable to the program or legislative body. These are important assessment situations in the lives of young children. It is important that their caregivers and teachers understand the stakes as they choose the technique to answer the questions. At best, an assessment not matched to purpose may just yield no important information related to purpose. At worst, assessment decisions based on incomplete, inaccurate, or otherwise technically flawed information may damage the life of a child.

Methods

The most basic technique that sustains most early childhood assessment is informed observation of the infant/toddler or child in action. To be an effective and accurate observer, the watcher must have the capacity to separate judgment from watching. For example: You look out your window and see several buildings of various ages. You describe the three brick buildings: one with concrete pillars and balconies, one with neo-classic

FIGURE 1.1 Essential building blocks for total assessment

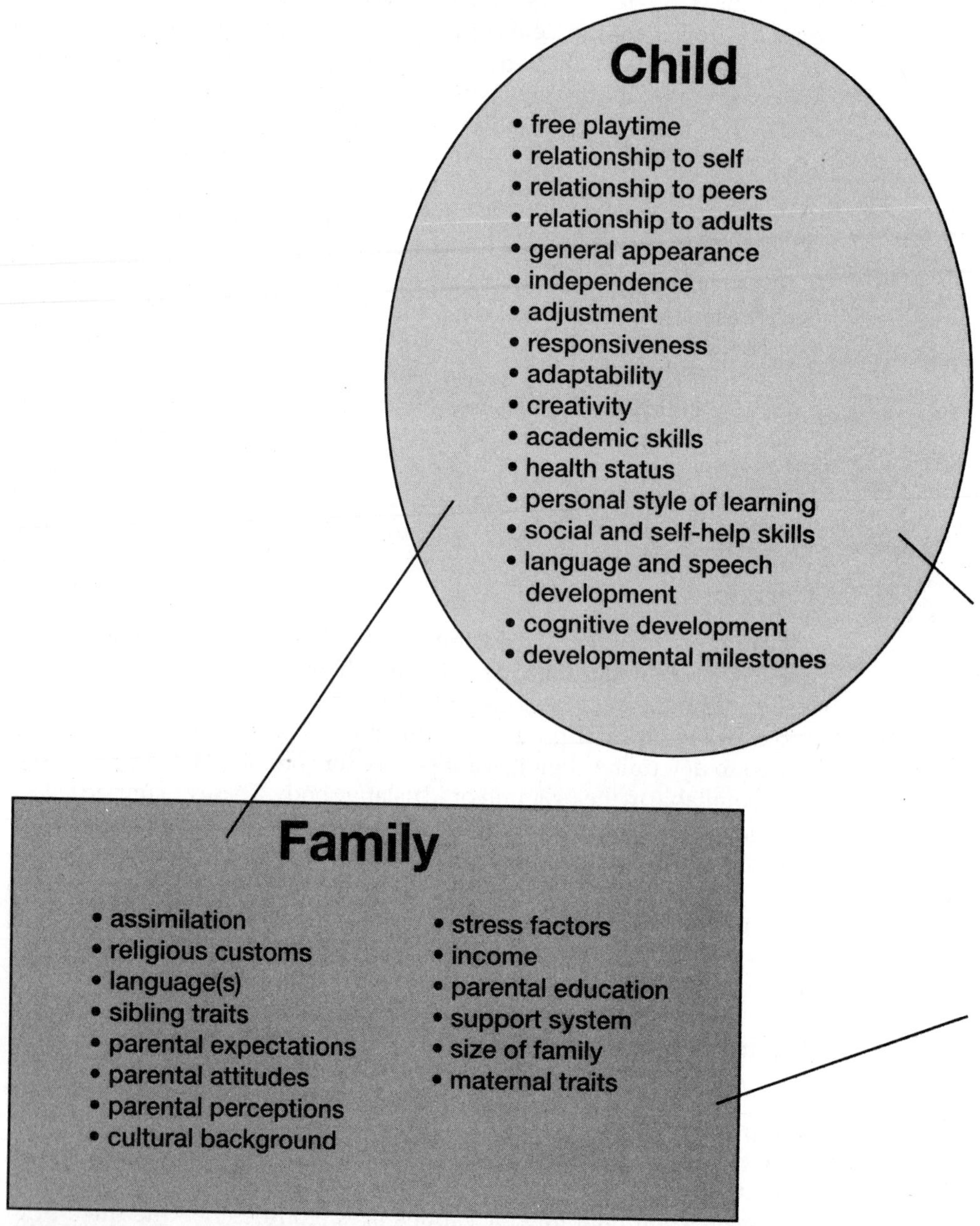

Child

- free playtime
- relationship to self
- relationship to peers
- relationship to adults
- general appearance
- independence
- adjustment
- responsiveness
- adaptability
- creativity
- academic skills
- health status
- personal style of learning
- social and self-help skills
- language and speech
  development
- cognitive development
- developmental milestones

Family

- assimilation
- religious customs
- language(s)
- sibling traits
- parental expectations
- parental attitudes
- parental perceptions
- cultural background
- stress factors
- income
- parental education
- support system
- size of family
- maternal traits

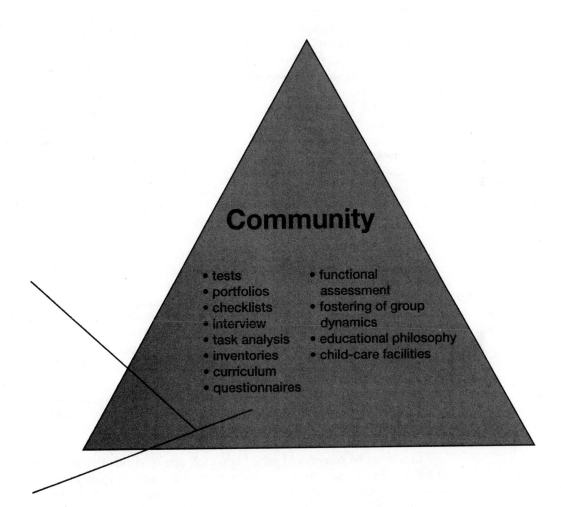

Community

- tests
- portfolios
- checklists
- interview
- task analysis
- inventories
- curriculum
- questionnaires

- functional assessment
- fostering of group dynamics
- educational philosophy
- child-care facilities

Greek ornamentation, and one with a chain link fence on top of it. You judge the one with the fence on top as "ugly," according to criteria (previously defined) for "ugly" city skyscrapers. Contrast this with saying simply, There are three brick buildings outside my window. One of them is ugly!

Notice the missing information in the two descriptions. If the observation report were on a child, much information would be lost and decisions would be made based on fragmentary information. Another important consideration for the teacher or professional observer is knowledge of child development and all the other variables that affect development.

In addition to observation, techniques of assessment include interview and presentation of task to individual or group. These may be structured or open-ended. There may be criteria for judging the information gathered or the assessor may be expected to bring clinical and contextual knowledge to bear when interpreting the way in which the child completes the interview or task. Some assessment procedures are specialized teaching techniques that permit you an opportunity to gather information to solve an individualization of instruction problem. These techniques are called *task analysis,* a procedure for gathering detailed information about the learning activity of a particular child, and *functional analysis,* a procedure for reviewing behavior that may be inhibiting learning for a particular child in a particular program. These methods are discussed in *Chapter Six.*

Finally, some techniques require that the child read, interpret, and solve paper and pencil activities that relate to definitions of development or curriculum. These measures are usually group achievement tests that are used primarily as **accountability** information, information gathered to see if the program is working. These paper and pencil measures are least appropriate for the youngest pupils in our age span. Issues surrounding the limitations, use, and misuse of these measures are discussed in *Chapters Five, Ten,* and *Eleven.*

Each of these techniques may be employed in a standardized or performance-based setting. The rules for interpretation and the limits for use of the results will vary accordingly. Each of these methods has strengths and limitations. Issues of accuracy, usability, defined limitations, and bias must be considered when applying one or another assessment technique. In all cases, the interpretation of an assessment measure must be related to the program and purpose for its use. For example, to be eligible for public services for children with special needs, standardized instruments must be used and applied with the appropriate limitations. This is the case, since eligibility for service definitions include test scores as one of the criteria. Of course, the score must be considered as only one of the pieces of information needed to make final determination for program placement and participation.

Whenever information is gathered by assessment techniques, the information must then be applied to practice. That is, the information gathered for the purpose of program eligibility in the example above becomes the baseline information that is used to plan intervention strategies. Interpreting assessment information and decision making is an on-going process. Information is continuously compared to standards, theory, and curricula so it can be evaluated. Evaluation occurs through matching information to standards for developmental and educational practice. The stakeholders in the assessment system then draw plans to advance and facilitate development. The assessors must remember that assessment results indicate the child's situation at only that moment in time. Further assessment may yield similar results, but only then is a pattern suggested. Even a pattern of assessment results, however, must be subjected to verification. For if the assessment measure is biased or if only some players in the system are in action, then the results may present only part of the story. "Any assessment results are like a photograph of a child: they only give one picture of the many-sided child." (Deno, 1990)

Table 1.2 lists some assessment decisions accompanied by examples of methods to address the questions. Column one lists some common assessment decisions. Column two lists methods for gathering information to make decisions for the questions. Column three raises contextual ambiguities that influence the choice of assessment method.

Assessment decisions are never as easy as they first appear. By keeping an open mind, an awareness of the complexity of the task, and your knowledge of child development, appropriate curricular implementation based on these principles will assist you in the development of a repertoire of assessment techniques to apply in the situations where you must determine child progress and report your decisions to parents and others. Throughout the book, you will be shown a range of assessment techniques appropriate for the children that you serve. After choosing appropriately from among these techniques, you will consider in *Chapter Seven* the issues of reporting to parents and others. Summarizing assessment information and planning for further assessment is discussed in *Chapter Eight*. Assessing children for teaching, for monitoring individual progress, and for the reports that you make are among your most important duties and responsibilities.

Ethics and responsibilities

The foundation of ethical behavior is personal recognition of the rights of children and families, the limits of personal knowledge, and the choice of appropriate assessment methods for programmatic decisions. Another key

TABLE 1.2 Assessment decisions

Decision	Methods to consider	Contextual ambiguities
1. Shall I introduce a new food to baby Shiloh?	observation of adjustment to previous foods; expert consultation	For Shiloh, critical variables are which stakeholder is making the decision and how old is Shiloh? The decision is appropriately made by parents. If she is one month old, hopefully, the parents will consult an expert. If she is 18 months old, previous experience and knowledge of the expert's previous advice may guide the decision.
2. Is baby Nicholas getting a long enough nap?	observation of waking state and comparison to knowledge of his previous patterns	Nicholas and the nap is an assessment decision that may be made by parent or caregiver, based on knowledge of Nicholas. Even then, issues of teething, over stimulation, and other variables may come into play here. Care interventions will vary depending on the available information. An on-going adjustment to the routine for Nicholas' sleeping routine will be made.
3. Is toddler Debbie talking, as expected, developmentally?	observation of Debbie in various situations requiring conversation; interview of Debbie's parents; developmental screening	If Debbie is saying only a few words, the assessment decision may seem to point to developmental screening. The decision changes, however, if the context includes a bilingual situation. Intervention and teaching activities will then support both languages and haste to judge as deficient will be curtailed.
4. Are the children in my preschool group playing cooperatively?	observation and comparison to definition of cooperative play; performance task	Group process evaluation seems to contain no ambiguity for the assessment decision maker. However, definition of cooperation and previous experiences of children influence the context of this decision. Teachers must provide descriptors for those tasks that they wish to use as evaluation markers. If the purpose of the assessment is to judge whether more experience is needed, then teachers observe and intervene accordingly.
5. Are the children tired of easel painting?	collection of paintings; frequency checklists	No one is easel painting. What is the reason? Maybe you need to change the paint colors. Maybe you need to see what else is available. Maybe it is not important that no one is painting. You make a teaching decision for yourself based on reflection about these and other hypotheses.

TABLE 1.2 (continued)

Decision	Methods to consider	Contextual ambiguities
6. Shall the preschool class study "our families"?	review of curricular goals; evaluation of child interest through discussion	Several children in your class report that they will soon have new brothers and sisters. Your program guide calls for the inclusion of a theme on families. You make teaching plans based on this and other information.
7. Is Oswald's conflict with peers, as expected, developmentally?	observation of Oswald in diverse settings; interview of Oswald's parents; developmental screening; diagnostic assessment by specialist	Oswald is indeed combative. He kicks, screams, bites, spits, and throws toys. This pattern of behavior has been consistent since September. In conversations with his mother, you note that she is similarly bothered at home with these outbursts. It is indeed time to seek an expert. If, however, Oswald started this stream of acting out following a major life crisis (new sibling, loss of family member, move, etc.), you may first plan intervention in the program geared toward reassuring Oswald.
8. Do the first graders in my program have the concept of a story?	review of checklist record according to criteria for the definition; performance task	Concept of a story, as empirically defined by your program, seems to be a critical piece of information that most first grade teachers will need to know. You choose an appropriate technique, e.g. story map, to gather the information and plan further teaching for those who have not developed an awareness or mastery of this concept. The contextual variables include definitions of the task, child experience with stories, and language development.
9. Are the third graders mastering the mathematical knowledge required by the state goals?	checklist comparison to the state goals; performance tasks	Third grade teachers are indeed responsible for state learning goals. So you plan to meet the goals through the implementation of a curriculum that is derived from these as well as other goals. You teach, you assess, you reteach. But, what if the goals are unrealistic. You do not have an assessment question; you have a policy problem that you and other stakeholders, parents, principals, and others, must solve in the best interest of the children.

TABLE 1.2 (continued)

Decision	Methods to consider	Contextual ambiguities
10. Is Louis demonstrating a talent for visual arts?	collection of art products; expert consultation	Louis seems to produce paintings and drawings unlike any that you have seen in second grade. You can enjoy these paintings, assist Louis in developing his talent, or refer to an expert. You must consider the wishes and interests of Louis and his parents before following up, since there may be important sociocultural variables that influence whether Louis should be encouraged in artistic activities.

factor is keeping personal biases out of the process. This is particularly important when serving children whose social and cultural experiences may be different than your own. You must keep in mind that your sociocultural lens may affect your objectivity when you interact with children and families from diverse cultures. You must also remember that families do not exist in a static definition of a particular culture. Our society is composed of socioeconomic variables that impact family identification as well as the "traditional" cultural norms. In addition, families choose, on the basis of their experiences, whether or not to identify with "mainstream American values" some or all of the time. Thus, it is crucial to take your cues from the family when considering issues of culture, social class, and ethnicity that may affect an assessment plan. Failure to consider the complexity of the social cultural context can result in serious damage.

The dreadful history of improper decisions for children include mismatch of method to purpose, interpretation of results beyond the limits of the technique employed, and failure to consider the role of contextual factors. Currently, early childhood educators must wrestle with the demands for accountability and whether or not the measures employed are appropriate for the children and families that they serve. The risk in ignoring this responsibility is lifetime stigmatization of young children, the foreshortening of educational opportunity. These issues are discussed in greater detail in *Chapter Five* and in the special issues in *Chapters Nine, Ten,* and *Eleven*.

An important responsibility of child care and teaching personnel is providing information to parents and others about the developmental process and progress of individual children. This information must be held and shared in confidence.

In addition, teachers have a central role in Child Find. This means that teachers must screen and refer children in their care who may need special intervention. Equal protection under the law requires that they must use

techniques appropriate for the situation and the child, as well as participate in the multidisciplinary team who plans for the Individualized Educational Plan (or the Individualized Family Service Plan for children birth
to three). Federal legislation (Section 504 of PL 93–112, PL 94–142, PL
99–457, IDEA, and the ADA) delineates the rights of children for entitlement to special intervention and education to meet special needs so that
they may have an equal educational opportunity. These topics are discussed in *Chapters Seven, Eight, Nine, Ten,* and *Eleven.* Special educational
decisions will involve you, the classroom teacher, as a member of a team.
You will have help in assuming these responsibilities.

In your own program, however, you must assume the responsibility of
the *match of* child, curriculum, and assessment technique. You must apply
the current knowledge of early childhood education theory and principles
in making this match. "Above all, we shall not harm the child. We shall not
participate in practices that are disrespectful, degrading, dangerous, ex-
ploitative, intimidating, psychologically damaging, or physically harmful
to children." This principle has precedence over all others in the NAEYC
Code of Ethical Conduct and Statement of Commitment (Feeney & Kipnis,
1989).

In the past, good intentions regarding the gathering of assessment information about children have resulted in inappropriate evaluation decisions. This has happened in large part because one or more elements of the
comprehensive assessment system have been ignored or unknown to the
individual making the judgments. For example, IQ tests, a form of structured interview and tasks presented individually to children, have often
been applied as single-technique options for assessment and placement
decisions. The factor of English language facility has sometimes been ignored. Life chances for children have been affected. In the present, early
childhood educators tussle with some of the same issues.

Current issues in the assessment of young children

An early childhood assessment system has many players. The central figure is the infant/toddler/child who can participate in more informed self-
conscious ways as maturity and experience are acquired. The second
crucial players are the child's parents. Parents have expectations and personal social/cultural knowledge and information to add to the assessment
mix. Teachers, childcare providers, and related service personnel enter as
important figures in children's lives and contribute to the information
pool. Administrators and boards, as those responsible for program excellence and evaluation, participate in the system. Finally, a society that cares
for the youngest of our citizens—babies, toddlers, and young children—
participates as standard setter and judge. Who are our children? What are

their skills, knowledge, and attitudes? The players in the assessment system grapple with many current assessment issues. These include accountability, high-stakes decision, authentic and portfolio assessment, and school readiness. None of these issues is simple, many overlap in their origins and complexity. In the next section, each is briefly outlined. These issues are addressed throughout the book as they impact the assessment system described.

Accountability

Stakeholders most concerned with broad social interests, in the provision of equal opportunities for all and the problems inherent in such efforts, have concerned themselves with **accountability.** Educational accountability is not a new term (Flesch, 1955) and professionals have usually made their best effort to teach "all" the children. Efforts have sometimes fallen short, as highlighted in the 1983 report, *A Nation at Risk.* This report suggested that large numbers of American youngsters were being miseducated. In response, across the country, states enacted legislation to "check-up" on school districts. These checks are shown in the form of state-mandated testing and state-mandated learning goals and learner outcomes. School districts respond to these demands in diverse ways. Many seek curricula that will "train" children to perform well on state-mandated tests. Other districts seek to deliver the best curricula, geared to appropriate practice for individual and group-suggested norms (Bredekamp, 1987). As teachers, you must be aware of the larger social issues or the context for assessment of young children and the role that you assume when participating in district and state-mandated assessment plans. With the understanding of the background for the present accountability movement, knowledge of appropriate practice, and knowledge of where assessment fits into a comprehensive programmatic approach to the education of young children, you are an informed stakeholder who can function as an advocate for the children you serve. Consult *Chapters Five, Nine, Ten,* and *Eleven* for elaboration of these issues.

High-stakes decisions

Accountability decisions become high stakes when funding is appropriated based on results of tests and when the names of schools "not achieving" are published in the newspaper. Such efforts are thought to call attention to educational malpractice. This may well be so in some cases. Often it is a case of not considering the context of the learning environment, not matching the assessment instrument to the curriculum, interpreting tests beyond their limits, or other errors of measurement application. In early childhood, the error most commonly made is the use of screening and readiness tests to deny kindergarten entrance; retention in kindergarten on the basis of test scores; and choice of primary curriculum based on test scores. Historically, tests have placed children in special education programs on the basis of IQ alone. These decisions are not only wrong, they have lifelong consequences for the individuals involved—affecting the opportunity for education, self esteem, and chances to change life goals. Moral issues involved in assessment such as this should always shape our actions and decisions.

Authentic assessment and portfolios

Many in the early childhood education field are concerned with appropriate practice. (Bredekamp & Rosegrant, 1992; Kamii, 1990; Meisels, 1987; Shepard & Smith, 1989) Many leaders have articulated the link from theory about child learning to the application for appropriate curriculum. In turn, assessment practices must be consistent with this theoretical knowledge. From the field of early childhood and elsewhere have come assessment activities that more closely resemble the activities of the preschool and primary classroom. This is part of the current trend toward authentic assessment, performance-based assessment, and portfolio assessment. While this trend is promising, the alternative measures are not without limits. Issues regarding these limits are discussed in *Chapters Three, Five, Ten,* and *Eleven.*

As a teacher, you will have the opportunity to participate in this trend for effective, efficient, and authentic assessment of children. The daunting questions for this effort are how to individualize, hold to standards, respect familial and cultural differences, and enhance opportunity for all? One concrete example where the field took a standard demanded by the federal government, examined the standard from the best interest of children, and redefined the criteria for accomplishment is Goal One of the National Education Goals (PL 103–227).

The first goal is that all children will come to school ready to learn by the year 2000. Three objectives for achieving Goal one are

▍ all children with disabilities and from less-advantaged families have access to good quality, appropriate preschool experiences.

▍ every parent devote time every day to help their preschoolers learn, and they have access to training and support needed to do that.

▍ children receive nutrition and health care needed to arrive at school healthy.
(Washington, Johnson, McCracken, 1995)

This goal has been variously interpreted by the stakeholders in the system. In the narrowest interpretation, young children will take a "test" to determine readiness for learning. In the broadest dimensions, every child will achieve their potential with these critical components:

- health
- nutrition
- family and community stability
- cultural competence
- self esteem
- quality learning experiences
  (Washington, Johnson, McCracken, 1995)

Early childhood educators will not measure the success of this goal on the basis of a "readiness" test. These broader principles will be considered. Early childhood educators will lay the foundation for "every adult literate and able to compete in the work force." (another of the important National Education Goals, PL 103–223). The implementation of early childhood ethical responsibilities toward respect for "childhood as a unique and valuable stage in the life cycle . . . paramount responsibility . . . provide safe, healthy, nurturing, and responsive settings for children . . . supporting children's development by cherishing individual differences, by helping them learn to live and work cooperative and by promoting self esteem" (Feeney & Kipnis, 1989) guide the accomplishment of these goals.

Summary

Each of the players (child, parent, caregivers, teachers, administrators, boards, legislators) in the rearing (care and education) of a child comes to the stage with a distinct knowledge base, potentially dissimilar goals, and often diverse notions of how to gather information for the purpose of judging developmental process and progress. Each of the players applies information to the standards/outcomes that relate to their ideas of important questions and issues to be documented, measured, or otherwise assessed and evaluated. Because of the complexity surrounding the interface of these various players, each must be considered separately, and each must be careful to practice responsible/responsive assessment so that children are treated fairly and equitably by the assessment system and the stakeholders individually and collectively.

ACTIVITIES

1. On your campus, ask students not enrolled in education to define assessment. With your classmates review the definitions collected. How do these definitions compare to those discussed in this chapter? What kind of public awareness plan should be made to address students on your campus?
2. Reflect on your own experiences with assessment. Which have you enjoyed the most? Which do you hope no one will ever have to repeat? How do your experiences influence what you believe should be done for young children?
3. Review the week's newspapers or television coverage on education. Note any stories that involve assessment. How are these stories treated? What would you do differently if you were the reporter or newscaster?

CHAPTER 1 Suggested further readings

Bergen, D. (1995). *Assessment methods for infants and toddlers: Transdisciplinary team approaches.* NY: Teachers College.

Gullo, D. F. (1994). *Understanding assessment evaluation in early childhood education.* New York: Teachers College.

Henning-Stout, M. (1994). *Responsive assessment: A new way of thinking about learning.* San Francisco: Jossey Bass.

Rossetti, L. M. (1990). *Infant-toddler assessment: An interdisciplinary approach.* Austin: Pro-ed.

Salvia, J. & Ysseldyke, J. E. (1995). *Assessment* (6th ed.). Boston: Houghton Mifflin.

CHAPTER 1 Study questions

1. Can you identify the issues related to the development of a comprehensive assessment system for the early childhood year?
2. Who are the important stakeholders? How are they involved?
3. For which assessment decisions must early childhood teachers assume primary responsibility? How is this assessment process developed?
4. Which techniques do early childhood teachers use in their assessment activities? What techniques are used by other stakeholders?
5. Where to teachers fit in the accountability process? What high-stakes decisions must early childhood teachers prepare for?

⊞ References

Berk, L. E. (1994). *Infants and children: Prenatal through middle childhood.* Needham, MA: Allyn & Bacon.

Bredekamp, S. (Ed.). (1987). *Developmentally appropriate practice in early childhood programs serving children from birth through age eight.* Washington, DC: National Association for the Education of Young Children.

Bredekamp, S. & Rosegrant, T. (1992). *Reaching potentials: Appropriate curriculum and assessment for young children* (Vol. 1). Washington, DC: National Association for the Education of Young Children.

Deno, S. (1990). Individual differences and individual difference: The essential difference in special education. *Journal of Special Education, 24,* 160–173.

Feeney, S. & Kipnis, K. (1989). The National Association for the Education of Young Children code of ethical conduct and statement of commitment. *Young Children, 45,* 24–29.

Flesch, R. (1955). *Why Johnny can't read.* New York: Harper.

Kamii, C. (1990). *Achievement testing in the early grades: The games grown-ups play.* Washington, DC: National Association for the Education of Young Children.

Meisels, S. (1987). The uses and abuses of developmental screening school readiness testing. *Young Children, 42,* 4–6, 68–73.

National Commission on Excellence in Education. (1983). *A nation at risk: The imperative for school reform.* Washington, DC: U.S. Government Printing Office.

Shepard, L. & Smith, M. L. (Eds.). (1989). *Flunking grades: Research and policies on retention.* London: Falmer.

Washington, V., Johnson, V. & McCracken, J. B. (1995). *Grassroots success,* Washington, DC: National Association for the Education of Young Children.

CHAPTER 2

Developing Parent Partnerships in Assessment

Terms to Know

- parent perspective
- parental reports
- parental questionnaires

- developmental questionnaires
- behavioral questionnaires
- parent interview

CHAPTER OVERVIEW In this chapter, the foundation role of parents in the assessment process is described. The crucial nature of this foundation in the lives of young children and their families is highlighted. The use of questionnaires and interviews with parents as part of an early childhood assessment system is described. Links to parent education programs and parent-teacher collaboration efforts are made.

Topics Discussed

- Parents' partnerships in the assessment system
- Methods for obtaining information from parents—questionnaires and interviews
- Parents' educational programs
- Parent-teacher collaboration

Parents' partnerships in the assessment system

When parents enroll their child in a program, a teacher, director, social worker, or other early childhood education professional interviews the parents, whether casually, formally, or informally. This interview forms the foundation of the group care and education process for the life of a child. That is, the first experience that parents have with intervention programs, child-care centers, or schools forms a lasting impression. As early child-hood professionals, it is our responsibility to appreciate the **parent perspective.** In this way we can care responsively for the young children and families who are served in our programs. When teachers begin the enroll-ment process, they need to keep in mind the parent perspective, as well as the infant program, child-care center, or school's "need to know."

Teachers want to know

Typically, teachers want to know what parents think about their child's de-velopment, learning, and education. Depending on the enrollment situa-tion, teachers and caregivers will need more information and will require special interview skills to acquire this information. Often the teacher is a member of a team in the more specialized situations. The information you need depends on your teaching role.

> Ms. Sprint, a home-caregiver requires basic health, safety, and emergency contact information when enrolling baby Leslie. In addition, she needs to know Mr. & Mrs. Jeffersons' preferences for nap, feeding, and any special toys that will comfort Leslie. If Ms. Sprint and the Jeffersons are neigh-bors, the need for additional formal interview may even be less.

As situations become more formal in group child-care settings, the teacher's need to know and the structure for obtaining information be-come more formal. In addition, the issues of cultural group values, lan-guage, and social class affect the initial trust of the budding partnership. When special needs are added, as well, the teacher needs to know more. In any of these more specialized situations, the teacher relies on consultation or social work intervention. Sensitive teachers are familiar, however, with the many facets that influence the giving and receiving of information (cf Berger, 1995; Berns, 1993; Gestwicki, 1992; Gonzalez-Mena, 1993).

Parent contribution

Parents can contribute critical information regarding their children's abil-ities, strengths, possible problems, and educational needs. Parents have observed their children's behavior in a wide range of situations over a long period of time. Their descriptions of what their child is doing can provide valuable information about that child's development and personal adjust-ment. Their questions, concerns, and interpretations regarding their chil-dren add an important perspective.

Parents of young children wonder about their child's development. "How is my child doing?" "Is my child doing well enough?" At a given time, the child's parents will be more or less satisfied with what the child is doing, perhaps concerned about the child's development, or may at least have questions regarding the child. Teachers need to know how satisfied the parents are and how and whether they are concerned about something. Often parents are the first people to recognize that their children are not developing well. Although parents recognize problems and potential problems, they may not be willing to share "everything" they know or "all" their worries. Skillful and sensitive interviews will permit parents greater opportunity for sharing their knowledge and concerns.

There is little question that "parents have the most information about the present functioning and past history of the child . . . the parent is the first and often best assessor of his/her child's functioning and problems" (Walker & Wiske, 1981). Over forty years ago, Gesell and Amatruda (1954) emphasized the importance of involving parents in diagnosing the developmental problems of young children. Even then, the point must have seemed self-evident.

Crucial importance of parent information

Information uniquely available to parents may help to compensate for the limitations of teachers' observations. Furthermore, only certain kinds of behavior can be evaluated by testing. Information gained from a test may be inaccurate and it is certain to be limited to a particular time. A child's parent, having observed how the child actually behaves in many different situations—from the supermarket, to the supper table, to the trip on the subway—can supply information that a teacher or test cannot provide.

Information from parents may cover a wide range of material—medical history and any current symptoms; the child's current developmental functioning and developmental history; personality and social–emotional adjustment, including behavioral/emotional problems; family information, including relevant stress factors such as loss of a parent through death or divorce; and other situational factors that might bear on the child's functioning.

Although parents possess a wealth of information about their child, one critical question is whether their reports are reliable or accurate. **Parental reports** are not uniformly dependable; some parents are better observers of children than others. Also, some parents may give biased responses due to their own personal needs. The accuracy of parental information is related to a number of factors, including (1) the parent's willingness to participate, (2) the parent's ability to comprehend the request for information and to provide accurate data about the child, and (3) the professional's ability to create useful parent-involving ways of obtaining information from parents.

Research demonstrates that parental reports of children's current behavior are usually reliable, especially when these developmental reports are obtained through structured interviews or inventories (Liechtenstein and Ireton, 1984). Parents have been asked to provide information about their young child's developmental abilities (e.g., Can your child draw pictures that can be recognized?) in screening and follow-along programs. In some of the first research of this type, Knobloch and others (1979) used a parent-completed questionnaire including items taken from the Gesell Developmental and Neurologic Evaluation to follow high-risk newborns for the first two years of life. In this study, parents' reports were quite similar to the results of professional evaluations. However, parental reports of past history or early developmental milestones are not as reliable. Parents' concerns about their child's present development and behavioral problems are found to be reliable indicators of problems (Glascoe, MacLean, & Stone, 1991).

Involving parents in the assessment process

Despite the increasing recognition that parents are the "true experts" about their children, this has not always been easy to translate into involving them in the assessment process. Professionals continue to devote considerable effort to selecting or creating psychological and educational tests to assess a child's developmental functioning, while paying relatively little attention to parental information.

There appear to be two interrelated reasons for this. First, some professionals may not be oriented toward working with parents in a collaborative manner. Parents may be relegated to the role of passive observers while professionals exhibit their polished skills in assessing, teaching, or treating children. Professionals thus assume the role of being experts on the child, both in their own eyes and in the eyes of the parents. Second, some professionals consider parents to be subjective, biased, and even untrustworthy in providing information about their children. While these attitudes exist, many professionals who routinely work with parents whose children have developmental problems acquire great respect for parents' knowledge and insight.

The challenge is how to obtain accurate information from parents in practical ways that contribute to building a working relationship with them.

⊞ Methods for obtaining information from parents— questionnaires and interviews

Information from parents comes to teachers in a variety of ways: informally, in parents' comments about the child; in casual conversations; and in the questions parents ask and the concerns they express. More in-depth information may come in response to the teacher's questions at parent-teacher conferences. Parents may be asked to provide information more systematically through interviews and by completing **parental questionnaires.**

When a child-care center is the first point of entry for a child into the care and education systems, teachers may find an enrollment questionnaire appropriate. An example of a questionnaire is shown in Box 2.1. These questions could be asked in a systematic interview or the parent could complete the questionnaire. Then the parents' answers would be discussed with the parent in an interview conference.

Parent questionnaires

Parent questionnaires are designed to obtain information similar to that obtained through interviews. Questionnaires completed by parents prior to children's enrollment in a program are typically extensive including questions about the child's health, development, personal habits, and preferences, family information, etc. Usually, such questionnaires include present status and past history, such as medical history. Typically, they do not provide any guidelines for interpretation. Briefer questionnaires have been devised to determine more narrowly the child's present development, learning, or adjustment.

Parent questionnaires can be used routinely in advance of parent-teacher conferences and selectively, with parents of children whose development is in question or whose behavior is problematic.

Using parent questionnaires can benefit parents and teachers in the following ways:

- Parents have an opportunity to thoughtfully describe their child, answer questions, and express questions and concerns.
- Teachers have advance information, so surprises may be limited.
- Teachers can assess whether the parents and teacher are on the same wavelength.
- As a focus for a later discussion, it may help and thus save time.

BOX 2.1

Program Enrollment Questionnaire

Date _____   Time _____

Child's name _____

Nickname (preferred name) _____

Parent(s) name(s) _____

Address _____

Phone Number _____

Parent(s) present _____

With whom does the child live? _____

What do you expect your child to learn and do in preschool?_____

Have you or has your child lived in or visited other places?_____

What types of things do you do together as a family? (vacations, celebrating birthdays and holidays) _____

Of these, what does your child enjoy most? _____

What does your child do with free time? (favorite activities and interests, likes and dislikes) _____

Has your child had experience with scissors _____ paint _____ Playdough _____?

Does your child listen to stories? _____

Do you spend time reading with your child _____ coloring _____ drawing _____ making things _____ cutting things out _____ cooking _____?

Does your child know colors _____ numbers _____ write _____ emergency procedure _____ phone number and address _____?

Does your child have brothers or sisters? _____

Name(s)
Age/Grade

_____   _____

_____   _____

_____   _____

_____   _____

How does you child get along with siblings? _____

How does your child get along with other children? _____

BOX 2.1 (continued)

Has the child been to a babysitter, preschool, or religious school? _____

What is the child's reaction when you leave? _____

How does your child respond to new situations and people? shy ____ bold ____ curious ____ slow to warm up ____ initiates conversation ____

Are there other significant adults in the child's life? (grandparents, aunts, uncles) _____

Does your child pretend in play? Does the child make up friends or places? _____

Is your child attached to a favorite toy, blanket, or stuffed animal? _____

Name of toy? _____

Is your child easily upset? By what kinds of things? Emotional? Fearful? Temper tantrums?

_____

What do you do for discipline for misbehavior? _____

How does your child respond? _____

Does your child have chores or other responsibilities? _____

Are there any changes in family—expecting, separation, or divorce—that could affect your child? _____

Are there any physical limitations? (sight, hearing, walking, speech) _____

Is your child frequently ill? (colds, flu, earache, allergies) _____

Does your child take a nap? ____ Sleep patterns: early or late riser? ____

What are your child's eating habits? (meals, snacks, small or large appetite, uses fork and spoon or hands) _____

Does your child have toilet training problems (accidents, bed wetter) _____

In what ways can we help your child this year? _____

Is there anything else you would like us to know about your child? _____

- Teachers have an opportunity to educate or communicate program goals to parents.
- Parents may feel included and respected by having the responsibility for completing the questionnaire.

Developmental and behavioral questionnaires

A number of **developmental questionnaires** focus on the child's present development and include norms and guidelines for interpreting results. One example is the Denver Prescreening Developmental Questionnaire–

revised (PDQ–R) (Frankenburg, Fandal, & Thornton, 1992; Frankenburg, van Doorninck, Liddel, & Dick, 1976). The PDQ–R covers the first six years and consists of a series of brief age-related questionnaires that cover four areas of development: personal–social, gross motor, fine motor, and language. The Infant/Child Monitoring Questionnaires (IMQ) (Bricker & Squires, 1989; Bricker, Squires, Kaminski, & Mounts, 1989) have a similar format and cover the first three years of life. The IMQ questionnaires are designed to be completed by parents at home and can be distributed in a postage-paid, mail-back format. The PDQ–R and IMQ questionnaires were designed for screening and for early identification of children with developmental disabilities by pediatricians and school Child Find programs.

Behavior problem questionnaires

Behavior problem questionnaires are designed to give parents an opportunity to report any behavior problems, usually not to describe the child's overall adjustment. They typically are couched in terms of problems or symptoms and may include a few related questions (Perrin, 1995; Carey, 1992). Usually these brief **behavioral questionnaires** do not have norms but may be useful in pediatric practice and possibly in early childhood settings.

One limitation with most of these questionnaires is that they address one primary area (e.g., development or behavior problems) to the exclusion of other areas. Comprehensive questionnaires that address children's development, learning, adjustment, health, etc., including both strengths and problems, are more useful for teachers.

Child development review–parent questionnaire

The Child Development Review–Parent Questionnaire (CDR–PQ) (Ireton, 1990) is a comprehensive survey of the child's present functioning that covers development, learning, adjustment, including behavior problems, health, vision, and hearing, etc. The CDR–PQ includes six open-ended questions and a 26-item problems list. The sample questionnaire shown in Figure 2.1 includes the results for a three-year old. The parent's replies to the questions and problem items picture the parent's view of the child, including strengths and possible problems, and the parent's questions and concerns. Finally, there is information about how well the parent is doing.

The CDR–PQ is standardized and includes norms for parents' responses to the six questions and the frequencies of the problems items by age and sex. Validity studies have shown that certain problems items are associated with placement in early childhood/special education: speech is difficult to understand; clumsy—walks or runs poorly; does not seem to understand well; immature; acts much younger than age. (Ireton, 1994).

FIGURE 2.1 Child development review

child development review

Harold Ireton, Ph. D.

Child's Name _____ Sex ☐ Male ☐ Female
　　　　　　　　Last　　　　　　　　First　　　　　　Initial

Birthdate ☐☐ ☐☐ ☐☐☐☐　Today's Date ☐☐ ☐☐ ☐☐☐☐　Age ☐☐ ☐☐
　　　　Month　Day　Year　　　　　　　Month　Day　Year　　　　Years Months

Your Name _____ Relationship to Child _____

A WORD TO PARENTS: Your answers to these questions can help us to understand your child. They also let us know what questions and concerns you may have about your child. The possible problems list at the bottom of the page provides another way of knowing your concerns about your child.

1. Please describe your child briefly? *Friendly, affectionate, but sometimes very aggressive.*	4. Does your child have any special problems or disabilities? What are they? *Speech*
2. What has your child been doing lately? *Talking a lot more, asking for things. Sits still longer.*	5. What questions or concerns do you have about your child? *Sometimes overly aggressive.*
3. What are your child's strengths? *Usually happy, good helper, good physical coordination.*	6. How are you doing, as a parent and otherwise, at this time? *My hectic schedule. Gets pretty crazy, but I will survive.*

The following statements describe possible problems that your child may have. Read each statement carefully and check (✓) those statements that describe your child.

1. ( ) Health problems.
2. ( ) Growth, height, or weight problems.
3. ( ) Eating problems — eats poorly or too much, etc.
4. ( ) Bowel and bladder problems, toilet training.
5. ( ) Sleep problems.
6. ( ) Aches and pains; earaches, stomachaches, headaches,etc.
7. ( ) Energy problems; appears tired and sluggish.
8. ( ) Seems to have trouble seeing.
9. ( ) Seems to have trouble hearing.
10. ( ) Does not pay attention; poor listener.
11. (✗) Does not talk well for age.
12. (✗) Speech is difficult to understand (Age 3 and older.)
13. ( ) Does not seem to understand well; is slow to "catch on."

14. ( ) Clumsy; walks or runs poorly, stumbles or falls (Age 2 and older.)
15. ( ) Clumsy in doing things with his/her hands.
16. ( ) Immature; acts much younger than age.
17. ( ) Dependent and clingy.
18. ( ) Passive; seldom shows initiative.
19. ( ) Disobedient; does not mind well.
20. ( ) Temper Tantrums.
21. (✗) Overly Aggressive.
22. ( ) Can't sit still; may be hyperactive.
23. ( ) Timid, fearful, or worries alot.
24. ( ) Often seems unhappy.
25. ( ) Seldom plays with other children.
26. ( ) Other?

STOP

FIGURE 2.1 (continued)

Child Development in the First Five Years

Harold Ireton, Ph.D.

Age	SOCIAL	SELF-HELP	GROSS MOTOR	FINE MOTOR	LANGUAGE
5-0 yrs.	Shows leadership among children	Goes to the toilet without help	Swings on swing, pumping by self	Prints first name (four letters)	Tells meaning of familiar words
4-6	Follows simple game rules in board games or card games	Usually looks both ways before crossing street	Skips or makes running "broad jumps"	Draws a person that has at least three parts - head, eyes, nose, mouth, etc.	Reads a few letters (five+)
4-0 yrs.		Buttons one or more buttons	Hops around on one foot, without support	Draws recognizable pictures	Follows a series of three simple instructions
	Protective toward younger children	Dresses and undresses without help, except for tying shoelaces			Understands concepts - size, number, shape
3-6	Plays cooperatively, with minimum conflict and supervision	Washes face without help	Hops on one foot, without support	Cuts across paper with small scissors	Counts five or more objects when asked "How many?" / Identifies four colors correctly
	Gives directions to other children	Toilet trained	Rides around on a tricycle, using pedals	Draws or copies a complete circle	Combines sentences with the words "and," "or," or "but"
3-0 yrs.		Dresses self with help	Walks up and down stairs - one foot per step	Cuts with small scissors	Understands four prepositions - in, on, under, beside
	Plays a role in "pretend" games - mom-dad, teacher, space pilot	Washes and dries hands	Stands on one foot without support	Draws or copies vertical (	) lines	Talks clearly - is understandable most of the time
2-6	Plays with other children - cars, dolls, building				
	"Helps" with simple household tasks	Opens door by turning knob	Climbs on play equipment - ladders, slides	Scribbles with circular motion	Talks in two-three word phrases or sentences
2-0 yrs.	Usually responds to correction - stops	Takes off open coat or shirt without help	Walks up and down stairs alone	Turns pages of picture books, one at a time	Follows two-part instructions
	Shows sympathy to other children, tries to comfort them	Eats with spoon, spilling little	Runs well, seldom falls		Uses at least ten words
	Sometimes says "No" when interfered with	Eats with fork	Kicks a ball forward	Builds towers of four or more blocks	Follows simple instructions
18 mos.	Greets people with "Hi" or similar	Insists on doing things by self such as feeding	Runs	Scribbles with crayon	Asks for food or drink with words
	Gives kisses or hugs	Feeds self with spoon	Walks without help	Stacks two or more blocks	Talks in single words
	Wants stuffed animal, doll or blanket in bed	Lifts cup to mouth and drinks	Stands without support	Picks up two small toys in one hand	Uses one or two words as names of things or actions
12 mos.	Plays patty-cake	Picks up a spoon by the handle	Walks around furniture or crib while holding on	Picks up small objects - precise thumb and finger grasp	Understands words like "No," "Stop," or "All gone"
	Plays social games, peek-a-boo, bye-bye		Crawls around on hands and knees		Word sounds - says "Ma-ma" or "Da-da" as name for parent
9 mos.	Pushes things away he/she doesn't want		Sits alone . . . steady, without support	Picks up object with thumb and finger grasp	Wide range of vocalizations (vowel sounds, consonant-vowel combinations)
	Reaches for familiar persons	Feeds self cracker	Rolls over from back to stomach	Transfers toy from one hand to the other	Responds to name - turns and looks
6 mos.	Distinguishes mother from others	Comforts self with thumb or pacifier	Turns around when lying on stomach	Picks up toy with one hand	Vocalizes spontaneously, social
	Social smile	Reacts to sight of bottle or breast	Lifts head and chest when lying on stomach	Looks at and reaches for faces and toys	Reacts to voices / Vocalizes, coos, chuckles
Birth					

The CDR–PQ is one element in an overall system that includes three main elements:

1. Parents' Report, including the CDR–PQ
2. Early Childhood Teachers' Observations
3. Parent-teacher Conference

During the parent-teacher conference the parent's observations, questions, and concerns are the initial focus. This is followed by the teacher's observations of the child, then discussion of how the child is doing, and the child's educational and other needs. Most important, the teacher has reviewed the parent's report before the parent-teacher conference.

One early childhood teacher has used this systematic approach with over 100 parents of three- to six-year olds in her preschool program (Ofstedal, 1993). She found that parents welcomed the opportunity to complete the questionnaire, that completing it contributed to rapport, and that many more issues were talked about and dealt with than in past conferences. Parents' reports were used to help the teacher prepare for the conference, including bringing along relevant materials for parents. One example is the following situation:

> Bill was four when he started at our center. I immediately noticed how bright and curious he was. I was interested to see how his parents filled out the Review, wondering what they thought about their son's progress. As I read the report, I saw that Mom had addressed so many concerns. We met soon to sort out her thoughts. I gathered information for the parents concerning disobedience, poor listening skills, and hyperactivity. Mom was excited to have concrete methods for handling situations. I assured her that Bill was busy, but delightful, in school. He just needed structure and guidelines. The parents and I met several times and they soon began to see positive changes in their son at home. They spent some "quality time" each day with him and established "rules" for him to follow.
>
> Bill is the type of child a teacher loves to have in school. He is excited about everything and anything and flourishes in a structured environment. Our conference could have been 20 minutes of me praising their son without hitting on any of the serious problems they were having at home.

This example illustrates the importance of knowing something about how parents are doing with their children.

Limitations of the questionnaire process

Use of parent questionnaires depends on how comfortable and able parents are to respond to paper and pencil forms. One advantage of questionnaires is that they provide advance information that can help focus an interview with the parents. Another advantage is that they may save some professional time since teachers can read the questionnaires more quickly than they can ask questions and listen for responses. However, questionnaires are a one-way communication device. That is, the teacher cannot observe the parent response. Thus, valuable clues about comfort with the questions and knowledge of their purpose may be lost.

In addition, questionnaires have serious limitations when parents and teachers are communicating in different languages. Paper forms may inhibit the candor with which parents approach the center when parent literacy is a factor, when cultural norms find paper and pencil "less than friendly," or when parents are enrolling children for less than "choice" reasons.

For example, Susan Teenager has been advised that she must enroll her three-year old in the local "at risk" program and attend classes to secure her GED. This direction has come from her public aid case worker. Susan may have many mixed reactions about "the fact" of her child, sending her baby to school, attending school, and not the least—"growing up" as another single parent in her peer group. A questionnaire may heighten her feelings of vulnerability or attack her autonomy. After all, she may feel uncertain of her mothering capacities, as well. Susan may choose to haphazardly answer the questions or not answer them . . . then starting the baby's career with "a bad taste" toward teachers in the early childhood setting. A paper cannot answer her questions, comment on what a happy baby she seems to have, etc.

In addition, many questionnaires lack any kind of standardization. Standardization of formal assessment instruments is an important issue that you must consider when choosing questionnaires, as discussed in *Chapter Four.* You must ask yourself "Why am I asking the questions?" "Will the information help me teach Johan better?" "Am I just being nosy?" If Johan is allergic to chocolate, this is an important piece of information . . . so asking about allergies is important. Who lives in the home may be an interesting fact to know about, but Johan's parents may find it intrusive. Maybe this information can be obtained later in the collaborative partnership.

Not everything must be known immediately. Teachers and parents can communicate regularly and elaborate their partnership. One of the ways that this may happen is through the interview process.

Parent interviews

Conversations with parents are the most natural approach for teachers to talk with parents about their child. There is no substitute for talking with parents about their children. Parents usually enjoy this, if they feel comfortable and respected. Sometimes a more systematic **parent interview** can provide a survey of what the child is doing and tentatively determine how well the child is doing. The interview needs to be keyed to parental perceptions, concerns, if any, and questions about the child.

For example, Ms. Hawk, a teacher at Corporate Center Child Care, is curious about Tina. Tina entered Corporate Center Child Care about a month ago. She is making some friends and has explored the room and the activities with enthusiasm. Ms. Hawk wants to meet with Tina's mother, Ms. Banker, to check out Ms. Banker's perceptions and to sustain the budding teacher/parent partnership. Ms. Hawk asks the following questions:

- What has Tina been doing lately?
- Please describe Tina for me, the way you see her.
- What do you see her strengths to be? How is she special?
- What questions or concerns do you have about her development? Learning? Behavior? Health? Other?
- How are you doing as a parent?
- Is there anything else you can tell me that would help me to understand Tina?

It is usually best to begin by asking parents for their observations of what their child has been doing lately. Asking for their questions and concerns helps to determine how satisfied or concerned they are about their child. When there are concerns or problems, asking them for their ideas about what is wrong and what might be needed, involves them in all aspects of the assessment and educational process. Parents' spontaneous observations of their children may include three kinds of "observations":

1. Descriptions of what the child is doing, including comments about what the child is not doing yet.
2. Questions and concerns regarding whether this is "normal" or not.
3. Attempts to explain "why" this is the case.

For example, for a two-year old child, his mother may say "He is not talking a lot yet, not as much as he should be, but his big sister is always there, handing him things when he makes noises." Please notice that parents engage in the same processes of observation and interpretation that professionals do.

Accuracy of parent observations

Parents' descriptive observations are usually accurate while their interpretations of these observations are less accurate (Coplan, 1982; McCormick, Shapiro & Starfield, 1982). This is not surprising because parents' "norms" and their sense of the range of normal are less sophisticated than for early childhood professionals.

Interview formats

Formats differ in the amount of structure prescribed and the amount of latitude that is allowed the interviewer and the parent. Even a so-called "open-ended" interview has a limited purpose and encompasses a finite amount of territory. Within these boundaries, the interviewer begins with fairly broad questions and continues with questions that are tailored in consideration of the preceding replies. The selection, phrasing, and sequence of questions in an open-ended interview is up to the interviewer. No two interviews proceed exactly the same way.

In a structured interview, the interviewer asks a predetermined set of questions, usually with the same wording. Some flexibility may be built into the structured interview with a branching procedure. For example, if the parent answers "yes" to a question about noticing unusual speech behavior, the interviewer would then ask "What seems to be unusual?" or a related series of questions, e.g., "Is your child's speech intelligible? Does your child speak in sentences?", according to some pre-established rule. A structured interview requires less interviewing skill than an open-ended interview, where the professional is simultaneously interpreting data and deciding what to ask next.

Structured developmental interview

A structured developmental interview covers specific areas of development—social development, self-help, gross motor, fine motor, and language—in a systematic fashion. The interview is conducted in a step-wise fashion, moving from general questions to questions about specific behaviors. Ireton (1994) developed the approach for the *Child Development Review* using a chart of typical developmental milestones in the first five years. As the teacher interviews using the steps that follow, notes of milestone progress are unobtrusively made. Any milestone or curricular goal list can be used in this fashion.

Step 1: "Please tell me what your child, (name), has been doing lately?"

The parents' spontaneous response gives them a chance to talk about their child in their own way. It also gives the interviewer an opportunity to note behaviors that are spontaneously reported and to determine tentatively the age level of behaviors that may need to be surveyed.

Step 2: "Please tell me more about. . . ."

Begin the second level of questioning by asking for more information in the area of development that the parent has said the most about. For example, gross motor: "Tell me more about how your child is getting around from place to place." The specific wording of the teacher's questions is less important than a natural approach that is comfortable to the parent.

Step 3: "Does your child . . . specific behavior, (e.g., walk alone)?"

At the third level of questioning, within the given area of development, the teacher asks specific questions about the presence of behaviors expected for a child this age. For example, "Does your child . . . ?" and state the behavior. Using a developmental chart, the teacher can check the behaviors the parent answers "YES." The teacher may also mark some behaviors with a "B" for "just beginning to."

This two-three step sequence is repeated for each area of development. When asking about specific behaviors, the teacher must be careful not to create expectations or to ask leading questions that would influence the parent to answer based on what the child "should be" doing. The teacher asks these questions in a "Does . . . ?" or "Is . . . ?" form, not "Can your child . . . ?"

Standardized developmental interview

These interviews provide not only a specified set of questions to be asked, but also standards for scoring the answers and norms for the interpretation of the results. The Vineland Adaptive Behavior Scales (Sparrow, Balla, and Cichetti, 1984) is probably the best-known measure of children's developmental skills based upon a parent's or other caretaker's report. The Vineland measures adaptive behavior from birth to adulthood in six areas: self-help, locomotion, occupation, communication, self-direction, and socialization. The Developmental Profile II (DP II) (Alpern, Boll, & Shearer, 1980) is similar to the Vineland. The DP II format and content provides for a structured interview with the parent or other caretaker and may also be administered as a test to the child. The DP II measures adaptive functioning for ages birth through nine years in five areas: physical, self-help, socialization, academic, and communication. The authors of the DP II recommend its use for screening children, deciding program placement, writing Individualized Educational Plans (IEPs), assessing a child's progress, and making program evaluation.

These instruments are appropriately used by teachers and others who are trained in their use. The results obtained from these standardized interviews must be interpreted in accordance with the directions in the manuals. Careful attention must be paid to appropriate groups of parents for the use of these materials. Violation of the conditions for use and interpretation may present serious consequences for the unwary teacher and the families involved.

Parents' educational programs

When talking with parents about their children, teachers also learn a lot about how they are doing as parents. The teacher gets a sense of how much they enjoy their child or how frustrated or discouraged they are. When trying to appreciate how well a parent is doing, it is wise to avoid "diagnosing" them. Instead, try to appreciate their efforts and strengths as well as recognize their difficulties. This knowledge can form the backdrop to develop parent-education programs. Such programs are best developed in collaboration with parents. Traditionally, parent education has been offered "for" the parent. More appropriately, parents assess their own needs, seeking assistance from teachers and others when needed.

The following example shows parents' responses to different parent programs. Inner city preschool program A offered "parent education programs" on topics selected by the staff. Topics included "Discipline for three year olds," "Nutritious Snacks," etc. Two parents of 40 came to each of the sessions. Inner city preschool program B scheduled a Craft Making meeting. Informally, while making "bleach bottle" baskets for their children, the 20 (out of 40) parents shared experiences and discussed alternatives. Topics ranged from child discipline, managing coupon shopping, and new ways to make macaroni. The parents planned to meet again and asked the teacher to schedule a child literacy expert as speaker.

The difference in the scenarios was that parents were in power. They were assessing their own needs and seeking resources as necessary.

Of course, there are times when the family is the client, but even in these situations, the parent must be empowered to prioritize the family intervention plan in collaboration with the relevant professionals (cf Cataldo, 1987; Powell, 1989).

Parent-teacher collaboration

Knowing the parents and their priorities, as well as their child, contributes to effective collaboration. As parents contribute to the assessment of their child, the stage is set for ongoing collaboration. "Parents who have been interviewed about their child's developmental competence . . . have, in many instances, spontaneously suggested remedial action or shown increased acceptance of recommendations for remediation. They recognize that the data generating the recommendations have come from them rather than from an assessment of which they had no part" (Boll & Alpern, 1975).

The importance of working with parents in meeting the educational needs of their children has long been recognized. The challenge of finding ways of involving parents in the assessment of their children's developmental and educational strengths and problems has only been partly met. While useful methods for obtaining developmental information from parents do exist, professionals' skepticism regarding parental ability to be objective about *their* children have limited the use of this information source. It does appear that parents have been given less credit than they deserve for providing valuable information regarding their childrens' development.

Collaboration at the assessment level sets the stage for collaboration at other levels. Parent involvement begins by providing the parent with an opportunity to report on the child's development and to raise concerns or questions, if any. Assessment data based both upon parent information and on teacher observation and any testing of the child then provide a sound basis for appreciating the child's abilities and educational needs. A positive, informative relationship with parents will be helpful to the parents as well as the child. A school program with these elements optimizes the prospects for making appropriate decisions and lays the groundwork for effective parent-school relationships.

Summary

When embarking on the road to parent partnerships, teachers must remember that reciprocity is implied in the word *partner.* Respect and appreciation for the complex roles of parents will ensure the beginning of a smooth and productive relationship in the best interests of children. Parents must be involved in providing information about their children so that teachers may effectively care for and educate them. Child care and school settings must understand the values and conventions that shape parent practices and perceptions. Together, parents and teachers nurture children so that they may grow to be self-confident, happy, and capable young students.

CHAPTER 2 Suggested further readings

Croft, D. J. (1979). *Parents and teachers: A resource book for home, school and community relations.* Belmont, CA: Wadsworth.

Gonzalez-Mena, J. (1993). *The child in the family and the community.* Columbus, OH: Merrill.

ACTIVITIES

1. Visit a child-care facility in your community. Ask for a description of enrollment policies and procedures. How are parents involved in the process? Do you think the procedures match the potential population?

2. Choose a questionnaire or structured interview. Try it out on a volunteer parent. Summarize the results of your experience. What conclusions can you draw about the parent and about the process? Compare your experiences to those of your classmates.

3. With permission, review the entrance forms or other parent-interview material in the files of two children. Observe the children. Make a tentative judgment about the progress of the children from time of entrance into the program. Discuss your assessment with the classroom teacher.

Hale, J. (1995). *Unbank the fire*. Baltimore: Hopkins.

Polakow, V. (1993). *Lives on the edge: Single mothers and their children in the other America*. Chicago: Chicago.

CHAPTER 2 Study questions

1. What factors must an early childhood teacher consider in order to develop a "fair" understanding of the parent perspective?

2. What are the key elements of parent reports? How can these instruments be used in early childhood programs? What are their limitations?

3. Describe developmental questionnaires. What role do these instruments play in an assessment system? What advantages and limitations are applicable to these?

4. When and how may an early childhood teacher use behavioral questionnaires? How do these instruments affect the parent partnership?

5. When do early childhood teachers use parent interviews in the assessment process? What factors influence the perceived parent/teacher partnership when interviewing is a part of the assessment process?

References

Alpern, G. D., Boll, T. J., & Shearer, M. (1980). *Developmental Profile II*. Aspen, CO: Psychological Development Publications.

Berger, E. H. (1995). *Parents as partners in education* (4th ed). Columbus, OH: Merrill.

Berns, R. A. (1993). *Child, family, community: Socialization and support* (3rd ed.). New York: Harcourt.

Bjorklund, B., & Burger, B. (1987). Making conferences work for parents, teachers, and children. *Young Children, Jan.* 26–31.

Boll, T., & Alpern, G. D. (1975). The developmental profile: A new instrument to measure child development through interviews. *Journal of Clinical Child Psychology, 4,* 25–27.

Bricker, D., & Squires, J. (1989). A low-cost system using parents to monitor the development of at-risk infants. *Journal of Early Intervention, 13*(1), 50–60.

Bricker, D., Quires, J., Kaminski, R., & Mounts, L. (1988). The validity, reliability, and cost of a parent-completed questionnaire system to evaluate at-risk infants. *Journal of Pediatric Psychology, 13*(1), 55–68.

Carey, W. B. (1992). Pediatric assessment of behavioral adjustment and behavioral style. In M. D. Levine, W. B. Carey, & A. C. Crocker (Eds.), *Developmental-behavioral pediatrics* (pp. 609–616). Philadelphia: Saunders Company.

Cataldo, C. Z. (1987). *Parent education for early education: Child rearing concepts and program content for the student and practicing professional.* New York: Teachers College.

Coplan, J. (1982). Parental estimate of child's developmental level in a high risk population. *American Journal of Disorders in Childhood, 136,* 101.

Frankenburg, W. K., van Doorninck, W. J., Liddell, T. N., & Dick, N. P. (1976). The Denver Prescreening Developmental Questionnaire. *Pediatrics, 57,* 744–753.

Frankenburg, W., Fandal, A., & Thorton, S. (1987). Revision of the Denver Prescreening Developmental Questionnaire. *Journal of Pediatrics, 57,* 744–753.

Glascoe, F. P., MacLean, W. E., & Stone, W. L. (1991). The importance of parents' concerns about their childs' behavior. *Clinical Pediatrics, 30,* 8–11.

Gesell, A. L., & Armatruda, C. S. (1954). *Developmental diagnosis* (3rd ed.). New York: Hoeber.

Gestwicki, C. (1992). *Home, school and community relations* (2nd ed.). Albany, NY: Delmar.

Gonzalez-Mena, J. (1993). *The child in the family and the community.* Columbus, OH: Merrill.

Ireton, H. R. (1994). *The child development review manual.* Minneapolis: Behavior Science Systems.

Ireton, H. R. (1992). *Manual for the child development inventory.* Minneapolis: Behavior Science Systems.

Ireton, H. R. (1990). *Child development review–parent questionnaire.* Minneapolis: Behavior Science Systems.

Knobloch, H., Steven, F., Malone, A., Ellison, P., & Risemberg, H. (1979). The validity of parental reporting of infant development. *Pediatrics, 63,* 873–878.

Lichtenstein, R., & Ireton, H. R. (1984). *Preschool screening: Early identification of school problems.* New York: Grune & Stratton.

McCormick, M., Shapiro, S., & Starfield, B. (1982). Factors associated with maternal opinion of infant development. Clues to the vulnerable child. *Pediatrics, 69,* 537.

Morrison, G. S. (1978). *Parent involvement in the home, school, and community* (p. 163). Columbus, OH: Merrill.

Ofstedal, K. (1993). Parent-teacher conferences using the child development review-parent questionnaire. (Personal communication).

Perrin, E. C. (1995). Behavioral screening. In Parker, S., & Zukerman, B. (Eds.). *Behavioral and developmental pediatrics: A handbook for primary care* (pp. 22–23). Boston: Little, Brown and Company.

Powell, D. (1989). *Families and early childhood programs.* Washington, D.C.: National Association for the Education of Young Children.

Sparrow S. S., Balla, D.A., & Cichetti, D. V. (1984). *Vineland adaptive behavior scales, interview edition.* Circle Pines, MN: American Guidance Service.

Walker, D. K., & Wiske, M. S. (1981). *A guide to developmental assessments for young children* (2nd ed.) (p. 32). Boston: Massachusetts Department of Education, Early Childhood Project.

CHAPTER 3

Observing as the Key Method in the System

Terms to Know

- observations
- observation records
- anecdotal notes
- running records
- checklists

- frequency records
- event sampling
- time sampling
- rating scales
- portfolios

CHAPTER OVERVIEW   In this chapter, child observation is described as the cornerstone of an assessment system. The chapter describes the observational process, methods for recording information, and procedures for interpreting and using the results of observation. The role of observation in the development of portfolios is descried.

Topics Discussed

- Observation in the assessment system—planning, deciding, and recording
- Portfolios
- Limitations of the observational method
- Planning and scheduling observations

⊞ Observation in the assessment system—planning, deciding, and recording

Teachers make many important decisions that affect the lives of children. Teachers decide what to teach on a day-to-day basis for a group of children and how to individualize activities for particular children. Teachers decide what kinds of materials and equipment to use to carry out the curriculum. Teachers decide whether to use themselves in the teaching process as model, as guides, or as directors of the learning task. Teachers set up rules and expectations about how the children will interact with each other.

Teachers are decision makers

Observations of the children in the program inform the decisions of teachers. Observations are the most important assessment tool, more so than any book or set of packaged tests. Teachers spend several hours a day with the children they teach. Teachers who regularly and systematically observe young children use the soundest informational basis for curricular and instructional planning. By knowing what to look for and how to observe children, teachers make accurate inferences regarding the needs of children.

The observation process is used by both preschool and primary teachers to learn more about young children. By keeping their eyes open, teachers gather the information needed to assess developmental progress. They find out how well the children in the program are learning and how they get along with other children, teachers, and other adults. Teachers decide whether to begin, continue, or change an activity. They decide which children to group in various activities based on what they see.

It is the keeping of the records of these observations that allow teachers to reflect and to inform decision making. Thus, early childhood education programs must include all of the following forms of **observation records:**

- Brief, casual anecdotal observations of various children throughout the day, perhaps recorded on Post-it notes;
- Daily logs written at the end of each day;
- In-depth running record observations, about ten minutes long, of particular children or situations.

Regular, data-based decision making is important to the early childhood program. Teachers want to avoid "hit or miss" decisions so that they do not misjudge children and their progress. All teachers want to help children learn and adjust. No one wants to be judged on the performance of their "off days." Nor do teachers want to base all curricular decisions on performance of "peak performance." Spotty observation notes may not catch the whole picture of the child. Think of observation notes and records as snapshots in the classroom lives of children. Teachers want notes to show all the angles: front, side, back, and 3-D. Choosing one or several ways to record observations suggested here and using them regularly for all the children in the program ensures "full color portraits."

In summary, the questions teachers ask and answer while teaching include the following:

What does Jon know about the alphabet?

What can Freddy do in math?

How does Marvin get along with other children?

How does Paul get along with teachers?

How does Brad get along with his parents?

How can I help Juanita learn to tie her shoes?

Shall I put all the three year olds together for finger painting?

Should I put the story time before lunch?

My class seems to be humming along, shall I make any changes?

The answers to these questions come from observing the children. In fact, teachers make assessment decisions daily.

Insights from observation are the basic early-childhood, education-assessment tools. Further testing of a formal nature may be necessary sometimes. Insights gained through observation will help decide when, whether, and how to use formal tests as part of the program. Teachers gather important insights from observations to share with parents in conferences and in reports. With parents, teachers use observational insights to decide whether to refer an individual child for further assessment that may lead to the provision of special services for a particular child.

Observational information on all the children in the program can be summarized to provide important evidence for administrators and other decision makers. Such material can help in program evaluation that shapes and directs plans for the future. These summaries can serve as documentation of effective practice and to prove the need for continued or enhanced funding of programs.

Since teachers want to make these decisions and reports effectively, they must develop assessment plans that are comprehensive, yet realistic. Not every procedure suggested in this chapter is necessary for every child. However, the plan for each child must represent techniques that will provide insights on all aspects of each child's development and learning in the program. To ensure that a plan is comprehensive, use many ways (multiple measures) to observe each child in multiple settings. This also enables the teacher to gather insights about how the group is behaving and learning. For each child, report on the basic areas of development: motor skills, language, intellect, social skills, and self-esteem. More detail will be required if there is a particular concern about David, Walter, Jose, Esther, or Enora.

Practicing being a better observer

Observation is a skill sharpened with practice. Teachers have already had considerable practice in it. Teachers observe children in a variety of situations throughout the day. To practice observing more keenly, begin in a small way by watching the children's interaction—for instance, in the block corner—for five or ten minutes a day.

Ms. Wolf watches and records what she observes in good detail. She asks Ms. Brown to observe the scene with her—a second teacher, a supervisor or a teacher aide—and to listen to the report. Through the discussions, Ms. Wolf sees whether she observed similar behavior as the second adult and whether their conclusions match. This is a good check on the accuracy of the data. Almost certainly one of them picked up a detail or two that the other missed.

To sharpen your observation skill, imagine that you are looking at a video recorded on your first birthday. At first the camera showed the whole party scene: the balloons, grandparents laughing and watching, and the older children at play. Then it moved closer to capture you diving into the cake with two hands. With this favorite scene on film, you can review it and enjoy the experience all over again, seeing things that you may have forgotten—the color of the napkins, balloons, the exact expression of Aunt Mimi, etc.

Think of yourself as that camera. First note the complete "party" of your classroom. Then observe smaller groups of children involved in various activities. Then move in on the group in the doll corner, with close-ups of the individual children. At even closer range you record one child's facial expression and wonder about the emotions reflected. At this natural level of observation, you are primarily noticing and describing. Your observations will be of great use when it comes to discussing a child with parents. But your observations will be of use long before that. Observations will reinforce (or perhaps lead you to question) your general impression of the child—individual style, peer relationships, problem-solving skills, etc. Observations will contribute to your appreciation of each child in your care as a unique individual, and to your empathy for each child—even for a misbehaving child. Too, the observations will teach you much about your class as a group, material that can be applied to future planned activities. Your observations help you to read situations and children.

Planning for observations

First list your questions. Decide what insights you want to be able to write down about all the children in your program. Decide which children you may want to learn more about. Here you are defining what to observe and the focus of your observation. Is Jeanie really in constant motion? Can Elton work by himself on a writing project? Is Anita pinching other children? How long does Johnny work in the block corner? Is Julie directing the play in the doll corner? How is Wayne doing as chair of the social studies project? Decide what you want to be able to tell parents at report time. Decide what information your principal or director will require about the children in your class. After you have the questions, choose the ways to record that will give you the insights you want.

The outlines in Box 3.1 and Box 3.2 highlight the kinds of questions you may want to keep in mind so that you can report completely on each child. You do not have to answer all questions for every child, but use the questions to help you pinpoint descriptions for each child.

Recording observations

There are many ways to record observations, varying from brief notes to extensive running records. Some ways require lots of time, so teachers need to plan what the children will be doing while observing. For example, it is very hard to record detailed observations while you are telling a story, leading a song, or taking children on a walk. The detailed observations are best conducted during free play or while primary children are engaged in project work. If there is extra help in the classroom, a teacher can sit and record details during large group time. Also, teachers can train assistants and others to help in this kind of observation or invite a supervisor or colleague to help with the task.

Some observational records can be done more casually and even by reflection. In planning for observational assessments, a teacher needs to be sure that different kinds of observations for each child are planned. The *first rule* of any assessment plan is to make multiple measures, so be sure to collect several samples of observations on all the children. Three of the most common methods for recording observations—anecdotal notes, running records, and logs or notebooks—are described in the next section.

These are naturalistic observations: "live" recordings that allow you opportunities to look at the same notes at different times and to gain new information or insights about what you saw each time. The following guide in Box 3.3 is created from ideas presented in various forms by early childhood professionals who have worked hard to make observation a skill that is available to our field. Included are ideas from Almy and Genishi (1979); Cohen, Stern, and Balaban (1983); Cook, Tessier and Klein (1992); and Greenspan (1987).

BOX 3.1

Suggested Observation Outline

General Overview

- Expressions: cheerful, bland, angry, etc.
- General tempo: active, plodding, etc.
- Alert, energetic, or listless and apathetic? Variable? If so, why?
- Dressed well or disheveled?
- Runny nose, eyes, etc.
- Specific personal habits you notice (e.g., chewing hair, sucking thumb, etc.)?

Gross-Motor Skills

- Seems agile?
- Uses climbing apparatus well?
- Runs smoothly?
- Jumps on two feet?
- Hops on one foot?
- Gets up and down stairs?
- Throws and catches a ball?

Fine-Motor Skills

- Strings beads?
- Grasps a crayon, marker, or pencil well?
- Stacks a tower of blocks?
- Manipulates a puzzle?
- Chooses small manipulatives to work with (small blocks, etc.)?

Speech and Language

- Uses language to express needs?
- Speaks clearly or mumbles?
- Speaks both to children and adults?
- Understands what you say?
- Follows directions?
- Answers questions?
- Speaks only one language or parts of two languages in a bilingual home and/or school environment?

BOX 3.1 (continued)

Cognitive Skills

- Can identify objects?
- Can identify objects in pictures or books?
- Can name some colors?
- Can count to two? ten? twenty? one hundred?
- Can learn new words quickly?
- Can recognize letters or numbers?
- Can solve problems: reflective, impulsive?

Relationship to Adults

- Discriminates between teachers and visitors?
- Calls teachers by their names or calls them "teacher"?
- When asked, knows teacher's name?
- Seems overdependent on adults?
- Appears defiant toward adults?
- Is cooperative, resistant, too compliant?

Relationship to other children

- Plays cooperatively?
- Shares materials?
- Becomes anxious when other children want to share?
- Teases or provokes other children?
- Hits or behaves in an aggressive manner?
- Is withdrawn or uninvolved?

Relationship to Self

- Appears self-confident?
- Appears to know who he/she is?
- Can tell own full name?
- Can tell about own likes and dislikes?
- Can tell about own family? house?
- Possesses self-help skills?

Free Play or Self-Selected Activities and Interests

- Finds occupations during free time or self-selected time?

BOX 3.1 (continued)

- Plays with other children (solitary, parallel, cooperative, games with rules, rough and tumble)?
- Stays with activity or flits frequently?
- Uses materials appropriately, creatively?
- Requires an adult to initiate activity?

Group Activity

- Makes required oral or movement tasks?
- Sits with group during activities?
- Is attentive and cooperative?
- Needs the help of an adult to attend?

Transitions

- Moves easily from one activity to another?
- Requires frequent reminders from adults?
- Responds to prewarnings or announcements that a change of activity is coming?

Routines

- Follows schedule?
- Is self-reliant?
- Remembers structure?
- Challenges rules and expectations?

General Impressions

- General areas of strength?
- Any weakness?
- General areas of skill?
- Any particular impressions?

(Modification of Baumann, McDonough, & Mindes, 1974)

Anecdotal notes

Anecdotal notes are brief notes made of significant events or critical incidents in a particular child's day. For example, a child who has never talked in class begins speaking. The teacher writes down what she said and under what circumstances she has said them.

BOX 3.2

Infant and Toddler Observation Categories

Object Manipulation

- ▌ Play, with toys? Which toys? How?
- ▌ Uses specific features of the toy (pulls string, pushes buttons)? Which? Ignores other features (e.g., lifting lid)?
- ▌ Combines toys or real objects (spoons, cups) in pretend play? How?
- ▌ Imitates actions observed in the environment? (pushes stroller with dolls)? How? What kind?
- ▌ Uses any strategies to solve problems? How? What persistence?

(Derived from Higginbotham & Pretzello, nd)

Valerie, age three, arrives breathless, having run from the corner of the street. Her mother is a few steps behind, smiling broadly. Valerie jumps up and down in front of you, yelling "puppy, puppy." Her mom confirms that indeed the family now has a new puppy at home. Valerie's teacher, Ms. Sizemore, records this dated and timed note on the notebook in her pocket and makes a note to add books about puppies to the book corner. She does all of this while listening to Valerie, her mother, and the other children who are arriving. Or Ms. Sizemore records the incident as soon as she can, keeping track of all the relevant details for Valerie's file.

In another case, Ms. Weffer is working with Maureen who hits other children often. One day Maureen and Peg are playing in the block corner. Maureen has used almost all of the blocks of the foot-length size for her house. Peg has been asking her for some of them to complete her own house structure. She gives up on asking and begins to put her foot back, as if to swing at Maureen's house. Maureen screams at Peg, "STOP, don't you dare knock my house down! I told you to get out of my way." Maureen starts to march toward Peg with her hand outstretched. Peg, anticipating the slap, retreats hastily away. Ms. Weffer moves quickly to the block corner before Maureen has a chance to swing. She commends Maureen for talking about the problem (though it was at scream pitch) and tries to help the girls figure out an agreeable way of sharing the blocks. Ms. Weffer records this *anecdote* as soon as possible for Maureen's record, so that she can begin to mark her progress toward verbal problem-solving strategies.

BOX 3.3

What Should I Do to Record Anecdotes and/or Running Record Observations?

1. Look at one child or situation. Be sure to observe all children at different times in the day over the course of the year. By the end of the year, you can probably answer questions about each child and how the child fits into the routine of your classroom. Questions that you may wish to answer to give a complete description of Gene, Lorraine, Bernadine, or Stephen include the following:

   a. description: physical appearance, expressions, agility, general tempo, moods, problem-solving style, and communication style

   b. attendance and arrival: start of the day, response to overtures from friends and teachers

   c. relationship to teachers and children

   d. relationship to materials

   e. relationship to routines

   f. approach to tasks

2. Write down exactly what a child is doing. You should be like a camera, recording what you can see. All the details should be recorded so you can remember later what happened and can interpret the behavior. For example, Joshua played in the block corner for 20 minutes is a sparse note. All that you can interpret from this note is that Joshua can concentrate. Details describing what he built, whether he constructed things by himself, whether he was using a theme, or merely stacking blocks and knocking them down gives you much more information to work with in figuring out later what Joshua's development is like.

3. Focus on one child at a time, recording peer interactions as they affect the focus on that child. It may be hard to write down the language of several children. They are all talking at once and may not be talking to each other. It is also easier to file materials about one child and to be sure that you have a range of material on one child if you focus on one child at a time. Occasionally, however, when two children interact, the observation can serve a dual purpose.

4. Be sure to record the observation in the same order that events occurred. For example, Sara cried, threw a doll at Marcia, and grabbed her arm in pain. What really happened is that Marcia socked Sara. Sara grabbed her arm in pain, cried, and then threw a doll at Marcia. The interpretation of Sara's behavior will be different depending on the order in which the events are recorded.

5. If group dynamics are the focus of the observation, do not try to record every word said. Record key phrases and use arrows to show action between children. You probably will use this approach when you are trying to solve a classroom grouping problem or a social-behavior problem. That is, can Kevin and Arthur ever be placed in the same small group? How can I get Sylvia and Rose to broaden their jump rope group to include Suzanne?

6. Record in a style that is convenient for you. You may wish to develop your own abbreviations and symbols to help you in writing quickly. For example, T for teacher, first initials for children's names, and shorthand for objects (e.g. hse for house, blk for block, bk for book, etc.).

BOX 3.3 (continued)

The purpose of the observation will shape the way you record. For example, if you wish to keep a record of all your 35 third graders using art media, you will need to know which students you have observed. One way to remember is to write each child's name on a flag that you put around a pencil—one pencil for each child. Place all the pencils in a cup on your desk; have an empty cup beside the full one. As you record a note on each child, move the pencil to the empty cup. Watch your progress as one cup fills and the other empties (Greenberg, 1991).

The major advice in keeping observational records is to make the system easy for you. Keep pens and pencils handy—in your pocket, around your neck, in magnetic boxes attached to furniture, etc. Notebooks and papers of various kinds should be readily available. Some teachers like to use Post-it notes on the spot and place them on paper for filing. Various-sized cards can be arranged and rearranged with notes for the summarization process.

Letter-size paper can be divided into sections for four to six children. After observations are entered, the paper can be cut into pieces for filing.

Dot	Harold
Ryan	Elsie
Jon	Gavriela

7. Collect regular information on a child; observe the child at different times in different settings. Avoid recording only negative incidents or only positive behaviors.

BOX 3.3 (continued)

8. Be sure to schedule observations. Plan to observe only a few children each day. It is too hard to teach and record lots of observation notes each day. You want to participate in the play or discussion, so you have to think about what you are teaching, as well as the effect of the teaching on each child. Four children are a suggested number to observe in a whole day. Four observations on each child each month will give you 36 to 48 notes for the year. You then have many rich details to share in reports to parents and information on which to base trend statements about each child in your program. Veronica enjoys putting puzzles together. She has put puzzles together every day for the last six weeks. Donna organizes the play in the housekeeping corner. She decides whether the girls will be ballet dancers or whether they will be psychologists and then gives everybody a part to play. The girls cooperate with her.

Avoid recording running records on stressful days, e.g., parent night, first day after vacation, field trip days, etc. Of course, if a critical incident occurs, by all means jot down the anecdote.

9. Another way to organize the scheduling aspect of observations is to pick a subject. Observe art one week, science the next, math the next, etc. Collect information on Keisha, Andy, Arnold, Alex, and Otto for each subject.

10. Be discreet when observing. That is, record your notes so that the child's work or play is not disturbed. If children ask what you are doing, you can say that you are writing, because you like to write about children's play or work, and you are making notes to help you remember.

11. Be aware of your reactions as you are observing. What are you feeling about the action that is occurring? In a separate section of the notes, jot down these notions. Refer to them later as you try to understand what your opinion is about an individual child. For example, as I watched Luzmarie struggle to communicate with Tom, I felt pleased that she was making an effort to make herself understood. Or, as I watched Leo flit round and round the room, bumping into things, I felt exhausted and frustrated. These notes to yourself will help in the interpretation of the observations.

12. When you finish an observation session, jot down any questions, ideas, and conclusions that pop into your mind about the observation. These notes will be useful for the summarization and planning process.

13. Maintain confidentiality of notes. Don't leave them out where the casual visitor can find them. Stress the need for confidentiality to all staff and volunteers who may be involved in recording observations.

Running record

Running records are notes made of routine functioning of an individual child or a small group of children. For example, Ms. Ryan plans to observe Rachel for 10 minutes during free-play period. Then she writes down everything that Rachel does or says. The record is collected at different times throughout the year. Ms. Ryan saves each record for later analysis.

In another instance, a group of second graders are planning a way to use attribute blocks for a new game. As they establish rules, Mr. Solis observes and records the process. When he analyzes this record, he makes decisions about child progress and grouping plans and also gains information about what further details he should provide to the group about attribute blocks, game development, etc.

Recording narrative notes.   Before beginning to record an observation on a child or a situation, you should make a few notes that will help in remembering important issues and details. This includes a sketch or mention of the part of the room where the action takes place and a note about the context, i.e., who is playing, acting, where, etc. Record the date, time, and any relevant preceding events. For example, if you are recording that Theda is crying, note what happened before—Ronald hit her, she smashed her finger, or you saw nothing that tells you why she is crying. Box 3.4 illustrates a naturalistic observation.

Impressions from this observation.   Ronald seems to have had an "off day"; that is, he was quiet and subdued and tried to resist offers of others to play. He is usually so peppy. (Is he feeling well? Did something happen at home?) Brad finally succeeded in dragging him into play. He seems to have a way of pulling Ronald out of his withdrawn mood. The other children really seem to depend on Ronald's leadership skills. Both boys could pull themselves together when the play was beginning to get out of hand. They are developing good self-control. Ronald's play shows a good imagination (use of dishes as gas); Brad is more concrete in his play (dishes as symbols of food).

The teacher, Ms. Perez, saves this *running record* for Ronald's file. Ms. Perez may also summarize her impressions of Brad and place it in his file. When doing this, Ms. Perez will want to protect Ronald's and Brad's privacy as she uses the files. She collects notes on each child in the program once or twice a month for each child. At the end of the year, or when she wishes to report to parents, she reviews the notes to help clarify her thoughts about the developmental progress of each child in the program. Running record observation is the most time-consuming kind of observation. As you can see from the above example, Ms. Perez's primary occupation during the 10 minutes is recording notes about Ronald and Brad. She sits close to the boys and watches and records their play. The rest of the group is playing in their respective areas of the classroom. Ms. Cobbler, the assistant teacher, is keeping an eye on the total group. This kind of observation may not always be possible in a program. The children in the class may need all the adults in the room to help them maintain smooth play. Sometimes, teachers may also need to collect observations while they are one of the participants in the action. Running records will not work

BOX 3.4

Sample Observation (in a Child Care Center)
Two Boys at Play

This center is in a large house. It is a cozy, warm old house with many nooks and crannies for children to explore. During the free-play period, children can be inside or outside as their play takes them.

On this day, Ronald is inside in the living room of the house. This is the area where the house-keeping equipment is set up. Besides the standard equipment of wooden stove, refrigerator, and sink, there are large cardboard boxes set up in the area. The boxes are there to invite creative play. The boxes vary in size, but most will easily hold one or two children.

Ronald is a tall, slender, well-coordinated four-year old. He is dressed in a tee-shirt and comfortable cotton pants. Ronald is always clean and neat. He is regarded as a leader in this program. Most of the time he leads children in a play activity of his choice. Today, he is playing alone in the housekeeping corner. His expression is bland today, usually he is peppy, expressive. He appears to be a little bit tired, not his usual energetic self.

9:09 Ronald is sitting on the table pulling knobs off the stove. He is waving the knobs in the air, as if they were airplanes. He announces, "Take off, take off."

He pauses in his play to command Jon, who has strolled near Ronald at the stove, "You ain't playing here." He states this, not in an angry way, but to clearly show that he wants to be alone and that he has the authority to direct the play of his peers.

Brad tries to join the play by handing Ronald a large cardboard box the size of an orange crate. Ronald tosses the box back to Brad.

Brad kicks the box around the housekeeping area. He really seems to want Ronald's attention. They usually play together. Ronald continues to ignore Brad and Jon. Jon wanders away.

Ronald continues his airplane play alone, with much buzzing sound.

He then declares, "Take off, man." He continues "flying" the stove knobs. He is becoming more excited and enthusiastic about the flying. His voice is louder, clearly imitating his notion of airplane sounds.

9:11 "BBBBBBBBBBBBBBBB"

"uum oo oo"

"Buzz—"

"5 4 3 2 1 blast off." (Have the knobs become a rocket?)

Brad, who is sitting near Ronald in one of the boxes, turns to Ronald and entreats, "Pow, your turn to drive. Ronald, your turn to drive the car."

Brad with resignation, says, "OK, I'll drive one more time."

Brad continues to badger Ronald, "Your turn to drive the car."

Pleadingly, Brad turns to Ronald, "Would you drive the car for me?"

Ronald finally climbs into the box with Brad. (Brad smiles broadly. He seems pleased to have finally recruited his friend Ronald into play.)

Ronald asks, "Where we going to—your house?" (He seems to be enjoying himself and seems good naturedly going along with Brad in the shift to the car play.)

Brad exclaims, "Go real fast." They scoot around the floor in the box. Ronald hops out.

9:15 Ronald grabs some dishes from the stove.

Brad asks with puzzlement, "Ronald, what are you doing?"

BOX 3.4 (continued)

Ronald responds, matter-of-factly, "Putting gas in it."
Brad pronounces, "Just drive the car." Ronald hops back into the box.
Ronald sits in the box with Brad, but does not begin to drive. He turns his hands over and over (like wings).
Brad, frustrated, says, "Will you drive the car?" Ronald ignores Brad, continues making wing-like movements.
Brad agrees reluctantly: "OK, I'll drive the car."
Ronald jumps out of the box.
9:16 Ronald throws more dishes into the box.
He turns to Brad and announces, "OK, we'll throw these out as we go."
Brad says excitedly, "I got my foot on brake. We gotta get more food."
Ronald adds more dishes to the box.
Brad drops in a telephone.
Ronald throws in another phone.
Ronald shouts, "Get cover, get cover."
Both boys throw blankets in the box. (They seem to be getting a little silly. They are giggling and laughing. The play has shifted from driving a car, to throwing things into the box.)
9:17 Ronald turns to Brad and shouts as he gives him toy fruit, "Here, Mr. Smith. Here Mr. Smith."
Brad rejoins, "My name is cool Joe."
Ronald says commandingly to Kevin, "Don't play with us." (Kevin has come in and sat on the table.)
Brad falls on Kevin and laughs. Kevin joins the laughter. Brad and Kevin are rolling playfully on the floor.
9:20 Ronald threatens Kevin, "You better not laugh, kid."
Tony calls Kevin from across the room. He runs to join Tony.
Ronald and Brad settle back to the initial car game. They seem to have calmed down. Together, they plan a trip in the car to Brad's house.

---

then. Alternatives include making notes in logs or notebooks or on Post-its or cards as soon as possible after the action, discretely during the action, or asking an assistant, volunteer, or child to help remember an incident. For example, you turn to the four-year old at your elbow during story time and say, "Keisha, let's write down your comment. It added so much to our discussion." Then jot a note on the Post-it in your pocket. This serves to remind you of the high-level cognitive functioning of Keisha that you want to note with examples.

Log or notebook
These are records accumulated throughout the year on each child. For example, Ms. Myers gets spiral notebooks for each child. She keeps the

notebooks in a basket on the side of the room with a pen handy. Nearby, she hangs a calendar with the names of four children written on the days of the week when the program is running regularly. The calendar is her appointment schedule for recording observations for the children in the program. So, she does not schedule observations on days when the class will be on a field trip, the day before or after vacation, or at other high-stress times in the life of the program. Throughout the year, Ms. Myers collects observations on each child in the various areas of the room. The log is a *developmental progress record*. Ms. Myers records in her lesson plan book when she will collect these developmental progress records (Figure 3.1).

Some teachers like to make notes about each child on each day of the year. These daily logs are completed at the end of each day, then summarized at the end of each week. These are collected *anecdotes* like the examples above. They are brief and can be filled with one's own notes and abbreviations, sketches, etc. You write enough information so that you can remember the event, but the notes do not have to be so complete that by doing this, they wear you out. These are impressions or memories of what children have been doing for the day rather than live observation notes. The impression or memory material can be useful, but "live" observations must be included as well. Keep in mind that impressions and memory material have already been interpreted or filtered—conclusions have been drawn.

Writing notes are not the only observational methods for the busy teacher. Some additional methods for recording information are described in the following sections. These methods do not provide the rich insight data, but they do help teachers collect information. For example, Mr. Psujek, the third-grade teacher, plans a science project. He wants to be sure that everyone in the class uses the telescope at some point in the eight weeks. It is not necessary for him to record anecdotes or running records to assess the accomplishment of this goal. He can keep a checklist. As teachers, we do not always need to use the most complex method to assess children. We must match the knife to the purpose: a butter knife for bread, a steak knife for steak.

Checklists as records

Checklists are useful for recording skills or attributes of the children in your class. Choose checklists that are commercially available, if these are compatible with your instructional goals. Make checklists that match your teaching plans for the class. Make checklists to record progress that Zachary is making toward the goal you have set for him.

Frequency records.   **Frequency records** are teacher-developed or commercially designed checklists which teachers use to record the presence or absence of selected behaviors, how often a certain behavior occurs, or the

FIGURE 3.1 Observation in the teacher's schedule

Time	Week of Jan 3 '96					
	Mon	Tues	Wed	Thurs	Fri	Notes
9:00– 10:15	Indiv. Activities				→	Observe Anthony
10:15	Snack				→	
10:30	Story Time				→	Observe Lakesha
10:45– 11:30	Outdoor Play				→	
11:30	Dismissal	*Call Ms. Johnson	Bring Fish Food		Look for Pix for Train Theme	

quality of the behaviors. For example, you want to know how often Mary Irene drinks milk at lunch. You make a list for this and check off the days Mary Irene drinks milk. Your colleague wants to know which students can add single-digit numbers. As she observes their play at the math center, she can check off which children can accomplish this task (Figure 3.2).

As teachers develop checklists, they must be aware that these are developing "assessment" instruments. So the instruments must be derived from the philosophy and curriculum. The lists must describe skills (Figure 3.3) or target behaviors in a way that reflects appropriate developmental sequence and subject matter progression. Otherwise, these seemingly benign lists become a biased instrument. Sources for the development of checklists include program goals, child development milestones, and district-wide scope and sequence charts.

Because we value the program goal of independence, we operationalize the goal for the age of the child we teach. For example, Ms. Potenza, a second-grade teacher operationalizes the independence goal for her students as follows: Second graders arrive, hang up their coats and choose an activity from their file of "things to do." Children may work together on their projects and share experiences. During this time, Ms. Potenza collects lunch money, conducts writing conferences, and provides individual

FIGURE 3.2 Addition skills checklist

		Yes	No
Adds single digits:	Ellen	X	
	Toni	X	
	George		X
	Albert	X	
	Bernard	X	

FIGURE 3.3 Self-help checklist for the Main Street School

Teacher's Name _____   Week of _____

	Puts jacket in Cubby					Washes hands before lunch				
	M	T	W	T	F	M	T	W	T	F
Name										
Shirley	X	X	X	X	X	X	X	X	X	X
Elly	X	absent				X	absent			
Laurita	X	X	X	X	X	X	X	X	X	X
Charles	X					X				

guidance for those requesting assistance. At 9:45 the class meets to review the status of projects, to plan the day's agenda, and to listen to a story.

Modesto teachers want to asses the development of the children referred to their early intervention program. They check a child development milestone list to remind themselves of the typical sequence for the development of communication skills. They use the list as one indicator of progress, with interpretation dependent on the nature of each child's particular special need and with understanding of the issues involved in bilingual language development.

Math teachers at Middle Sized City have studied the National Council for Teachers of Mathematics Guidelines and invited experts to visit. They create a chart that shows which skills will be developed at each age level, K–12. Ms. Park uses the Kindergarten list to record which skills Kelly has developed. She finds that Kelly has mastered all of the skills. It is October. What next? Ms. Park can consult the first-grade scope and sequence material. She can use the first grade list to record Kelly's accomplishments.

Activity checklists.   Activity checklists are lists of activities that teachers prepare to record who is doing which activity during a given period. For example, you wish to know who is using puzzles, clay, blocks, the easel, books, geoboards, etc. List the activity across the top of the page. Then, down the side of the page, list the children in your class. You check or date when each child is doing one of the activities (Figure 3.4).

Event sampling

Event sampling is a record of skills or behaviors that you want the children in your class to know or to do. For example, you want to know how often William asks to share a toy; how often Lonnie is writing at the writing table; and how often Perry is at the computer center. Additional skills and attributes that can be observed and recorded in this way include:

- *Social skills*: cooperation, group cohesion, sense of fair play, competitiveness, loyalty;
- *Affective expressions*: joy, pleasure, satisfaction, self-confidence, shyness, fear;
- *Cognitive attributes*: decision making, problem solving, expressive language, exploration;
- *Creativity*: divergent response, fluency of ideas, spontaneity, flexibility, originality;
- *Enhancement to self*: sense of humor, leadership, curiosity.

Note that these skills and attributes are important life skills—ones not assessed with tests. Observation, therefore, is a critical method for assessing

FIGURE 3.4 Activity checklist

Name	Puzzles	Small Blocks	Books	Clay	Geoboards								
Laurita	1/2	1/3			2/15								
Regina			3/1	1/3									
Cheryl			3/2										
Mary			2/4										
Lisa			1/2										
Larissa					2/10								
Nancy				3/15									
Jack	2/1												
Dennis		1/4	3/5										
Duncan		2/6											

developmental progress. For example, Mr. Friedman, a second-grade teacher, values creativity. He wants to assess whether children in his room are showing creative behavior. (See Box 3.5.)

Time sampling

Time sampling is a way to check to see what is happening at a particular time with one or more children. For example, you wish to know what is happening between 1:00 and 1:15 on Mondays. You collect this information by using a running record on Martin or you use a checklist to record the activities of several children. This technique may be helpful when you feel that the program is not working smoothly. There may be a lot of running about, bickering, or waiting in line. By sampling the time period, you get an idea of who is where and begin to make some different plans. This technique also works to assess concentration and persistence for Mari.

BOX 3.5

Cognitive Event Sample Record				
Name	Divergent	Fluency	Spontaneity	Original
Arthur	3/5	3/6	3/8	3/12
Herb	3/5			
James	3/5	3/9		
Tom				
Betty				
Susan		3/6		
Dick			3/12	
Jane				3/12
Sally				
Frances				
Joey				
Marilyn				
Debbie				
Billy				
Shawn				
Sharon				
Tony				
Melissa				
Deanne				
Alan				
Tiffany				
Angela				
Jeff				
Linda				
Rick				
Joye				
Bob				
Christie				
Michael				
Brian				

BOX 3.6

Time Sample Record   *Week of April 15, 1996*

   Playground Activities for the Humming Bird School

Fifteen-minute record. Observer samples once each minute.
Observer watches one child at a time.

Child's Name	Big Wheel	Climber	Ball	Jump Rope	Not playing
Judy	x----15				
Vincent	xxxxx		x-10		
John		xxxxx	x-10		
Mari	xx	xx	xx	xx	x-6

Ms. Carr is curious whether Mari can stick to one activity on the playground, so she makes the time sample chart in Box 3.6 to check whether Mari can concentrate in outdoor play.

Rating scales

These require judgment of predetermined behavioral description. They are frequently used as part of a report card. As teachers, we are asked to decide whether an individual child possesses a particular skill or attribute and to what extent. For example, Clarence turns in homework on time (always, often, seldom, never); Arnetta writes clearly (excellent, satisfactory, needs improvement). Such procedures are subject to error and bias. For example, as teachers, you may hesitate to use the extreme positions of never and always. Unless, of course, Clarence, a third grader, needs to get a "wake up call." Never turning in homework may be a serious problem. It also may mean that the homework is irrelevant, and Clarence knows it. These rating scales may lack a common definition in the minds of teachers. What does it mean that Gloria, a four year old, has emerging or accomplished conversation skills. What exactly is expected in conversation for a four year old? Do all the teachers in the center have a shared definition? Do Gloria's parents know that "emerging" may be a problem at age four? Is it a problem at age four?

When developing or using **rating scales,** look for well-defined categories and those that are observable behaviors. For example, "recognizes five words (yes, maybe, not reading)," or "asks questions about the story (often, sometimes, never)." You can quickly observe each of the children in your class and "rate" each child's performance on these criteria. Keep in mind, then, that the more complicated the behavior is to rate, the greater the chance of error unless you and your colleagues have participated in extensive training to learn the definitions for the complicated behaviors to be rated.

Using photographs, videotapes, and audiotapes

Observational notes can be enhanced with photographs. These are particularly useful in recording sculpture, block designs, and group dynamics. Videotape and audiotape are very helpful in recording storytelling and dramatic play. However, tapes should be used sparingly, especially if the material will need to be transcribed to paper when the material is used for accountability. Transcription frequently takes two to three times as long as the original observation. For instance, a 10-minute observation may take 20 to 30 minutes to transcribe. As a permanent record of child work, tapes can be a rich source of information, since not only the words are recorded, but the affect and group dynamics as well. The environment is as important as the players in video recordings.

Portfolios

Technically speaking, **portfolios** are one type of performance-based assessment, a strategy for deciding the competency of children in a particular area or areas. The portfolio is the place to keep all the information known about each child. Observational notes form the foundation of the portfolio. To enrich the observational record, add to the collection of each child's work. A collection of children's paintings, drawings, stories, lists of books read, and other products throughout the year provides a good progress report. These materials are saved in places such as individual file folders, portfolio envelopes, file boxes, scrap books, or other convenient containers. The materials are collected to answer questions about progress in developmental areas: social/emotional skills and attitudes, language/cognitive knowledge, and gross- and fine-motor coordination. Pictures and sketches of projects that you make aid in illustrating child progress. Interviews of children about their interests, such as their favorite books, games, and activities add details of each child's year in the program. Notes of parent conferences and questions add to a well-rounded picture of each child.

Involving children in the portfolio process

As children grow older, they will want to be involved in the process of portfolio development. When you hold writing conferences with them, you can ask them to select writing samples for their permanent record. Marcia can choose which math paper shows that she has learned to add single digits. Eloise can select the painting that shows a complete story. At conference time with children, you can involve them in writing notes about their progress in social studies. Jacob may tell you that he is more comfortable in his assigned social studies project than he was at the beginning of the assignment. This gets translated into a note that says, "Jacob is feeling more comfortable in small group assignments." Harvey may tell you that he enjoys reading "bigger" or "longer" books. A conference note is included that says, "Harvey is reading books of 15 pages now." By involving the children in the selection of work to be included in a portfolio and by showing them some notes that you make at individual conferences, you are showing how assessment should be conducted. You are collecting samples of work that show skills; you are collecting *multiple* pieces of information. You are demystifying the assessment process for children. You are showing them how to assess their own progress. Regularly examining the portfolio and setting new goals shows children that learning evolves. Children can be proud of past accomplishments and help decide where they want to go next.

⊞ Limitations of the observational method

Appropriate use of observational methods depend on skillful, knowledgeable teachers. Teachers must know and understand child-development milestones. They must be sensitive to cultural, individual, and situational variations for the attainment of these milestones. Teachers must know curriculum and instruction principles. That is, they must know how children learn and how subject matter is organized.

Teachers must also avoid the following observer traps:

▌ Overinterpretation of behavior

> During an hour visit in a day-care home, Otto cried the entire time. He cried when the caregiver held him.

> *Interpretation:* Otto is ill.

Not enough information is given to sustain this interpretation. If the observer considers other factors: too many children in this facility, five infants and one caregiver; length of time in the setting and other unknown factors, Otto may be behaving appropriately for a stressful situation.

■ Making inferences from global behavioral descriptions

> While the children were reviewing their Japanese words, Barbara was excited to answer the questions, but during free play when she was playing in the doll corner, she wanted to play alone.

Interpretation: Barbara seems to be an outgoing person when it is necessary, but when she has more of a choice, she prefers to be by herself.

Answering questions in large group is not necessarily "outgoing"; nor is playing alone a reflection of isolation. There is no information about antecedent events. Did Barbara fight with friends? Do her classmates function cognitively at a different level? Is this behavior a regular occurrence?

■ Observer's personal bias

> Maria, age four, chatted with friends at the kitchen table in the house corner. Alicia suggested that the table become a diner. Maria, "No, I was here first and I want it to be my home."

Interpretation: Maria sure is bossy. Alicia is much more cooperative.

It sounds like this observer expects girls not to be assertive. The observer may not like Maria as well as Alicia and interprets Alicia more favorably.

■ Wrong focus

> David, age three, is playing with blocks. He is talking very softly to himself. Occasionally, he directs a remark to his companion, Air, in the block area. He has built a large structure. Now he seems to be hiding the small cars and animals in the structure. Air asks him what he is doing. David doesn't answer.

Interpretation: David is an isolated child who is not social.

Other possibilities: David is absorbed in the play. He is concentrating. He doesn't hear Air. The cognitive sophistication of what he is doing is missed, because the language is missing.

■ Inaccurate recordings

> George ran around the room, dumped blocks of Sally and another girl who were playing at the small group table. Then settled to work on a puzzle.

Interpretation: George is hyperactive and aggressive.

Other possibilities: George is playful. Sally and Keisha dumped his puzzle immediately before. The three engage in playful teasing and cooperative assistance in picking up puzzles. The three are working on learning to cooperate.

Failure to record times of beginning and ending of behavior

Failure to show the names of all the children involved in a segment of behavioral observation

■ Preconceived notions

Ms. Clark is sure that Danny is hyperactive. She wants his parents to take him to the pediatrician to get a pill to calm him down.

Interpretation: Danny is a problem.

Ms. Clark records notes on Danny when he is very active in the room. She does not record Danny at times when he is absorbed in an activity, even while he is moving. She neglects the language and cognitive aspects. She does not look at her schedule and routines.

⊞ Planning and scheduling observations

"Appropriate curriculum planning is based on teachers' observations and recordings of each child's special interests and developmental progress. Realistic curriculum goals and plans are based on regular assessment of individual needs, strengths, and interest. Curriculum is based on both age-appropriate and individually appropriate information."

(NAEYC, 1987, p. 3)

Your observations naturally include brief, casual observations of various children throughout the day. You adjust your teaching based on these causal observations. Significant events are recorded as *anecdotal notes* on children. Periodically, you need more in-depth *running record* observations. Finally, you need a *systematic plan* for observing and recording the behavior of all children within your program.

Your assessment plan must include regularly scheduled *running records* so that you can plan appropriate learning activities based on the needs, strengths, and interests of the children in your program. *Anecdotal notes* document special events in the lives of individual children. *Reflections* of conversations and interactions with children allow you opportunities to think about individual strengths and interests of the children in your program. *Checklists* of developmental milestones help you see progress of individual children and provide a group summary. *Records of conferences* with parents assist you in building a total picture of each child in the context of family.

In these ways you are constantly gathering observational information to provide the best program possible for all of the children. This is a difficult and exhausting task. It is not the only task that a teacher faces. You must make, set up, and prepare materials. You must talk to children, help them settle into routines, and empathize with them. You must lead the group in song, story, and fun. You are a model of curiosity, good humor, and enthusiasm. You must set the tone for your assistant and parent volunteers. You must meet with parents. You must handle crises as they emerge.

The real world of everyday teaching

Observation is the partner of instruction. You can't teach well without observing. For example, as you set out the finger paints every day for a week, you notice that Jimmy won't touch them. Popping a Post-it note out of your pocket, you record an *anecdote*.

Six weeks after the beginning of the year, you sit one afternoon with your favorite checklist. For the next week, while the children are napping or participating in an informal group activity at lunch or recess, you reflect on each child and check the list accordingly. When you run into questions you can't answer, you plan to find out whether a particular child "uses two or more sentences to tell me something" by engaging this child in conversion.

Using the schedule you have made for yourself, you systematically gather *running records* on everyone throughout the year. You file them away, to use as you prepare reports and meet with parents. Obviously when an emergency occurs and staff is short, the schedule gets changed.

In summary, you have a responsibility to plan systematic observation for each child in your program. Just as you plan what you teach—which activities, structure of the room, schedule for the day, and staff interactions with children in a developmentally appropriate way—you must collect observational information on each child regularly, covering all aspects of development. Some information must be written down. Your plan must reflect the philosophy and realities of your program. Practical suggestions for collecting the information have been included in this chapter. You must decide how many running records, anecdotes, logs, and checklists to collect on each child. You will need a balance of observations for each of the methods so that you will have the material you need to confer with parents and to write developmental reports.

Summary

Keeping track of your observations on the children in your class makes it easier for you to teach them well. Recording observation notes and using

ACTIVITIES

1. With a partner, go to the cafeteria or other busy place on campus. Each of you should watch the action for ten minutes at a time. Record the details. Discuss your results with your partner. What were the similarities and differences? Which presents the more accurate picture? See what you missed and try again.

2. At the local supermarket on the weekend, station yourself in the cereal aisle. Watch parent and child interactions. Record details. Develop a checklist based on your initial observations. Collect information on several children. What patterns did you observe?

3. Go to the park or other community location where primary-aged children can be found. Draw a sketch of the area. Develop a checklist of the areas: basketball, climber, swings, benches, etc. Record ages and sex of children who participate in the diverse areas of the playground. Use this information to make after-school teaching plans based on your observations of the usage patterns and the goals for the after-school program.

4. Interview teachers in preschool and primary settings about how they use observation and records in planning for instruction. List each specific type and the purposes related to each type. Discuss ways that they use the material to solve teaching problems, to talk with parents, and to refer young children for any special intervention that may be necessary.

checklists takes time in an already busy day, but it makes you a prepared teacher.

Observation is the tool you use to make teaching decisions whether you write them down or not. Writing the notes, making the checks, or otherwise keeping track of your thoughts on the children in your class helps you be the best teacher for all the children in your care. In the end, you'll be better organized. You'll know which methods are working with which children. You'll be able to answer questions about cognitive, social/emotional, motor and language development, and academic progress with precision and examples. You'll feel more confident about your judgments and insights, since you have organized and planned for your assessments. You've made the link from the curriculum to assessment and completed the circle—teach, evaluate, reteach.

⊞ CHAPTER 3 Suggested further readings

Almy, M., & Genishi, C. (1979). *Ways of studying children* (rev. ed.). New York: Teachers College.

Beaty, J. (1994). *Observing development of the young child* (3rd ed.). Columbus, OH: Merrill.

Bentzen, W. R. (1993). *Seeing young children: A guide to observing and recording behavior* (2nd ed.). Albany, NY: Delmar.

Cohen, R., Stern, V., & Balban, N. (1983). *Observing and recording the behavior of young children* (3rd ed.). New York: Teachers College.

CHAPTER 3 Study questions

1. Why is observation the cornerstone of an early childhood assessment system? What are the diverse ways to record observations? How do early childhood teachers decide which is the appropriate method for a given situation?

2. How does observational information fit into the portfolio process in early childhood programs?

3. What is an anecdotal note? Which assessment situations are most suited for the use of this method?

4. Under which conditions should early childhood teachers consider using running records?

5. When is a checklist appropriate for early childhood teachers to use in an assessment program? How can teachers construct their own?

6. What assessment information can be collected by event sampling? frequency recording? time sampling? How do these records compare to anecdotal notes and running records?

7. Rating scales are most appropriate for which early childhood situations?

References

Almy, M., & Genishi, C. (1979). *Ways of studying children* (rev. ed.). New York: Teachers College.

Baker, E., O'Neil, H., & Linn, R. (1993). Policy and validity prospects for performance-based assessment. *American Psychologist, 48*(12), 1210–1218.

Baumann, E., McDonough, S., & Mindes, G. (1974). *Classroom observation guide for head start teachers.* Chicago: City of Chicago, Department of Human Services.

Bredekamp, S. (1987). *Developmentally appropriate practice in early childhood programs serving children birth through age 8.* Washington, DC: National Association for the Education of Young Children.

Cohen, D., Stern, V., & Balaban, N. (1983). *Observing and recording the behavior of young children* (3rd ed.). New York: Teachers College.

Cook, R. E., Tessier, A., & Klein, M. D. (1987). *Adapting early childhood curriculum for children with special needs* (3rd Ed.). Columbus, OH: Merrill.

Greenberg, P. (1991). personal communication.

Greenspan, S. I. (1981). *The clinical interview of the child*. New York: McGraw-Hill.

Higginbotham, M. L. O., & Pretzello, L. (nd). *Observation: Implications for appropriate early childhood assessment*. Unpublished manuscript. Louisiana State University Medical Center, New Orleans.

Phinney, J. S. (1982). Observing children: Ideas for teachers. *Young Children*, pp. 16–24.

Wortham, S. C. (1995). *Measurement and evaluation in early childhood education*. Columbus, OH: Merrill.

CHAPTER 4

Using Basic Concepts of Measurement

Terms to Know

- mean
- raw score
- range
- standard deviation
- normal curve
- standardized test
- norm-referenced test
- population
- normative sample
- norms
- criterion-referenced test
- derived scores
- age-equivalent scores
- grade-equivalent scores
- interpolated score
- extrapolated score
- percentile ranks
- deviation quotients

- normal-curve equivalents
- stanines
- reliability
- test-retest reliability
- interscorer reliability
- correlation coefficient
- standard errors of measurement (Sem)
- validity
- face validity
- content validity
- criterion-related validity
- concurrent validity
- predictive validity
- sensitivity
- specificity
- construct validity

CHAPTER OVERVIEW In this chapter all the basic concepts needed to use tests and other measurement devices in a developmentally appropriate manner are fully described so that teachers and childcare workers can communicate confidently with parents, administrators, psychologists, and other professionals about all aspects of tests and other assessment tools and what they mean in the lives of young children.

Topics Discussed

▮ Importance of basic concepts of measurement for teachers

▮ Terminology

▮ Standardization and norms

▮ Different types of test scores—developmental, percentiles, standard scores

▮ Reliability

▮ Validity

▮ Guidelines for test evaluation

⊞ Importance of basic concepts of measurement for teachers

Most teachers believe that understanding basic principles of measurement is an important aspect of classroom teaching and evaluation (Borg, Worthen, & Valcarce, 1986). But what exactly is "measurement"? According to Goodwin and Goodwin (1982), it is "the process of determining, through observation or testing, an individual's traits or behaviors, a program's characteristics, or the property of some other entity, and then assigning a number, rating, or score to that determination" (p. 523). In order for you, as a teacher, to understand how to evaluate tests, interpret test results adequately, and make appropriate use of other types of assessment (inventories, observation techniques, functional assessment, portfolio, authentic assessment, etc.), you should be familiar with some concepts and terms of measurement. Some of them will already be familiar to you from other contexts; others are more specific to tests. You will need to understand this vocabulary to be a good consumer of tests. By understanding tests and their properties, you will know when it is appropriate to use one and whether you have found a good one.

According to the National Association for the Education of Young Children (1988), while school principals, superintendents, or state school officials are responsible for decisions of "whether to use standardized testing, how to critically evaluate existing tests, how to carefully select appropriate and accurate tests to be used with a population and purpose for which the test was designed, and how to use and interpret the results yielded from standardized tests to parents, school personnel, and the media, . . . *teachers are responsible for administering tests and, therefore, have a professional responsibility to be knowledgeable about appropriate testing and to influence, or attempt to influence, the selection and use of tests"* (p. 43). (Emphasis added).

⊞ Terminology

Mean

Everyone is familiar with the word "average." The average is also known as the **mean**, the arithmetic average of a group of scores. To calculate the mean age of one of your reading groups in which the children are 70, 72, 73, 76, 78, and 81 months old:

1. add all the ages (450)
2. divide by the number of children (6)

Thus the mean of these numbers is 75.

$$70 + 72 + 73 + 76 + 78 + 81 = \frac{450}{6} = 75$$

Let's say that you want to check the understanding that your second graders have of the subtraction facts. Over a number of days you establish how many of the facts each child knows. You record their names and total facts known as shown in Figure 4.1. You add their total scores (624) and divide by the number of children in your class (24). Now you know each child's score and the mean for the group (26). You can also see if each child is above or below the mean.

Raw score

The first score one usually obtains on either a published test or a teacher-made test is the **raw score,** the number of items that the child answered correctly. To know each child's raw score is important when you wish to increase that score in comparison to the child's previous scores. However, raw scores provide little information about a child's performance in comparison with other children.

Range

When you are dealing with the scores of your class, the next measure you want to determine is based on the variability of the scores, how different they are from each other. The **range** is the "spread" of the scores or the difference between the top score and the bottom score. In the example where

FIGURE 4.1 The number of subtraction facts known by children in Miss Take's class

Child's name	# of facts	Child's name	# of facts
Alex	25	Lola	19
Ben	27	Maria	15
Christina	20	Martin	30
David	29	Norris	18
Dina	29	Paul	22
Ilana	31	Peter	12
Jerry	28	Ruth	28
Josiah	32	Sam	33
Juan	36	Sarah	11
Katie	30	Tara	17
Kim	40	Winston	29
Liz	23	Yolanda	40

we calculated the mean chronological age of the reading group, the range is 11. This is the difference between the lowest number (70) and the highest number (81) in the group or *distribution* of scores (81 − 70 = 11). The range is not a very sensitive measure because it is dependent on only two scores in the distribution, the highest and lowest.

Standard deviation

A very important measure which helps us quantify the "spread" of the distribution is the **standard deviation.** It measures the distance scores depart from the mean. If a distribution of scores is large enough, the scores will usually form a bell-shaped curve, known as a normal distribution (Figure 4.2). This bell-shaped or **normal curve** represents the distribution of a large number of human attributes including height, weight, and for our purposes, test scores. A normal distribution is hypothetically the way scores on a test would cluster if the particular test were given to every single child of the same age or grade in the populations for whom the test was designed. The pattern shows that most children are about average, a few are slightly above or below average, and even fewer have extremely high or low scores. The mean score, by definition, is in the middle of this hypothetical normal distribution so that half of the scores will be higher than the mean and half will be lower. The standard deviation is a unit of mea-

FIGURE 4.2 Different types of standard scores on the normal curve

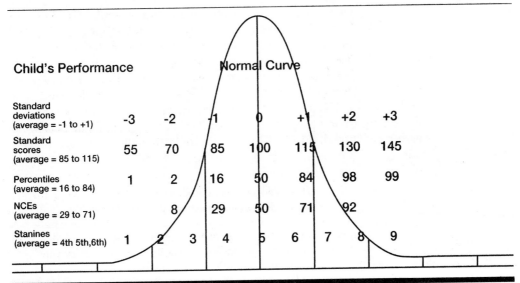

surement that represents the typical amount that a score can be expected to vary from the mean in a given set of data or on a particular test.

Looking at Figure 4.2, we can see that a large number of the scores fall near the mean or the "hump" part of the curve. Approximately 34% of the scores fall between the mean and one standard deviation above the mean; approximately 34% of the scores fall between the mean and one standard deviation below the mean. Thus, two-thirds of the scores (68%) fall between one standard deviation above the mean and one standard deviation below the mean. This means that two out of every three scores are within this range; this is certainly the "average" or to use another term frequently applied in early childhood education, the "normal" range. Approximately 14% of the scores fall between one and two standard deviations above the mean and another 14% fall between one and two standard deviations below the mean. If we go from two standard deviations below the mean to two standard deviations above the mean, we have taken into account approximately 96% of all scores (14% + 34% + 34% + 14%). That leaves only two percent at the low end and two percent at the high end of distribution.

Later in this chapter we will apply your understanding of these terms and their importance will become even clearer.

▦ Standardization and norms

Unlike teacher-made tests, most published tests are **standardized tests** or **norm-referenced tests,** which means they have undergone a lengthy and often costly process in their development. While standardized tests are indispensable for clinical and psychoeducational assessment (Sattler, 1988), they play a less important role in most early childhood and primary grade settings. However, early childhood educators should understand how such tests are developed and when they are needed. When they are properly designed and properly used, standardized tests eliminate bias in the assessment of individual children and provide data that can be combined, allowing comparisons of groups to a standard (Hills, 1992).

According to Green (1981),

> A standardized test is a task or a set of tasks given under standard conditions and designed to assess some aspect of a person's knowledge, skill, or personality. A test provides a scale of measurement for consistent individual differences regarding some psychological concept and serves to line up people according to a concept. Tests can be thought of as yardsticks, but they are less efficient and reliable than yardsticks. . . . A test yields one or more objectively obtained quantitative scores, so that, as nearly as possible, each person is assessed in the same way. . . . to provide a fair and equitable comparison among test takers (p. 1001).

Thus, a standardized (norm-referenced) test interprets a child's performance in comparison to the performance of other children with similar characteristics.

In designing a standardized test, test developers must first determine its rationale and purpose. Secondly, they must explain what the test will measure (there are many types of standardized tests such as achievement tests, readiness tests, developmental screening tests, diagnostic tests, and intelligence tests); whom the test will be given to; and how the test results will be used. Test developers try to adhere to the standards developed by the American Educational Research Association, the American Psychological Association, and the National Council on Measurement in Education (1974, 1985) which sets standards for test users as well as test developers. According to the National Association for the Education of Young Children (1988), while "the burden of proof for the validity and reliability of tests is on the test developers . . . the burden of proof for the utility of tests is on administrators or teachers of early childhood programs who make decisions about the use of tests in individual classrooms. Similarly, the burden of responsibility for *choosing, administering, scoring, and interpreting a score from a standardized test rests with the early childhood professional and thus demands that professionals be both skilled and responsible*" (p. 47). (Emphasis added.)

FIGURE 4.3 Relationship between a population and a sample

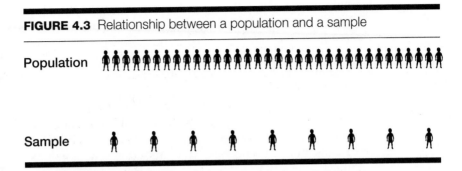

The **population,** or group of individuals, on which the test is normed is of utmost importance. Even if it were possible, it is not necessary to test everyone in a particular population to make the norms applicable. The characteristics of a population can be accurately estimated from the characteristics of a subset of the population as long as the subset closely resembles the population in terms of specific characteristics. These characteristics must also be present in the subset in the same proportion that they are present in the population for this subset to be representative. Such a subset is called the **normative sample**. Inferences based on what has been learned from the sample (subset) can be extended to the population at large so that inferences can be made about the population (Salvia & Ysseldyke, 1991). Figure 4.3 illustrates the relationship between a population and a sample.

Norming is the process of administering a test in a systematic and consistent way to a large, representative sample for the purpose of preparing comparative scores. **Norms** are the scores obtained from testing the normative sample (Hammill, Brown, & Bryant, 1992). The adequacy of these norms, according to Salvia and Ysseldyke (1995), is dependent on three factors: the *representativeness* of the norm sample, the *number* of children in the sample, and the *relevance* of the norms in terms of the purpose of the test.

When looking at the representativeness of the norm sample, it is common to look at the following factors: age, grade (for children in kindergarten or above), gender, geographic regions, socioeconomic status (which has a consistent relationship to how children perform on intellectual and academic tests), and racial or ethnic cultural differences. The importance of this last factor cannot be over-emphasized. "Assessment strategies that are not sensitive to cultural differences in learning style and rate and those that are not designed for children from linguistically diverse backgrounds cannot provide an accurate picture of children's strengths and needs"

(Hills, 1992, p. 48). Public law 94–142 mandates nondiscriminatory assessment; this requires fair and objective testing practices for students from all cultural and linguistic backgrounds.

The number of children in the normative sample is also important. One hundred subjects per age or grade is considered to be the minimum as an acceptable size.

The test user must be prepared to determine the relevance of the norms for his or her group of children or population. Generally speaking, for early childhood educators working with children in regular classrooms, nursery schools, or daycare settings, national norms would be the most appropriate.

The date of the norms is also significant because we live in a rapidly changing society. For a norm sample to be appropriate, it must also be current. Norms that are more than fifteen years old are considered out-of-date (Salvia & Ysseldyke, 1995).

There is another category of standardized tests, a **criterion-referenced test,** that compares a child's performance to his or her own progress in learning a set of skills or behaviors that can be arranged according to difficulty level. Such a test does not need to be normed.

Different types of test scores—developmental, percentiles, standard scores

When we try to determine if a child has learned all the addition facts of single-digit numbers, it is relatively simple to determine this through direct assessment in the classroom since there is a finite number of these facts. However, most information that we wish to assess is not finite, even for young children, so we are forced to ask a few questions and base our decisions on the assumption that what we learn from assessing a sample of behavior will give us an accurate picture of performance for the entire topic.

The most important reason for assessing a child's performance or behavior is to enable the teacher to develop appropriate lessons based on what the child can and cannot do. Since the teacher needs to know if the learning activity is suitable for a child of a particular age, test scores enable the teacher to determine the amount of difference that the child exhibits in a particular area from the expected level for his or her age or grade. In addition, the teacher must understand how to use information provided in test manuals.

Remember, the first score obtained from a test is the raw score, the number of items on either a published test or a teacher-made test that the child answered correctly. When you are using a standardized test, this score must be compared with the performance of a group of children of known characteristics (age, sex, grade, etc.) that are described in the test manual. These comparison scores are **derived scores** and are obtained by using the raw scores along with tables in the manual. Three types of derived scores are frequently used with young children: developmental scores (age-equivalent and grade-equivalent scores), percentiles, and standard scores.

Developmental scores

Developmental scores—**age-equivalent scores** and **grade-equivalent scores**—have been widely used in the past and are reported in test manuals mainly because they enjoy a false reputation as easily understood and useful scores (Hammill, et al., 1992). An example of a developmental age-equivalent score is 3–2. This score means that the child's performance on the test is considered to be the same as an average child who is three years, two months old. This score would then have to be compared with the child's actual chronological age. An example of a developmental grade-equivalent score is 3.2 (the same numerals as the above example but separated by a decimal point instead of a hyphen). This score means that the child's performance on the test is considered to be the same as an average child who is in the second month of the third grade. This score would then have to be compared with the child's actual grade placement. Developmental scores are obtained by computing the mean raw score made by children of a given age or grade. That point is recorded on a graph that has raw scores along one axis and age or grade levels on the other axis. Points are plotted for the scores obtained at different ages or grades and a line is drawn to connect these points so that one can easily determine what age or grade corresponds to each raw score. Figure 4.4 shows a graph for assigning raw scores to children in kindergarten, grade one, and grade two on the fictitious Amerikan Reeding Test.

The graph in Figure 4.4 indicates that only children at the beginning of the school year, three months into the school year, and six months into the school year participated in the norming. The asterisks indicate the mean score of the children in the normative sample. This information would be found in a table in the manual so you would know, for instance, that the derived grade-equivalent score for a raw score of 11 is 1.4. Such scores obviously are not based directly on evidence collected for children of a particular chronological age or grade but are interpolated or extrapolated. An example of an **interpolated score** would be if we tested a child whose derived score is between two points where data were actually collected, as in the above example. The derived score in the manual is interpolated because no children at that grade placement (1.4) were actually tested to establish that score. An example of an **extrapolated score** would be if we

FIGURE 4.4 Raw scores earned by K-2 samples on the Amerikan Reeding Test

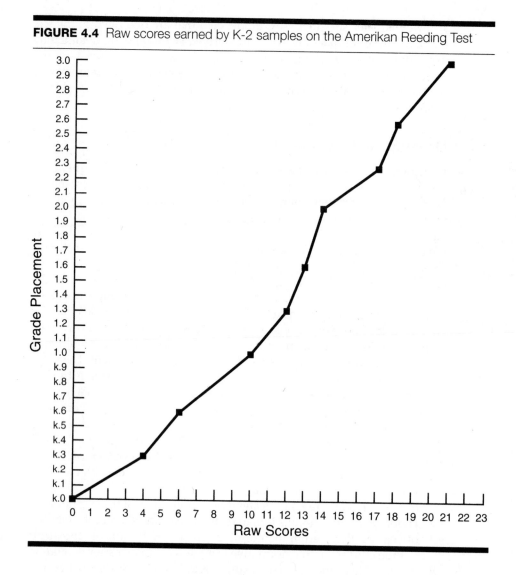

used this test with a child whose raw score was beyond 21. We would have to extend the hypothetical line to determine the grade placement.

According to Salvia and Ysseldyke (1995), there are at least four other types of problems with using developmental scores. For example, there is no such entity as an average 3–0 child (a child three years old) or an average 3.0 child (a child entering third grade) just as there is no such entity as an average family of 1.2 children. They are merely statistical abstractions and should be dealt with as such. In fact, both the International Reading Association (1980) and the Committee to Develop Standards for Educational and Psychological Testing (American Educational Research Association, American Psychological Association, and National Council on Measurement in Education, 1985) have recommended that developmental scores be abandoned. However, if you are going to deal with developmental scores, remember that age-equivalents are written with hyphens (2–3, 4–11, 6–9, etc.) to represent number of months in a year whereas grade-equivalents are written with decimal points (k.7, 2.3, 3.5, etc.) to represent months in a grade, which assumes that the school term is ten months long.

Percentile ranks

On the other hand, **percentile ranks** are more useful scores. They are derived scores which indicate the percentage of individuals in the normative group whose test scores fall at or below a given raw score. The percentile rank should not be confused with percentages; it is *not* the percentage of correct answers. Rather it is based on the percent of people who obtained the same number of correct answers. For example, if a child in your class receives a percentile rank of 84 on a particular test, it does *not* mean that she knew the answers to 84 percent of the problems on that test; it means that she scored as well as or better than 84 percent of the children in the sample for that test. Looking at Figure 4–2, you can see that the 84th percentile is at the top end of the average range.

Percentile ranks are not equal distances from each other. If we were to draw 100 vertical lines through the normal curve, with each line representing a percentile rank, the lines would be very close to each other near the center of the curve and get progressively further apart from each other as they moved to either end. Thus, there is a big difference between being in the 98th percentile as opposed to the 99th percentile while there is a very small difference between the 50th percentile and the 51st percentile. In addition, because they do not represent equal differences, they cannot be added, subtracted, multiplied, or divided.

Standard scores

A standard score, on the other hand, is the general name for any derived score that has been transformed or changed in some way so that the mean and standard deviation have predetermined values. Unlike percentiles, these derived scores are equal distances on the normal curve. Although there are five commonly used standard score distributions (z-scores, T-scores, deviation IQs, normal-curve equivalents, and stanines), only the last three will be discussed since these are the three most commonly needed by early childhood educators.

A deviation IQ is a misnomer because it is a derived score obtained from many different types of tests, not just an IQ or intelligence test. It has this name merely because it was first transformed for this type of test. More recently, this type of score is called a deviation quotient. **Deviation quotients** are standard scores with a mean of 100 and a standard deviation of (usually) 15. This type of score is widely used on *individually* administered tests of all types (intelligence, achievement, motor, language, etc.)

Normal-curve equivalents (NCEs) are standard scores generally found on *group* tests. Unlike percentiles, this scale divides the normal curve into 100 equal intervals with a mean equal to 50 and a standard deviation equal to 21.06. Figure 4.2 indicates that NCEs within the average zone range from 29 to 71.

Stanines are also standard scores which are less precise than the other two standard scores just described. The word "stanine" is a blend of standard and nine. Stanines divide the distribution into nine parts or bands. The middle stanine, the fifth, is .25 standard deviation above the mean and .25 standard deviation below the mean. The second, third, and fourth stanines are each .5 standard deviations in width below the mean, respectively, and the sixth, seventh, and eighth stanines are each .5 standard deviations in width above the mean, respectively. Finally, the first and ninth stanines are each 1.75 standard deviations or more below and above the mean, respectively. As a rule of thumb, the first, second, and third stanines represent below average performance (23%); the fourth, fifth, and sixth stanines are average performance (54%); and the seventh, eighth, and ninth stanines represent above average performance (23%). Parents may understand stanines easier than any other type of standard score by using the following scale to describe a child's performance:

9 Very superior
8 Superior
7 Considerably above average
6 Slightly above average
5 Average
4 Slightly below average
3 Considerably below average
2 Poor
1 Very poor

(Psychological Corporation, 1984, p. 4)

Thus, although it is not as precise as other standard scores, the usefulness of the stanine lies in the fact that it is a single-digit score and easily understood by parents.

⊞ Reliability

Reliability refers to consistency, dependability, or stability. A test needs to be reliable so that teachers and others can generalize from the current test results to other times and circumstances. If a test can generalize to different times, it has **test-retest reliability**. We can assume that we would get the same results tomorrow or next week. The typical length of time between the first test administration and the second is two weeks.

If a test can generalize to other similar test items, it has *internal consistency*, *split-half*, or *alternate form* reliability. We can assume that different test items would give us similar results.

If a test can generalize to other testers (people who administer the test), it has inter-rater or **interscorer reliability**. We can assume that if other testers would administer the test, they would obtain the same results.

These different types of reliability are reported in the test manual as correlation coefficients so you need to know what a correlation coefficient is. Without knowing how to compute it, it is still possible to understand it. A correlation is simply a measure of how things are related to one another; it is a measure of whether there is an association between two variables and if so, how much. The degree of relationship between two variables is called a **correlation coefficient** that can range from $+1.00$ to -1.00; no relationship at all is in the middle or .00. The number of the correlation coefficient tells us the strength of the relationship (the closer it is to one, the stronger it is) and the sign ($+$ or $-$) tells us the direction of the relationship. If the relationship is positive ($+$), as one variable goes up, so does the other. On the other hand, if the relationship is negative ($-$), as one variable goes up, the other goes down. An example of a positive relationship is the age of a child and his or her height. Generally speaking, as the child gets older, the child gets taller. An example of a negative relationship is the distance between the source of a sound and the ability to hear it. As the distance you are from a ringing phone increases, the ability to hear it decreases. An example of no correlation is the number of permanent teeth a child has and readiness to read as reported by Gredler (1992). Most correlation coefficients reported in test manuals are positive.

When considering correlations, remember that correlations do not indicate causality. Just because two variables are correlated, it does not mean that one has caused the other. For instance, scores on intelligence tests and scores on achievement tests usually are positively correlated. In this case, one cannot say that high intelligence scores cause high achievement scores nor that high achievement scores cause high intelligence scores. It is possible that another variable may cause either or both of these results. As there are at least three possible interpretations, we should never draw causality conclusions from such data.

Another important statistic that should be reported in a test manual is the **standard error of measurement (Sem).** It is commonly acknowledged that no test, no matter how well it is designed, is free from error. The reliability of a test depends of the size of the Sem. The larger the Sem, the less reliable the test. That is because the Sem is the estimate of the amount of variation that can be expected in test scores as a result of reliability correlations. Let's say a child in your class took an individual intelligence test that yielded a standard score of 88. The mean of this test is 100 and the standard deviation is 15. At first glance this score suggests that the child is in the average range of 85 to 115 where 68% of the normative population would score. However, the Sem for this particular test is 10. That means the confidence band for this score is that two out of three times, this child's true score will be between 78 and 98 (88 + or − 10); one out of three times, it will be above or below this band. If the Sem for this test was 3 instead of 10, you would have more confidence in the results because then the confidence band would be 88, (+ or − 3) and the true score would fall between 85 and 91 two out of three times. The smaller the Sem, the more reliable the test is because the scores fluctuate less. Thus, you can have more confidence in its stability. Figure 4.5 illustrates this example with the two confidence bands.

The top line shows the derived standard score of 88 on the normal curve without considering any standard error of measurement (Sem). Above the second line, you can see the range where the child's true score would fall two out of three times if the Sem is 10. Below the second line, you can see the range where the child's true score would fall two out of three times if the Sem is 3.

There are several variables that affect reliability and can thus inflate or deflate the reliability coefficients. The longer the test, meaning that it has more test items, the more reliable it will be. That is one of the main reasons diagnostic tests are more reliable than screening tests which, by their very definition and purpose, are shorter tests with less items. Another factor that is very relevant to early childhood tests and test length is the fact that many tests for young children do not have enough items at the lowest age levels so that the child has fewer opportunities to demonstrate ability (Bracken, 1987a). In other words, the difficulty level at the beginning of the test is too steep, which affects its reliability. When standard scores increase or decrease as a function of a child's success or failure on a single test item, the test is less sensitive to small differences in the child's abilities. Thus, a test should have enough easy items to discriminate properly at the lower end of the range (Bracken, 1987b).

The shorter the time interval between two administrations of the same test, the higher the reliability coefficient. Thus, when looking at this statistic in a test manual, the amount of time between the two test administrations must be stated and taken into account.

FIGURE 4.5 The influence of confidence bands (Sem) on the interpretation of a score

55	70	85	100	115	130	145
−3	−2	−1	0	+1	+2	+3

Sem = 10
88 (+ or − 10)

78 79 80 81 82 83 84 85 86 87 88 89 90 91 92 93 94 95 96 97 98 99

Sem = 3
88 (+ or − 3)

The larger the norming sample, the more reliable the test will be which is a good reason for adhering to the minimum recommended size of the normative sample. Finally, the range of test scores obtained from the normative sample can also affect the test's reliability. The wider the spread, the more reliably the test can distinguish between them.

Validity

Validity refers to the extent to which a test measures what it is supposed to measure. It tells how meaningful the test results really are. The validity of a test is not measured per se; rather it is judged on the basis of its reliability and the adequacy of its norms. Although the different types of test validity will be discussed separately, in reality they are interdependent.

Face validity is whether the test looks as if it is testing what it is supposed to be testing. This type of validity is very superficial; yet it is important to both the child taking the test and the person selecting the test. For example, if a mathematics test did not have addition, subtraction, multiplication, and division problems, it would not have face validity even if it were a very valid mathematics test based on other types of validity.

Content validity is established by evaluating three factors: how appropriate the items are; how complete the item samples are; and the way in which the items assess the content (Salvia & Ysseldyke, 1995; Sattler, 1988). This type of validity is especially important for achievement and adaptive behavior tests. When utilizing this type of validity, the user must keep in mind the appropriate use of the test. For example, one would not use a mathematics test for determining reading ability.

Criterion-related validity is the relationship between the scores on a test and another (criterion) measure. Of course, this criterion must itself be valid if it is to be used to establish the validity of a test. This type of validity is usually expressed as a correlation coefficient between the test and the criterion. The criterion does not have to be a test but often is.

There are two categories of criterion-related validity that differ only on the basis of time. **Concurrent validity** is the relationship between a test and the criterion when the evidence is obtained at approximately the same time. For example, when a new test is developed, a portion of the normative sample is usually administered with a well-established test at the same time. During the development of the Kaufman Assessment Battery for Children (K–ABC), children in the sample were administered the Wechsler Intelligence Scales for Children–Revised (WISC–R), a well-established intelligence test for children. If the scores on the new test correlate highly with the scores on the well-established test, then the new test is said to have concurrent validity. The concurrent validity of a screening test is usually judged by the amount of agreement the scores have when a sample of children are administered an intelligence test. **Predictive validity** refers to how accurately the child's current test score can be used to estimate performance on some variable or criterion in the future. For example, you administer a reading-readiness test to your kindergartners. The test should have established predictive validity when it was designed so that you know, by means of a correlation coefficient, the relationship of your children's scores to reading scores at the end of first grade or second grade on a specific reading achievement test (the criterion). Predictive validity strongly suggests that if a child currently has a score that indicates a developmental delay, the likelihood is that the child is at risk of future school failure.

Developmental screening tests, widely used in early-childhood settings, should also report another important type of predictive validity that measures the test's accuracy in correctly detecting children with and without problems. If a developmental screening test under-identifies children with problems, it defeats the very purpose for which it was designed. If it over-identifies children, this results in needless parental anxiety and expense and wastes limited diagnostic resources (Glascoe & Byrne, 1993). Thus, developmental screening tests should report in their manuals their sensitivity and specificity. **Sensitivity** is an indicator of how well a test identifies children with delays (Glascoe, 1991). Quantitatively, it is the percentage of children with problems who are correctly identified (a rate of about 80% is considered preferable) (Glascoe & Byrne, 1993). **Specificity** is an indicator of how well a test identifies children without delays (Glascoe,

1991). Quantitatively, it is the percentage of children without problems who are correctly identified (a rate of 90% is expected here because there are so many more children without problems in the general population, usually 88 to 90 percent) (Glascoe & Byrne, 1993). Finally, the predictive validity of the test is measured by the percentage of children who failed the developmental screening test who have true developmental problems on a diagnostic test (the criterion). This rate should be 70–75% (Glascoe & Byrne, 1993).

It may be easier to understand sensitivity and specificity by looking at Figure 4.6 (Adapted from Lerner, Mardell-Czudnowski, & Goldenberg, 1987 and Cicchetti & Wagner, 1990). The results of the developmental screening test are found on the left-hand side of the box ("Yes" means to refer for further testing; "no" means the child passed the screening test.) The results of the criterion test, which is a more in-depth diagnostic test, are found at the top of the box ("Yes" means the child does have a problem; "no" means the child does not have a problem.) The top left-hand cell is the sensitivity or score or hits, the percentage of children who were correctly identified by the developmental screening test because the criterion test confirmed that there was a problem. The bottom right-hand cell is the specificity score or true rejections, the percentage of children who do not have problems according to both measures. When the developmental screening test indicates that a child has a problem which is not confirmed by the criterion, this is known as a false positive (over-referral) and would be the percentage found in the top right-hand cell. When the developmental screening test indicates that a child does not have a problem but the criterion test indicates that there is a problem, this is known as a false negative (under-referral), and would be the percentage found in the lower left-hand cell. As mentioned before, both types of errors are serious and affect the predictive validity of the developmental screening test.

Construct validity refers to the extent to which a test measures a theoretical characteristic or trait such as personality, intelligence, or creativity. These traits are considered theoretical because they are not observable behaviors that can be seen or measured directly. As such, this may be the most difficult type of validity to establish.

Just as there are factors which affect reliability, there are factors which affect validity. First, there are test-related factors such as anxiety, motivation, understanding of instructions, rapport between the examiner and the examinee, degree of bilingualism, unfamiliarity with the test material, and differences in other ways from the norm of the standardization group. Obviously the test is not valid for children who are uncooperative, highly distractible, or who fail to understand the test instructions (Sattler, 1988).

Secondly, validity is affected by factors related to the criterion used in establishing criterion-related validity. The length of time for establishing

FIGURE 4.6 Sensitivity and specificity diagnosis (the criterion)

	yes	no
yes	hits (true positives)	false alarms (false positives/ over-referral)
screening		
no	misses (false negatives/ under-referral)	correct rejections (true negatives)

$$\frac{\text{sensitivity}}{\text{(accurate referral)}} = \frac{\text{hits}}{\text{hits + misses}}$$

$$\frac{\text{specificity}}{\text{(accurate non-referral)}} = \frac{\text{true negatives}}{\text{false positives + true negatives}}$$

Adapted from J. Lerner, C. Mardell-Czudnowski, & D. Goldenberg, (1987). *Special Education for the Early Childhood Years*, p. 87, copyright 1987 by Allyn & Bacon, reprinted/adapted by permission; and D. Cicchetti, & S. Wagner, (1990). Alternative assessment strategies for the evaluation of infants and toddlers: An organizational perspective. In S. Meisels and J. Shonkoff (Eds.). *Handbook of early childhood intervention*. NY: Cambridge, University Press, p. 252. Reprinted with the permission of Cambridge University Press.

predictive validity is also a factor as well as intervening events such as special education.

Finally, validity is affected by the test's reliability. A test cannot be valid unless it is reliable so reliability is a necessary, but not the only, condition for validity.

Guidelines for test evaluation

Teachers are often expected to serve on committees for the purpose of selecting a standardized test, particularly a developmental screening test or a group achievement test. Early childhood teachers should be able to evaluate standardized tests, both in terms of their technical adequacy (norms, reliability, and validity) and their appropriateness for a particular group of children. The principles followed in the evaluation of a test should always be in congruence with the NAEYC Position Statement on Standardized Testing of Young Children Three Through Eight Years of Age (1988) and the Code of Ethical Conduct established by the National Association for the Education of Young Children (Feeney & Kipnis, 1989).

Evaluating tests is not a simple proposition. Even though there are standards which have been developed by a joint committee of three prestigious and knowledgeable organizations (the American Educational Research Association, the American Psychological Association, and the National Council on Measurement in Education, 1985), not all standards will be uniformly applicable across the wide range of instruments and uses that currently exist. However, just as test developers have responsibility to provide adequate information in the test manual, test users who need the scores for some decision-making purpose, such as teachers and administrators, have ethical responsibility in selecting appropriate tests that meet the necessary standards for making decisions about children.

The above committee that formulated the standards was joined by the American Speech-Language-Hearing Association and the American Association for Counseling and Development/Association for Measurement and Evaluation in Counseling to write a briefer document which differs from the Standards in both audience and purpose. The *Code of Fair Testing Practices in Education* is meant to be understood by the general public; thus, it is less technical than the Standards. It is limited to educational tests whereas the Standards apply to every type of published test. Finally, the primary focus is on those issues that affect the proper use of tests. Although the Code covers four areas—developing/selecting tests, interpreting scores, striving for fairness, and informing test takers—only the first area will be covered in this discussion. A single copy of the Code may be obtained free of cost from the National Council on Measurement in Education, 1230 Seventeenth Street, NW, Washington, DC 20036.

Using the above Standards and the Code as guides and recommendations from other sources (Hammill, et al., 1992; Salvia & Ysseldyke, 1995; Thurlow, 1988) for quantifying the Standards, criteria for evaluating the technical adequacy of norms are

1. Norms should be available in the manual or in an accompanying technical publication in the form of standard scores.
2. The test manual needs to define the standardization of the normative sample clearly so that the test user can determine the suitability for a particular population. Such defining characteristics should include five or more of the following variables: ages, grade levels, gender, geographic areas, race, socioeconomic status, ethnicity, parental education, or other relevant variables.
3. The norm-sampling method should be well-defined. If the norm sample is based on convenience or readily available populations, it is not acceptable.

4. For each subgroup examined, an adequate sample size should be used with 100 subjects per age or grade considered the lower limit. In addition, there should be 1,000 or more subjects in the total sample.
5. The test's norms should not be more than fifteen years old.

Criteria for evaluating the reliability of a standardized test are

1. The test manual should supply an estimate of test-retest reliability for relevant subgroups. A correlation coefficient of .60, .80, or .90 or better for group tests, screening tests, and diagnostic tests, respectively, is a current best practice criterion.
2. The test manual should report empirical evidence of internal consistency with a correlation coefficient of .90 or better.
3. Reliability coefficients as well as standard errors of measurement (Sems) should be presented in tabular format.
4. Reliability procedures and samples of at least 25 subjects should be described.
5. Quantitative methods used to study and control item difficulty and other systematic item analyses should be reported in the manual.
6. Measures of central tendency and variability (means and standard deviations for the total raw scores) should be reported for relevant subgroups during the norming procedures.
7. Empirical evidence of interrater reliability at .85 or better should be reported in the manual.
8. The steepness of the test items should be controlled by having a minimum of three raw score items per standard deviation. The range of items for the youngest children should span two or more standard deviations below the mean score for each subtest and for the total score of the test.

Criteria for evaluating the validity of a standardized test are

1. The test manual must define what the test measures and what the test should be used for.
2. Evidence of at least one type of validity should be provided for the major types of inferences for which the use of a test is recommended (i.e., content; criterion-related: concurrent or predictive construct).
3. For content validity, the manual should define the content area(s) and explain how the content and skills to be tested were selected. Tests that are based on content validity should update content on revised forms.
4. For both types of criterion-related validity, that is, concurrent and predictive, (a) the criteria should be clearly defined; (b) validity of the criteria should be reported; (c) samples should be completely

described; (d) correlation coefficients with other tests should be reported; and (e) for predictive validity, a statement concerning the length of time for which predictions can be made should be included.

5. For construct validity, the manual should clearly define the ability or aptitude measured. For tests for which there is a time limit, the manual should state how speed affects scores.

Other criteria include an adequate description of test procedures in sufficient detail to enable test users to duplicate the administration and scoring procedures used during test standardization and a full description of tester qualifications. The skills specific to a particular test should be enumerated. Evidence concerning the appropriateness of the test for children of different racial, ethnic, or linguistic backgrounds who are likely to be tested should be included. Due to the multicultural attributes of American schools, this is not easy. However, test developers must make every effort to avoid scores which vary as a function of race, ethnicity, gender, or language.

Besides using these criteria, formal evaluations of tests, written by experts, can be found in the Mental Measurements Yearbooks. The most recent yearbook (Kramer & Conoley, 1992) is even available on CD-ROM. Since the yearbooks do not appear annually, the Buros Institute at the University of Nebraska offers two other services for obtaining the latest test information and reviews of specific tests: an on-line computer database and a computerized test reference service. For more information about either service, you can write to them at the Buros Institute of Mental Measurements, 135 Bancroft Hall, University of Nebraska–Lincoln, Lincoln, NE 68588–0348 or call (402) 472–6203. Costs for both services are nominal.

Another source of objective information about the technical characteristics of norm-referenced tests is *A Consumer's Guide to Tests in Print* (Hammill, et al., 1992). Its purpose is to provide professionals with unbiased facts on tests they use daily or are contemplating using.

The importance of using only technically adequate tests cannot be over-emphasized. It is encouraging to note the trend to use more technically adequate tests when evaluating children. For instance, Mardell-Czudnowski (1980) documented that many of the most widely used tests lacked adequate norms, reliability, and/or validity data. In fact, when Mardell-Czudnowski and Lessen (1982) evaluated twelve of these widely used tests, only two met the standards of technical adequacy stated in the Standards for Educational and Psychological Tests (1974). In a more recent survey of widely used tests, Mardell-Czudnowski and Burke (1991) found that 11 of the 20 tests met all criteria for technical adequacy. This is a vast improvement that can be credited to both more sophisticated statistical skills of test developers and more importantly, more knowledgeable and demanding test users.

If a standardized test is not technically adequate, it should not be used no matter how well it meets the needs of your testing program from a non-technical standpoint. You may think that using a poorly normed test is better than making a decision without any comparative data. Salvia and Ysseldyke (1995) explain why this is not so.

> It is occasionally argued that inadequate norms are better than no norms at all. This argument is analogous to the argument that even a broken clock is correct twice a day. With 86,400 seconds in a day, remarking that a clock is right twice a day is an overly optimistic way of saying that the clock is wrong 99.99 percent of the time. Inadequate norms do not allow meaningful and accurate inferences about the population. If poor norms are used, misinterpretations follow. (pp. 117–118)

However, once it is deemed technically adequate, other considerations are appropriate before making a decision between one or more technically adequate standardized tests. Now is the time to consider administration and scoring characteristics such as time required to administer and score the test; age and/or grade range; ease of administration; the match between the content on the test and the content in your curriculum; examiner qualifications; and the appropriateness of the test format, how the items are presented and how the children are to respond, for your population.

According to the Code of Fair Testing Practices in Education (Joint Committee on Testing Practices, 1988), test users should select tests that meet the purpose for which they are to be used and that are appropriate for the intended test-taking populations. It is the responsibility of the test user to read the test manual, examine specimen sets, become familiar with how and when the test was developed and tried out, read independent evaluations of a test, ascertain if the test content and norm groups are appropriate, and select and use only those tests for which the skills needed to administer the test and interpret scores correctly are available.

Information on specific standardized screening and diagnostic tests used with young children is located in Appendix A. The names and addresses of test publishers are in Appendix B.

▦ Summary

This chapter emphasizes the importance of basic concepts of measurement for the competency of the professional working with young children. In order to increase that competency, basic terms are defined along with examples. Then more involved terms such as standardization, norms, validity, and reliability are fully discussed. These terms are then applied to the stan-

ACTIVITIES

1. Turn to the appendix on tests at the end of this text. Select two tests from any of the ten categories (e.g., screening, reading, giftedness). If possible, select two tests that are used in your school or community so that you can borrow the actual test and manual. Evaluate each test's technical adequacy following the guidelines in this chapter. Determine which of the two tests is more technically adequate. Check your decision with expert opinions from the most recent Buros Mental Measurements Yearbook in your university or community library.

2. Interview two experienced teachers working with young children of different ages who use tests for making decisions about children. Ask them which tests they use; which they like; and why. Later determine the technical adequacy of their choices.

3. Pretend that you are teaching a group of children in which a small subgroup speak Spanish both at home and with each other. Your administrator wants to use a standardized test with them which is not available in Spanish. Develop a list of arguments indicating that such a test would not be appropriate for these children and a list of possible solutions to resolve this problem.

dards for the evaluation of tests. Guidelines are listed so that teachers may determine the technical adequacy of the norms, reliability, and validity of any given standardized test.

CHAPTER 4 Suggested further readings

Bracken, B. (1991). *The psychoeducational assessment of preschool children* (2nd ed.). Boston: Allyn & Bacon.

Kramer, J., & Conoley, J. (Eds.). (1992). *The eleventh mental measurement yearbook*. Lincoln, NE: Buros Institute of Mental Measurement, University of Nebraska-Lincoln.

Lichtenstein, R., & Ireton, H. (1984). *Preschool screening: Identifying young children with developmental and educational problems*. Orlando: Grune & Stratton.

Meisels, S. (1989). *Developmental screening in early childhood: A guide* (3rd ed.). Washington, DC: National Association for the Education of Young Children.

Salvia, J., & Ysseldyke, J. (1995). *Assessment* (6th ed.). Boston: Houghton Mifflin.

CHAPTER 4 Study questions

1. What are the three roles of the teacher, according to the National Association for the Education of Young Children, in regard to tests and testing?

2. The child-care center director was very upset because half of the children in the center scored below the mean on a standardized screening test. Why was her behavior inappropriate?

3. Explain the differences between an age-equivalent score and a grade-equivalent score.

4. Name at least two problems with developmental scores.

5. Explain the difference of where a standard score of 85 (mean = 100, SD = 15) and a percentile score of 85 would fall on the normal curve.

6. Indicate whether the following would be positively correlated, negatively correlated, or if no statistical relationship exists:

    (a) the age of a car and its typical worth;

    (b) the number on a player's jersey and the number of points that player makes in a game;

    (c) the number of pages in a book and the thickness of the book in inches.

7. Name three factors that can affect the reliability of any test.

8. To which type of validity (a = content, criterion; b = concurrent; c = predictive; or d = construct) are the following situations referring?

    (a) A test is designed to distinguish between introverted and extroverted college students.

    (b) A guidance counselor wants to know how many kindergartners with high IQ scores will eventually succeed in college.

    (c) A new test correlates 0.63 with teachers' grades.

    (d) A teacher adheres closely to constructing test items that measure his stated objectives.

9. Name three factors that can affect the validity of any test.

10. Once a test has been evaluated as technically adequate, list five other factors that should be considered.

⊞ References

American Educational Research Association, American Psychological Association, & National Council on Measurement in Education. (1974). *Standards for educational and psychological testing.* Washington, DC: American Psychological Association.

American Educational Research Association, American Psychological Association, & National Council on Measurement in Education. (1985). *Standards for educational and psychological testing*. Washington, DC: American Psychological Association.

Borg W., Worthen, B., & Valcarce, R. (1986). Teachers' perceptions of the importance of educational measurement. *Journal of Experimental Education, 5,* 9–14.

Bracken, B. (1987a). Limitations of preschool instruments and standards for minimal levels of technical adequacy. *Journal of Psychoeducational Assessment, 4,* 313–326.

Bracken, B. (1987b). The technical side of preschool assessment: A primer of critical issues. *Preschool Interests, 2,* 6–9.

Cicchetti, D., & Wagner, S. (1990). Alternative assessment strategies for the evaluation of infants and toddlers: An organizational perspective. In S. Meisels & J. Shonkoff (Eds.), *Handbook of early childhood intervention.* New York: Cambridge University Press.

Feeney, S., & Kipnis, K. (1989). A new code of ethics for early childhood education. *Young Children, 45,* 24–29.

Glascoe, F. P. (1991). Developmental screening: Rationale, methods, and application. *Infants and young children, 4*(1), 1–10.

Glascoe, F. P., & Byrne, K. (1993). The accuracy of three developmental screening tests. *Journal of Early Intervention, 17*(4), 368–379.

Goodwin, W. L., & Goodwin, L. D. (1982). Measuring young children. In B. Spodek (Ed.), *Handbook of research in early childhood education.* New York: Free Press.

Gredler, G. R. (1992). *School readiness: Assessment and educational issues.* Brandon, VT: Clinical Psychology Publishing.

Green, B. F., Jr. (1981). A primer of testing. *American Psychologist, 36,* 1001–1011.

Hammill, D., Brown, L., & Bryant, B. (1992). *A consumer's guide to tests in print* (2nd ed.). Austin, TX: Pro-ed.

Hills, T. (1992). Reaching potentials through appropriate assessment. In S. Bredekamp & T. Rosegrant (Eds.), *Reaching potentials: Appropriate curriculum and assessment for young children* (Vol. 1). Washington, DC: National Association for the Education of Young Children.

International Reading Association Board of Directors. (1980, June). Board action. *Reading Today,* p. 1.

Joint Committee on Testing Practices. (1988). *Code of fair testing practices.* Washington, DC: Author.

Kramer, J., & Conoley, J. (Eds.). (1992). *The eleventh mental measurement yearbook.* Lincoln, NE: Buros Institute of Mental Measurement, University of Nebraska–Lincoln.

Lerner, J., Mardell-Czudnowski, C., & Goldenberg, D. (1987). *Special education for the early childhood years* (2nd ed.). Englewood Cliffs, NJ: Prentice-Hall.

Mardell-Czudnowski, C. (1980). The four W's of current testing practices: Who; what; why; and to whom—an exploratory survey. *Learning Disabilities Quarterly*, 3(1), 73–83.

Mardell-Czudnowski, C., & Lessen, E. (1982). Technical adequacy of assessment instruments: Can we agree? *Diagnostique, 7,* 189–202.

Mardell-Czudnowski, C., & Burke, L. (1991). Testing: Who, what, why and to whom a decade later. Paper presented at the National Association of School Psychologists, Dallas, TX.

NAEYC Position Statement on Standardized Testing of Young Children 3 Through 8 Years of Age. (1988). *Young Children, 45,* 42–47.

National Association for the Education of Young Children. (1988). NAEYC position statement on standardized testing of young children three through eight years of age. *Young Children, 44,* 42–47.

Psychological Corporation. (1984). *On telling parents about test results: Test service notebook 154.* New York: Author.

Salvia, J., & Ysseldyke, J. (1995). *Assessment* (6th ed.). Boston: Houghton Mifflin.

Sattler, J. (1988). *Assessment of children* (3rd ed.). San Diego: Jerome M. Sattler.

Thurlow, M. (Ed.). (1988). *Assessing young children.* Minneapolis, MN: Minnesota Department of Education, Special Education Section.

U.S. Government Printing Office. (1977). *Federal Register* (pp. 42496–42497). Washington, DC: Author.

CHAPTER 5

Testing in the Right Place

Terms to Know

- tests
- norm-based instruments
- screening tests
- inventory
- diagnostic tests
- curriculum-based measures
- criterion-referenced measures
- performance assessment
- portfolios
- technical issues
- rubric
- inter-rater reliability
- accountability
- authentic assessment

CHAPTER OVERVIEW This chapter begins with a brief history of the misuse of tests in special-education placement. Trends toward inappropriate practice in early childhood education are described. Appropriate uses of tests for screening, diagnosis, and individualized educational plans follow. There is a discussion of how performance-based measures can be used to answer the questions rather than tests. Technical issues regarding performance measures when these measures become tests is reviewed. Coordination of testing programs and cautions conclude the chapter.

Topics Discussed

- Tests in the assessment system
- Range of early childhood tests
- Individualized educational planning
- Coordination of testing programs
- Performance assessment

⊞ Tests in the assessment system

Tests serve an important function in early childhood programs when they are used for a specific, suitable purpose. Tests must be examined for their technical qualities. They must be appropriate for the children. Directions established in test manuals must be followed carefully.

Appropriate and inappropriate uses

Test scores must *not* be interpreted in isolation. That is, the information obtained from a test, is only part of the material needed to make an educational decision. Tests cannot be used casually. The impact of scores sets too many lifetime consequences in motion to consider the choice and use of tests lightly. Hobbs (1975) describes common offenses on labeling and classifying children based on test results:

> Large numbers of minority-group children—Chicanos, Puerto Ricans, blacks, Appalachian whites—have been inaccurately classified as mentally retarded on the basis of inappropriate intelligence tests, placed in special classes or programs where stimulation and learning opportunities are inadequate, and stigmatized.   (Hobbs, 1975, p. 3)

Early childhood teachers *must guard* against marching down the same path when seeking to meet the unique needs of children. Ponder the following cautions:

> Some early childhood tests have serious weaknesses, such as narrow focus on knowledge, inappropriate length, or developmentally inappropriate items. Group-administered tests are inappropriate for young children who are not accustomed to attending to a series of brief, uninteresting items. . . . testing . . . is a type of interaction that has few parallels in life and, thus, lacks ecological validity. Young children may not play the role of respondent, may become fatigued, and may try simply to please the adult tester. The idea is to use a benign, unobtrusive process to assess knowledge, but the testing process is neither benign nor unobtrusive because it is foreign to young children's experience.   (McNair & Schweinhart, 1990)

By focusing on *curricular-outcome measures and standardized tests* as the *only way* of judging child progress, we risk repetition of dreadful educational practices that stigmatize children. These include such practices as screening for readiness (Meisels, 1987), use of the Head Start Measures Battery to plan a curriculum with an emphasis on cognition (Raver & Ziegler, 1991), retention in kindergarten (Shepard & Smith, 1989), and tracking primary-aged children based on textbook or standardized achievement scores (Kamii, 1990).

Kamii (1990) calls for a halt to achievement tests commonly used in primary grades. She argues that achievement tests answer the wrong questions for us. They measure the child's ability to master educational content like everyone else. The emphases are on narrowly defined "right" answers. Teachers seek to help children become critical thinkers, to be responsible for themselves, their own learning, and to be creative—not to focus their energies on "one way" of viewing life.

Evidence of misuse mounts

Tests are used now in early childhood to monitor whether children move to the next grade, to determine eligibility for special programs such as Chapter 1 services, to determine teacher competence and school performance, and to allocate school funds. Teachers and students feel pressured. Some cheat to cope. Legislative pressure at the state and federal level for school reform places even more emphasis on standardized testing. Legislators are not educators; they typically do not concern themselves with the complexities of development and education. Early childhood professionals need to educate them about the limitations of tests, particularly when used to measure some aspects of young children's development. High stakes use of tests—life and opportunity options—must be carefully monitored with our youngest citizens (Charlesworth, Fleege, & Weitman, 1994).

Responsible use of tests

If you are going to use tests for an appropriate purpose, then you need to consider the following guidelines (Lictenstein & Ireton, 1984) for the process of administering scoring, and interpreting standardized tests. These guidelines help you think about the *responsibility you assume* when you seek to administer *any* educational test, no matter how simple it looks to you, as the adult. Think about all the skills and strategies that the child uses in completing each of the following typical test items:

- count to 3;
- find the broom;
- put the book on the table;
- close the door and then hop on one foot;
- day is to night as sun is to _____ .

Depending upon child experience and developmental status, these tasks become even more complex. Testing is neither as simple nor as straightforward as it may first appear.

Examiners must have an understanding of, and respect for, the importance of standardized testing procedures. That is, the exact instructions for administration and scoring must be followed to preserve the value of using standardized instruments.

The words *standardized test* describe the fact that test administration, scoring of results, and interpretations are done according to specific standards and in reference to a concept of *normal*. Everybody who administers a particular test is supposed to do it the same way.

Test instructions must be presented in a specified way, according to the manual. The child's responses to test items must be scored according to standards described in the test manual. Results must be interpreted according to the directions in the manual. Scores and statistics can only be derived from the procedures outlined in the test manual. Good tests include cautions and limitations in the manual.

Errors in testing that influence results

Inexperienced examiners often commit two types of *leniency* errors: (1) coaching—providing assistance to the child beyond that permitted by the instructions; and (2) giving the child a break on the scoring when the child seems to know an answer but cannot provide a creditable response. If teachers take liberties with administration and scoring procedures, the testing situation is no longer standard for each child and results are no longer comparable. Leniency errors in assessments may result in the failure to refer children who are in need of special help. Young children thus lose an opportunity for development.

To be effective, fair, and efficient, teachers must devote time to learning the administration and scoring rules for specific instruments they choose. Directions in the manual tell teachers to read instructions, word for word, but there are various other aspects of test administration—arranging materials, doing demonstrations, applying scoring rules, etc.—which must become second nature to the examiner. The teacher must practice doing the test before administering it to children so the test is administered smoothly and correctly.

While following standardized testing procedures, the examiner must also ensure that the child's optimal performance is elicited. Unless the child's cooperation is maintained by the examiner, a test will not yield a valid measure of performance. (Goodenough, 1949) notes that this will sometimes be the case "even under the best conditions and with the most skillful examiner" and proposes that "the safest procedure to follow is not to give any test at all, rather than to give a poor test." She suggests that the child return at a later occasion if the child doesn't cooperate.

Using test scores

Tests scores act to supplement information known about children. Tests are not infallible. Scores require interpretation in the context of the child's life.

This includes the personal, social, and emotional context, as well as the school context. Information gathered from a parent interview and teacher observation is the lodestone; test scores are the glittery specks. Unfortunately, teachers sometimes pay more attention to the glitter. A child is not a score on a test or a level of performance. A child is an individual: Lisa, Larissa, Peter, Jose, or Stephen, each with a particular family, a culture, and a personality, who uses diverse strategies to cope with the social/emotional and cognitive demands of the school setting.

Range of early childhood tests

Early childhood tests vary in many ways. The most important issues are their *content relevance* and *practical utility* to early childhood teachers. Some tests are *comprehensive*, covering all the major developmental domains including gross motor, fine motor, language, and cognition. Others are limited to one or only a few domains, such as tests of language development or understanding of concepts. Some educational tests are designed to measure the child's understanding of curricular content. Educational tests are *norm-based* or *criterion-based*. **Norm-based instruments** compare children to others of similar age, grade level, or other important characteristics, while *criterion-based* instruments identify the list of skills or milestone markers that *all* children will presumably pass on their way to successful mastery of the developmental stage or academic subject. Such tests evaluate a child's performance on a specific standard. A teacher checks to see whether a child can count to five, hop on one foot, etc. Some tests cover a broad *age range*, while others target a specific age group, such as infants or pre-kindergarten children. Tests vary greatly in length, and the time and skill it takes to administer, score, and interpret them.

Three purposes of tests

It is useful to think of tests as serving three purposes: (1) screening, (2) diagnosis, and (3) educational planning. Developmental **screening tests** are intentionally brief, designed to provide a global index of developmental delay or normality. Diagnostic level measures are more in-depth and time-consuming because they are designed to provide more specific information about a child's profile of abilities and disabilities and contribute to developmental diagnosis and identification of educational disabilities. The most in-depth measures are those instruments intended to provide specific educationally related information tied to curriculum goals and individual educational planning. For school-age children, academic achievement tests are the forerunners of these more complex measures.

In curriculum-based assessment, developmental benchmarks become integrated with specific educational goals and objectives. This is not an easy task to accomplish, by any means. At one extreme, screening instruments are brief, perhaps superficial, and may be invalid as measures of the child's functioning. At the other end are instruments that may be so detailed that they become cumbersome and may not be usable.

The cornerstone of test standardization is validity. The question is: "How well does the test do the job it claims to do?" For a developmental screening test, "How accurate are screening test results when compared to the results of more in-depth developmental testing?" For diagnostic measures, "How well do they relate to results of other test measures, to evaluation based on professional observation, parental reports, and school performance?" "Have trustworthy studies been done to decide these relationships?" Most detailed curriculum-based measures have not been studied in this way. They are presumed to be valid because they have been designed by educational specialists and are detailed. This assumption could cause problems, particularly when such instruments are chosen without consideration about how they match the philosophy, curricular goals, and developmental levels of the children in your program.

Choosing tests

To learn the relevance and utility of various measures for the children you work with, start by listing the characteristics of these children. Include age, sex, social-economic background, cultural and language backgrounds, and any other factors you consider relevant. Are these children assumed to be normal or are they "at risk" by virtue of environmental factors, developmental delay, or identified special disability? Next, why are you searching for a test? To help identify young children who may be in need of/entitled to early childhood special education services? To monitor the developmental progress of presumably normal children? To further assess children with identified developmental problems? Then ask "Is this test designed to serve the purpose I need to accomplish?" At the most basic level, "Is the item content of this instrument addressing the developmental issues that are appropriate for my program and the children that I serve?" "Are there sufficient numbers of items (questions-tasks) to adequately screen or assess these areas of development?"

Using screening tests

Tests are appropriately used for screening many children. In a screening situation, you are trying to take a quick look at many children. You do not know these children or their parents very well (or at all). You choose a technically sound test designed for screening. Most of the children you see will pass through the screen to the other side.

The following two example scenarios highlight issues that often arise during a screening process. Specialists conduct these screenings in consultation with early childhood teachers.

Routine vision screening

You want to know how many children in your class need glasses. A nurse asks all the four year olds in your class to identify letters or bunny rabbits, according to the directions she gives. Steven fails the screening. Before Mr. and Mrs. Green are asked to run out to get glasses for Steven, you consider whether Steven seemed to follow directions given by the nurse. If he did not follow directions easily, you might suggest a re-screening in six weeks. If he followed directions and his parents are concerned about his vision, you recommend that he be seen by an optometrist or opthamalogist for a diagnostic assessment.

Routine speech and language screening

At first grade level, a speech therapist comes to your class to screen children for articulation or other speech impairments. This is done to ensure that all children will have every available chance to continue early literacy development. You have been concerned about Carter who does not always speak clearly. Following the screening, you learn how to help Carter with articulation errors he makes. The speech therapist also decides, based on the results of screening, to come to your room Thursday afternoons to interact with Gregory, Laura, and Stephan to help them with articulation. She will see them in her office on Tuesdays.

Child find screening

Your educational screening is conducted the same way, using a technically sound instrument. You plan a day or more to screen three- and four-year-old children to find those children who may need a special service or to find out how the children in your community compare to the established curriculum. After screening 200 children, you find that 10 fall into the category of "risk" and 15 fall into the category of "watch." You let the parents of the 175 children who passed through the screen know that, "currently," readiness for learning seems to be in place for their children.

For the 15 children in the "watch" category, you look at the results of screening to see if there is one area of concern, or low performance areas across all the parts of the test, and compare the information that you have about each of the individual children and their families. You share the results of the screening with the parents personally and show that they can bring Robbin, Gloria, Constance, or Larry back for screening or seek diagnostic assistance, if they are still worried about progress in a few months.

For the 10 children who fell into the risk category, you look at all available materials and discuss the next step with each child's parents. For instance, Mr. and Mrs. Whitewater might be referred to Easter Seals for a diagnostic assessment for Ashley, since you are worried about Ashley's gross and fine motor performance. Luzmarie's mother might be referred to a bilingual preschool program, since you believe she may not have understood all of the English directions. Mitchell Oxford appears to be quite isolated in a world of his own. You refer Ms. Oxford to a mental health or child guidance clinic. Erick was a terror in the screening situation; Mrs. Ross, his mother, seemed frustrated and embarrassed that she could not calm him down. You refer her to a special education diagnostic team.

If 100 of the 200 children screened fail the test or are otherwise shown to be at risk of academic failure, you *change the curriculum*. Although such an event is unlikely, the point is that screening instruments are designed to catch the few who need special assistance. If many children are being caught by the screening net, then educational interventions or programs must be planned according to the needs of the children. Tests used in this way inform teachers as they make teaching decisions about how to carry out the curriculum. Screening can and should be done at all age levels.

Reading comprehension inventory

Third graders in your school are given a reading comprehension **inventory** by the reading specialist or by the third-grade teachers. Those who score below the school cut-off points are involved in special reading tutorials planned to bridge the reading gap, so that they will be successful in the independent work required in fourth grade. Only two or three in each class are found eligible for this special assistance. If 1/2 the class is found in need of remediation, the teachers will change the curriculum by examining the results of the test. That is, they look at the failure patterns and plan teaching strategies to help the children be successful.

These are screening situations in action. In these examples, tests are being used appropriately. The tests are gathering information quickly and in a standardized manner. The test score is only part of the data used to make a decision. Teachers are making decisions that affect the educational lives of children responsibly.

Diagnostic testing

Qualified professionals administer individualized intelligence tests, speech and language tests, and other specialized instruments based on a referral question from a parent, teacher, physician, or other person concerned with developmental progress of a particular child. Diagnostic measures provide an in-depth examination of a child's performance in cognition, language, hearing, etc. The psychologist, psychiatrist, speech therapist, physical therapist, or neurologist tries to answer the questions that lead parents, teachers, and others to seek further information to optimize child growth.

Teacher's responsibility on multidisciplinary team

The teacher's responsibility related to these tests is as a *multidisciplinary team participant.* Following the regular screening, a diagnostic evaluation, or watching the participation of children in their class, teachers raise questions about those children who seem to be significantly different in their functioning than other children. A plan for further evaluation is made and appropriate experts to conduct the diagnostic assessment are chosen. Teachers report observations, impressions, academic checklists, and academic test scores as the occasion demands in this process.

After the family is consulted and the tests administered, a plan is made to serve the child and family. Teachers serve as informed observers prior to individualized diagnostic assessment. Afterward, teachers are charged with the responsibility of carrying out the specialists' individualized recommendations for service to the child and the family.

Diagnostic curricular measures

Teachers in primary grades use individualized diagnostic procedures to solve teaching problems. Such instruments are generally individualized **curriculum-based measures.** For example, if Sally seems to read with great difficulty, Mrs. George, the third grade teacher, may use an individualized reading test to supplement her observations about the progress that Sally is making. She can then change her teaching approach.

Diagnostic tests are always used to help answer questions about children. Sometimes, they entitle children to services. For example, only children who are diagnosed with a particular condition, such as learning disabilities, are entitled to receive special assistance from the teacher of the children with learning disabilities. While the teacher of the children with learning disabilities might consult with other teachers about issues relating to learning, only diagnosed children are entitled to be included in the regular case load.

⊞ Individualized educational planning

Traditional academic achievement tests are the forerunners of curriculum-based assessment. Curriculum-based assessment arose from the recognition that diagnostic measures, such as intelligence tests, were too general and were not closely related to children's development and learning or to their learning-related abilities and problems. What was needed, then, were clearly defined educational outcomes (goals and specific behavioral objectives) so that teachers could measure each child's progress toward those specific objectives to evaluate both children's progress and the program's effectiveness; in other words, individual learner outcomes and general program outcomes (Deno, 1985).

Curriculum-based assessment

Over the years, Deno and his colleagues have incorporated two key assessment features in curriculum-based assessment: (1) "measurement methods are standardized; that is both the critical behaviors to be measured and the procedures for measuring those behaviors are prescribed" and (2) "the focus of the measurement is long term: the testing methods and content remain constant across relatively long time periods, such as one year" (Fuchs, 1993, p. 15).

As used in special education, this approach handles those situations in the primary years where teachers have specific academic goals that can be specified clearly, analyzed in component parts, and assessed. Such measures are similar in philosophy to performance measures. That is, the goal is to find a "test" that is "the same" as the "task." This is so that the learner will be treated fairly and so that the teacher will have concrete information about how to teach on any given day. The crucial difference between curriculum-based assessment and performance-based assessment is the underlying theoretical approach of the methods. Curriculum-based measures depend philosophically on the view of behavioral science as applied in seeable, measurable terms. Consider the following example:

> Ms. Mountain wants to know how Robert is progressing through the second grade reading program. The second grade program specifies many word attack and comprehension skills. Children work in workbooks and read with the teacher to develop these skills. Robert gets most of the pages wrong. Ms. Mountain chooses a curriculum-based reading test that evaluates the skills taught in the second grade. She gives the test to Robert, reviews the results, and revises her teaching strategies.

Performance-based measures depend philosophically on the view of a constructionist approach to education. An example of a performance-based measure follows:

> Ms. Knapp wants to know if Paul can complete a third grade project on pioneers. The project in part requires that each child read various materials and write a report at the end of two months. Ms. Knapp pulls a book from the third grade shelf, asks Paul to read a chapter, and to then write a summary. She observes how he handles the process and revises her subsequent teaching plan accordingly.

Curriculum-based assessment could be of value to young children, and in particular to young children with special needs, who require more specific individual educational planning (IEPs). If such an approach could truly bridge early developmental milestones and educational benchmarks and provide for instruction that was helpfully informed by relevant assessment/progress information, young children could benefit greatly. The *danger* in this approach is that the child and the broad understanding of how children develop might get lost in all the specifics and particulars and that teachers could be overwhelmed in the process. A comprehensive developmental perspective is basic to planning and implementing sound assessment and intervention strategies. Without this general knowledge, the specifics of any assessment or intervention plan are meaningless.

Curriculum-based assessment traces a child's achievement along a continuum of objectives, within a developmentally sequenced curriculum. In curriculum-based assessment, assessment and instruction are closely linked, both initially and over time, to find progress, or the lack of it, and to plan for appropriate educational help.

The foundation of curriculum-based assessment is a sequence of developmental objectives, sometimes called learner outcomes, which constitutes a program's curriculum. An objective may vary from landmark goals in a developmental domain, e.g., walks independently, to finely graded sequences of skills that lead to the achievement of the end goal. Such in-depth measures go beyond assessment for the diagnosis of some type of disability. They can pinpoint individual strengths and weaknesses and specific teaching objectives. Also, they provide for close monitoring of the child's progress under the program's effectiveness.

Criterion-referenced measures

In defining the curriculum, schools and programs identify certain skills that they believe should be mastered. In determining whether mastery has occurred, you compare each child to the yardstick that your philosophy deems important. Examples of these **criterion-referenced measures** in action include:

■ Kindergarten teachers specify self-help, beginning literacy, problem-solving, and social skills as the curriculum goals. They choose a published criterion-referenced instrument that provides a record-keeping system that matches these goals for recording child progress quarterly.

■ Third grade teachers choose a reading skills inventory that matches their goals for literacy instruction. The inventory includes a list of word-attack skills, writing-practice, and comprehension skills. They record child progress in six week increments and teach accordingly.

Sometimes school districts develop criterion-referenced procedures in district-wide curriculum committees. A committee establishes overall goals by reviewing the literature on the subject. They identify the component skills. This creates a criterion reference against which individual child progress is compared. It serves both as record keeper and standards list.

Coordination of testing programs

A plan is made for the responsible use of tests. Tests are matched to the purpose and to the population. Tests are considered from the point of view of usability for the faculty and staff. This includes factors such as special training required, possibility for breaking the procedure into several days, hand scoring, etc. Distinctions are made regarding screening, diagnosis, instruction, and accountability.

Teacher-observation and parent-interview sources are factored into the plan. Performance-based measures are included.

Performance assessment

A developmentally based view of the educational needs of young children does not lend itself to the formation of finite lists of skills to be assessed mechanically. You ask yourself: How will I know whether Pauline can read, compute, solve problems, and think creatively? How will I know whether Jeff can work cooperatively in a group? How will I know whether he can work independently? How will I involve Therese in the assessment of her own learning?

You can answer these questions based on observations of children in the classroom situation. In addition, you can plan special problems or situations that will tell you the answers to these and other important developmental questions. This approach to assessment is called authentic, direct, alternative, or performance since the child's "test" closely resembles the classroom situation (cf. Eisner, 1985; Kamii, 1990; Perrone, 1991; Puckett & Black, 1994). **Performance assessment** seems to be the broadest and most descriptive term.

Systematic collection of information

Teacher responsibility as educators, then, is not to just say *no* to testing and accountability requirements, but to develop measures that reflect and affirm your understanding of children and your philosophy of education. You do this through the *systematic collection* of information on each child in your care. You record through the use of checklists and interviews: child interests, thinking, conversations; children at play, children following routines and otherwise showing developmental progress. You keep anecdotal notes, logs, diaries, and samples of children's work.

Portfolios

You combine these materials into *comprehensive portfolios.* A **portfolio** is a folder, box, basket or other container that serves to collect work samples from children throughout the year. Wide variations of materials and procedures are used in the collection of this information. This topic is covered in more detail in the special issues chapters on preschool, Chapter Ten, and primary, Chapter Eleven. An example of this process in operation is found in the South Brunswick, New Jersey Schools. In achieving developmentally appropriate curriculum for K-3, the following performance-based materials were collected in *portfolios* for kindergarten and grade one.

- Self-portrait
- Child interview
- Parent questionnaire
- Concept About Print (Clay, 1989)
- Word awareness
- Reading sample
- Writing sample

Performance problems as measures

Since young children think differently than adults, you must watch them to see how they solve problems and set up assessment situations for them to display such skills. Examples of ways to assess naturally and to pose problems for assessment purposes are described in the following section. Seven common forms of performance assessment (Feuer and Fulton, 1993) are

- constructed-response items that require children to develop answers rather than to choose "the right one";
- essays that show analysis, synthesis, and critical thinking;
- writing that displays composition skills;
- oral discourse that includes interviews and recitations;
- exhibitions that require students to demonstrate;

BOX 5.1

1. To assess early literacy development, you might examine the way that children use written materials related to themes in the housekeeping corner. For example, you turn the housekeeping corner into a travel agency, bringing in travel posters, tickets, appointment books, etc. You observe how and how much written material each child incorporates into dramatic play. This tells you the child's understanding of the functions and uses of written language. Another place to observe early literacy is at the writing table. By looking at the child's drawings and stories, you assess each child's familiarity with the features of written language (e.g., vocabulary, devices, rhythm, and intonation), spelling and decoding strategies, and composing strategies. When you are reading stories to children, one on one, you see which children have the concept of a story and individual progress toward sound/symbol relationship, etc. (Teale, 1990, pp. 53–55).

2. To assess the mathematical understanding of young children, you might observe them during routines such as setting the table for snack. When a child must be sure that there is a cookie for everyone, he is showing you whether he has developed the concept of one-to-one correspondence. You could also introduce group games involving logico-mathematical thinking. For example, young children love to play card games like war (who has more cards), go fish, old maid, etc. You could watch them at play to assess math concepts. In discussions of numbers, you have a chance to see which children have developed some ideas about numbers. Examples of these opportunities include judging how many marbles are in a jar, graphing which children prefer red jelly beans, and how many people in my family. (Kamii and Rosenblum 1990, pp. 146–162).

3. Examples of science problems for primary grades include activities called Whirlybird and Sugar Cube (Educational Testing Service, 1993).

"Students watch an administrator's demonstration of centrifugal force and then respond to written questions about what occurred in the demonstration. Students need to make careful observations about what happens as the administrator puts the steel balls in different holes on the Whirlybird arms, and then infer the relationship between the position of the steel balls and the speed at which the arm rotates.

In the "Sugar Cube" experiment, students observe the effect of warm water on different states of sugar: cubes, raw sugar, and fine granules.

- experiments that include demonstration of hypothesis testing, experimenting and writing up findings; and
- portfolios that demonstrate student progress over time.

Technology has a role to play as well. Computer simulations offer the opportunity for multiple hypotheses testing, for teachers to monitor the work via print out.

Paired explanations—two students alternating listening and questioning roles—can be evaluated on the quality of their questions, ability to summarize, helpfulness in making ideas clear, and appropriateness of interruptions (ERIC, 1993).

Link to curriculum

Performance assessment is definitely linked to curriculum. That is, the kinds of activities in assessment problems are similar to what children are already doing in the classroom. For example, to assess third graders in science, the children are presented with a problem of a drop of water placed on different types of building materials. Children are asked to tell what will happen. The examiner observes and records each child's ability to observe, infer, and formulate hypotheses (Educational Testing Services, 1990). This is the same kind of activity that might occur in any classroom. For example, a teacher brings into a kindergarten class a piece of wool from a sheep, as part of a follow-up of a story read about sheep. She places the wool on a science table. Children examine the wool and discuss the properties between themselves and with the teacher. The teacher poses what if, why, and other stimulating questions. Children explain their thinking and their concept of wool is enlarged. The regular class activity and the experiment with the drop of water are similar activities. Children have an opportunity in both cases to think and express their ideas.

"The more we help children to have their wonderful ideas and to feel good about themselves for having them, the more likely it is that they will some day happen upon wonderful ideas that no one else has happened upon before (Duckworth, 1987, p. 14).

Technical issues

Technical issues regarding this kind of assessment are emerging. Just because these procedures seem user friendly and connected to a holistic philosophy of curriculum and assessment, the measures are not necessarily benign when used for accountability purposes. The variables of task, learner, and context are each multidimensional. Errors in the interpretation of results are thus geometric rather than linear in proportion. For example, if four year old Mona fails to give each child a napkin at snack time, does her teacher, Ms. Stone, assume on the basis of this one observation that Mona has not accomplished one-to-one correspondence? Most early childhood teachers would consider such an interpretation an over-interpretation and come up with several alternative reasons for the omission on Mona's part. This example is obvious and simple. In other instances, the accountability stakes are high and children may pass or fail based on the accumulation of evidence.

▌ Do kindergarten teachers agree on the definition of "conversational skills" as expected?

- Do third grade teachers know what "addition skills" are for the seven/eight year olds in their charge?
- Are expected self-help skills for three year olds uniform across cultural/family groups?

The point is that these items must be operationally defined. Teachers must be trained to agree on the definitions. To do less risks the repetition of the well-known abuses of standardized assessments in the performance arena. Consider the following analogy of two gardens. One garden has wild flowers with no path. There are also many weeds. The second garden is laid along defined paths with small stones to set off the flowers. There are no weeds. Which garden is beautiful? What definitions of garden and beautiful are used? Which garden should "flunk"?

Rubrics

One way to address the issue of operational definition is to create scoring criteria for the performance tasks that will be used for assessment. These scoring criteria are frequently called **rubrics.** Teachers and others who develop performance tasks create standards and rules for judging the performance. In some cases the criteria can be described as points along a scale so that the criteria guide the teacher and the student in the teaching and learning process (Marzano, Pickering, McTighe, 1993).

> Small school districts may decide to examine the way they teach and assess math in the primary grades. After reviewing curricula, consulting the learner outcomes for their state, and considering the National Council of Mathematics standards, the teachers choose a sequence of instruction for K–3. They match activities to the goals. As the teachers work, they choose tasks that they believe are check points along the continuum of problem solving. These will be the performance tests. When they choose the performance tasks as tests, they must identify clear criteria for judging performance and progress toward the "ultimate" or top performance: shows complete understanding of. . . .

To ignore the rubric development or to haphazardly adopt a task outside the philosophy—curriculum—assessment system offers serious opportunity for disaster. Vague, subjective, and unspecified criteria for evaluation result in unfair practices for children. In addition to clear, defined, and operationalized criteria, there are other technical issues that must be faced when using performance assessment.

Other technical issues

Other important technical issues include reliability, consistency of the application of standards, and intra-rater and inter-rater reliability. Standards such as **inter-rater reliability** must be established if performance assessment will be used for **accountability** purposes. If the procedures are used to guide teaching, there is little question of validity. Questions emerge in using the measures for high-stakes decisions. Such high-stakes decisions are those regarding promotion, placement in special programs, and identification as a special learner. This is due to the complexity of establishing reliability regarding these assessments.

Now, there is limited research on high-stakes performance measures that include questions of individual differences, task specificity, and the level of difficulty of the task (Elliott, 1993). While these issues affect formally identified children with special needs, they are important considerations for all children. When important decisions are made about children, you must be sure that every effort is made to protect the rights, the best interests, and the integrity of the individual child. The tests must match the purpose of assessment, no matter what the form. A performance measure is not inherently better, if the items are not congruent with the curriculum, if the child does not understand the directions, if the time limits are too rigid, or if the material is biased toward children with special needs, or along cultural or sex role lines.

"When used for accountability purposes, the assessments must be conducted with many students, there must be consistency in the domains of knowledge being assessed, and the assessments must yield adequate samples of student performance within those domains. Costs and time associated with administration of the assessments to numerous students are also major considerations" (McLaughlin and Warren, 1994, p. 7).

Some practical guidance for school districts that seek to begin the use of performance assessment is presented by Herman, Aschbacher and Winters (1992):

- Use the standards of NAEYC and applicable professional associations for defining expected performance at different age levels.
- Gather some definitions or descriptions of expected performance.
- Gather samples of children's work that illustrate varying quality.
- Discuss the work with colleagues.
- Write your own descriptions.
- Gather another set of student work samples.
- Discuss with colleagues and revise criteria for judging performance.

Seidel (1991) has identified five phases that teachers, schools, and/or school districts traverse before fully implementing performance assessment. These are

- looking for alternatives to traditional assessment,
- experimenting by teachers,

■ learning the vocabulary associated with alternative assessment,

■ developing clinical judgment skills, and

■ using the alternatives for instruction and accountability purposes.

Seidel (1991) suggests the following additional phases:

■ connecting alternative assessment to educational reform

■ developing guidelines for district-wide implementation of portfolio assessment

■ developing consistent scoring of portfolios and other authentic assessment formats

■ speaking to the public with performance assessment

These phases depend on the background and experience of teachers in the school systems. Early childhood and special education teachers have historically considered the individual, clinical approaches and multiple information sources. Therefore, the implementation of alternative assessment in early childhood settings may be more rapidly accomplished than in settings accustomed to the reliance on standardized measures.

"**Authentic assessment,** when compared to conventional testing, makes far greater demands on both students and teachers. Some critics believe that it takes so much time that instruction is short-changed. But this point of view misses the symbiotic relation between instruction and assessment. Within the best models of authentic assessment, teaching and evaluation become virtually indistinguishable: an assessment that teaches students how to monitor their work is a vital form of instruction" (Inger, 1993).

So that educators do not repeat the mistakes of the past when performance measures are used by school districts for accountability, the Urban District Assessment Consortium at the Boston College Center for the Study of Testing, Evaluation and Education Policy (n.d.) formulated a procedure to decide whether performance items should be used. Performance items are reviewed and the following questions are answered. Are the items

■ developmentally appropriate?

■ of interest and meaningful to children of diverse backgrounds—ethnic, socio-economic, gender?

■ opportunities for children to demonstrate their best work in their primary language?

- on the cutting edge of content area developments?
- promoting integrated curriculum?
- promoting complex thinking processes and skills?
- involving real situations or obvious simulations of real situations?
- reflecting exemplary instructional practices?
- offering opportunities for various solution strategies?
- permitting student reflection on previous knowledge, skills, and attitudes?
- providing clues that the task can be solved?

These criteria grew from the work that the Boston College Center for the Study of Testing, Evaluation and Educational Policy conducts in urban settings, where the abusive and inappropriate uses of tests and test scores occur most often. The Boston College Center hopes that debate of these criteria will result in the codification and acceptance of ethical criteria for school districts, states, test publishers, and educators. Children and families will be well-served by these efforts.

Summary

Consider these final comments about testing in early childhood education. Ask yourself, "Why am I doing this?" Remind yourself of the uses and limitations of standardized tests and of their possible misuses and abuses. One common abuse is the misuse of a developmental screening test as a basis, by itself, for making educational program-placement decisions. Remember that testing definitely does not equal assessment. Developmental assessment is a *process* for detecting the developmental progress of a child that may include testing. The child's parents know more about the child's development and functioning than any single test will ever reveal and so do you, as the child's teacher. Use the observations well in the service of both the child and the child's parents.

"No single score can give a full picture of the range of competencies of different students in different instructional programs. Accordingly, multiple sources of evidence—different question types, formats, and contexts—must be considered. Some of these will be broadly meaningful and useful; other will be more idiosyncratic at the level of the state, the school, the classroom, or even the individual student" (Mislevey, 1992, 73).

Teachers must turn tests from *Gatekeeper to Gateway* (National Commission on Testing and Public Policy, 1990). "Test scores are imperfect measures and should not be used alone to make important decisions

ACTIVITIES

1. Visit the child care center near you. Ask the center how they screen young children. Match their procedures to the outlined practices described here. Are there any missing pieces?
2. Interview the special-education coordinator in your area. Ask how tests are used in the community.
3. Examine the contents of screening batteries. Try one or more of the measures on your classmates and volunteer children. Discuss the problems you had in administering the measures and compare them with your classmates' experiences.
4. Visit a school or center that uses a portfolio assessment system. Ask how the material is collected and used, plus what role, if any, the child plays in the process. Discuss with classmates whether you found any potential technical problems in the system and whether high stakes are involved.

about individuals, groups, or institutions; in the allocation of opportunities, individuals past performance and relevant experience must be considered" (p. xi).

CHAPTER 5 Suggested further readings

Gullo, D. F. (1994). *Understanding assessment and evaluation in early childhood education.* New York: Teachers College.

Kamii, D. (1990). *Achievement testing in the early grades: The games that grown-ups play.* Washington, DC: National Association for the Education of Young Children.

Meisels, S. (1985). *Developmental screening in early childhood: A guide.* Washington, DC: National Association for the Education of Young Children.

Popham, W. J. (1993). *Educational evaluation* (3rd ed.). Needham, MA: Allyn & Bacon.

Salvia, J., & Ysseldyke, J. E. (1995). *Assessment* (6th ed.). Boston: Houghton Mifflin.

CHAPTER 5 Study questions

1. What is a test? How do early childhood teachers decide when to appropriately use tests?
2. How have tests been misused historically and currently? As a multidisciplinary team member, what is the early childhood teacher's role in preventing misuse?

3. Describe the appropriate role for screening, diagnostic, and performance measures. Which measures are most often used by early childhood teachers? How does a teacher incorporate test results from other professionals in planning?

4. How are tests involved in Individualized Educational Planning?

5. What are the technical issues that shape choice of tests that are appropriate for an early childhood assessment system?

6. When are criterion-reference and curriculum-based measures most appropriately used in an early childhood assessment systems? What are the limitations of such measures?

7. Where do tests fit in the portfolio process? What kinds of measures?

8. When using authentic assessment, why are rubrics and inter-rater reliability important considerations?

9. Under what conditions can performance measures become as inappropriate as norm-based measures? How does a multidisciplinary team guard against such eventuality?

10. Outline the role of tests in comprehensive assessment systems for the early childhood years birth through eight. Incorporate young children with special needs in your work.

References

American Educational Research Association, American Psychological Association, & National Council on Measurement in Education. (1985). *Standards for educational and psychological testing.* Washington, DC: American Psychological Association.

Charlesworth, R., Fleege, P. O., & Weitman, C. J. (1994). Research on the effects of group standardized testing on instruction, pupils, and teachers: New directions for policy. *Early Education and Development, 5,* 195–212.

Clay, M. M. (1989). Concepts about print: In English and other languages. *The Reading Teacher, 42,* 268–277.

Deno, S. (1985). Curriculum-based measurement: The emerging alternative. *Exceptional Children, 52,* 219–232.

Duckworth, E. (1987). *The having of wonderful ideas and other essays on teaching and learning.* New York: Teachers College.

Educational Testing Service. (1993). Learning by doing: A manual for teaching and assessing higher-order thinking in science and mathematics. In *Performance assessment sampler: A workbook.* Princeton: Author.

Educational Testing Service. (1990). Testing in the schools. *ETS Policy Notes, 2.3.*

Eisner, E. (1985). *The educational imagination: On the design and evaluation of educational programs* (2nd ed.). New York: Macmillan.

Elliott, S. N. (1993). *Creating meaningful performance assessments: Fundamental Concepts.* Reston, VA: Council for Exceptional Children.

ERIC Digest. (1993). Alternative assessment and technology. ERIC Clearinghouse on Information and Technology, EDO-IR-93-5.

Feuer, M. J., & Fulton, K. (1993). The many faces of performance assessment. *Phi Delta Kappan, 74,* 478.

Fuchs, L. S. (1993). *Connecting performance assessment to instruction.* Reston, VA: Council for Exceptional Children.

Goodenough, F. L. (1949). *Mental testing: Its history, principles, and applications.* New York: Rinehart.

Guskey, T. R. (Ed.). (1994). *High stakes performance assessment: Perspectives on Kentucky's educational reform.* Thousand Oaks, CA: Corwin.

Herman, J., Aschbacher, P., & Winters, L. (1992). *A practical guide to alternative assessment.* Alexandria, VA: Association for the Supervision of Curriculum Development.

Hobbs, N. (1975). *The futures of children.* San Francisco: Jossey Bass.

Illinois Association for Supervision and Curriculum Development. (1989). *Early childhood screening: Position statement by the IASCD early childhood committee.* Normal, IL: Illinois State University.

Inger, M. (1993). Authentic assessment in secondary education. *Institute on Education and the Economy Brief, 6,* 4.

Kamii, C. (Ed.). (1990). *Achievement testing in the early grades: The games grown-ups play.* Washington, DC: National Association for the Education of Young Children.

Kamii, C., & Rosenblum, V. (1990). An approach to assessment in mathematics. In *Achievement testing in the early grades: The games grown-ups play.* Washington, DC: National Association for the Education of Young Children.

Lichtenstein, R., & Ireton, H. (1984). *Preschool screening: Identifying young children with developmental and educational problems.* New York: Grune & Stratton.

McLaughlin, M. J., & Warren, S. H. (1994). Performance assessment and students with disabilities: Usage in outcomes-based accountability systems. Reston, VA: Council for Exceptional Children.

McNair, S., & Schweinhart, L. (1990). Assessment through observation of young children in action. Unpublished manuscript.

Marzano, R. J., Pickering, D., & McTighe, J. (1993). *Assessing student outcomes: Performance assessment using the dimensions of learning model.* Alexandria, VA: Association for the Supervision of Curriculum Development.

Meisels, S. J. (1987). Uses and abuses of developmental screening and school readinesss testing. *Young Children, 42.2,* 4–6+.

Mislevy, R. J. (1992). *Linking educational assessments: Concepts, issues, methods, and prospects.* Princeton: Educational Testing Service.

Mitchell, R. (1992). *Testing for learning: How new approaches to evaluation can improve american schools.* New York: Free Press.

National Association of Elementary School Principals. (1990). *Standards for quality programs for young children: Early childhood education and the elementary school principal.* Alexandria, VA: Author.

National Commission on Testing and Public Policy. (1990). *From gatekeeper to gateway: Transforming testing in America.* Boston: Author.

Perrone, V. (Ed.). (1991). *Expanding student assessment.* Alexandria, VA: Association for Supervision and Curriculum Development.

Perrone, V. (1991). A position paper of the association for childhood education international on standardized testing. *Childhood Education, 67.3,* 131–142.

Puckett, M. B., & Black, J. K. (1994). *Authentic assessment of the young child.* New York: Macmillan.

Raver, C. C., & Ziegler, E. F. (1991). Three steps forward, two steps back: Head Start and the measurement of social competence. *Young Children, 46,* 3–8.

Seidel, S. (1991). Five phases in the implementation of portfolio assessment in classrooms, schools and school districts. Project Zero, Harvard Graduate School of Education. Unpublished manuscript.

Shepard, L., & Smith, M. L. (Eds.). (1989). *Flunking grades: Research and policies on retention.* New York: Falmer Press.

Teale, W. H. (1990). The promise and challenge of informal assessment in early literacy. In L. P. Morrow & J. K. Smith (Eds.), *Assessment for instruction in early literacy.* Englewood Cliffs: Prentice Hall.

Urban District Assessment Consortium (n.d.) at the Boston College Center for Testing, Evaluation and Educational Policy. Boston College. Unpublished manuscript.

CHAPTER 6

Using Alternative Assessment Strategies

Terms to Know
- intrinsically motivating
- task analysis
- presentation mode
- response mode
- dynamic assessment
- mediated learning experience (MLE)
- functional assessment
- multiple intelligences theory

CHAPTER OVERVIEW This chapter surveys a variety of alternative assessment strategies that can be employed by early childhood teachers. The use of each strategy is dependent on the particular skill or skills being assessed, as well as a number of other variables such as the age of the child, the amount of time the teacher can invest in the assessment, etc.

Topics Discussed
- Why should teachers know about alternative assessment strategies?
- Play-based assessment
- Task analysis
- Dynamic assessment
- Functional assessment
- Assessment of multiple intelligences

⊞ Why should teachers know about alternative assessment strategies?

There are a number of reasons why early childhood teachers should be aware of alternative assessment strategies. First, there is little overlap between what is measured on many norm-referenced tests and what is taught in the typical classroom. Second, published norm-referenced tests are designed to measure relative standing, how a child compares to other children. This is different than measuring change, how a child develops over time. Teachers usually are more interested in the changes children demonstrate. Third, there is a wide variability in how children perform on published norm-referenced tests, depending upon the specific test used. For example, if a child has a chronological age of 6-0 and labels letters correctly but reads no words, the child's standard score can vary from one test to another. As a result, there is a high likelihood that intervention teams and teachers will disregard the data collected from published norm-referenced tests in educational planning. Yet educational planning is the ultimate reason for conducting an assessment. Finally, there are limited resources of time and personnel in most schools and child-care centers, requiring teachers to have their own strategies for teaching a particular child or until a child gets assistance outside the regular classroom.

⊞ Play-based assessment

Most teachers believe that they can recognize play when they see it. However, play is easier to recognize than it is to define (Johnson, Christie, & Yawkey, 1987).

Play is often thought to be the natural learning medium of the child. From a competence perspective, "play is defined as a complex process that involves social, cognitive, emotional and physical elements and relates to an aspect of reality as not 'serious' or 'real'. For the child this characterization makes it possible to relate to things that might otherwise be confusing, frightening, mysterious, strange, risky, or forbidden and to develop appropriate competencies and defenses. The active solution of developmental conflicts through play thus enables the young child to demonstrate and feel . . . competence" (Mindes, 1982, p. 40). Through play children develop many capabilities. Examples of child accomplishments are that they learn communication skills, physical agility, independence, social judgment, cooperation, impulse control, etc. Play activities must be voluntary and **intrinsically motivating** to the child, otherwise they are not play. By watching children at play, teachers can gain insight into the developmental competencies of infants, toddlers, and young children.

Play is systematically related to areas of development and learning (Linder, 1993). Play influences language usage, cognitive understanding, social-emotional development, and physical and motor development. This interaction forms the basis for using play as an assessment tool and an intervention strategy. Teachers may be able to understand play behavior better by using the model in Figure 6.1 that defines play according to three categories or types (Mindes, 1982, p. 41).

Using play as an assessment tool is not a new concept but what is new is that play scales are now refined enough that they have practical applications for young children (Weber et al., 1994). Three play assessment scales and procedures, presented in Table 6.1, are used by speech pathologists, school psychologists, and early childhood special educators. However, the best approach for regular early childhood educators would be informal assessment of play which is appropriate for the entire age range and utilizes ordinary but interesting and age-appropriate toys to assess general aspects of a child's development through direct observation. In addition, the detailed analysis of older children's conversations as they engage in collaborative make-believe can reveal information about interactive skills, social cognition in action, and the knowledge of practical language use that young children bring to their play (Garvey, 1993).

One of the easiest ways for early childhood teachers to begin assessing play behavior is to use lists of critical skills and to match these to the curricular plan. Van Hoorn, Nourot, Scales, and Alward (1993) provide several examples of these matches. (1) A play observation diary is keyed to learning contexts and social contexts. That is, where is a particular child playing in the classroom, and in each area is he alone, with one friend, or with several friends. Over time, the charts can be analyzed for patterns. (2) Block play stages from Hirsch (1984) are listed on a table with each child's name. The teacher keeps track of whether a particular stage is emerging or is at mastery level for each child in the program. (3) A chart for role play including the use of props, make-believe, interaction, and verbal communication allows teachers to keep track of child developmental progress through the stages of socio-dramatic play. These charts assist teachers in focusing observations, planning curriculum, and documenting child and program progress.

Bricker and Cripe (1992) offer similar suggestions for charts to use with infants and toddlers with special needs. Chart categories suggested include fine motor, gross motor, self care, cognitive, social communication, and social. A numerical rating adds the potential to assess progress of in-

FIGURE 6.1 A model for defining play categories

Social Play

Solitary Play

The child plays alone with toys different from those used by other children; although the child may be within speaking distance, there is no attempt at verbal communication with the peer group. The child is centered on his or her own activity.

Parallel play

The child plays independently but among other children. The child plays with toys that are similar to those the other children are using. In short, the child plays beside rather than with other children.

Group play

Associative play. The child plays with other children. The children are borrowing, following each other with play things. All engage in similar if not identical activity. There is no division of labor and no organization of activity.

Cooperative play. The child plays in a group that is organized for making some material product, striving to attain some competitive goal, dramatizing situations of adult or group life, or playing formal games. There is a division of labor, a sense of belonging, and an organization in which the efforts of one child are supplemented by those of another.

Cognitive play

Functional play

Simple muscular activities and repetitive muscular movement with or without objects are used in functional play. The child repeats actions or initiates actions.

Constructive play

The child learns use of play materials, manipulation of objects to construct something or create something. There is an attempt to create something (e.g., drawing a person, building a playdough house, measuring with water beakers).

Dramatic play

The child takes on a role; he or she pretends to be someone else, initiating another person in actions and speech with the aid of real or imagined objects.

Games with rules

The child accepts prearranged rules and adjusts to them, controlling actions and reactions within given limits.

Miscellaneous categories

Unoccupied behavior

The child is not playing in the usual sense but watches activities of momentary interest, plays with his or her own body, gets on and off chairs, follows the teacher, or merely glances around the room.

Onlooker behavior

The child watches the others play and talks to, questions, and offers suggestions to the children playing but does not enter into the activity.

Reading

The child is being read to by the teacher.

Rough and tumble

Children in a group of two or more run and chase each other or engage in mock fighting.

Note: The author wishes to thank Kenneth Rubin of the University of Waterloo, Waterloo, Ontario, for permission to use his working draft of this play observation scale.
Mindes G. (1982). Social and cognitive aspects of play in young handicapped children. *Topics of Early Childhood Special Education, 2,* 14. Copyright 1982 by PRO-ED, Inc. Reprinted by permission.

TABLE 6.1 Play assessment scales and procedures

Name	Age (months)	Description
Play Assessment Scale (Fewell, 1991)	2–36	Experimental measure of play development with 45 developmentally sequenced items. Opportunity to use verbal cues and modeling. Yields a play age.
Symbolic Play Scale (Westby, 1991)	9–60	Observation of 1–4 children interacting in a large room with five centers: infant stimulation, store, household, creative play, and motor. Developed to assess language acquisition and social play.
Transdisciplinary Play-Based Assessment (TPBA) (Linder, 1990)	6–72	Employs arena assessment techniques to assess cognitive, communication, social-emotional and sensorimotor development; learning style; and patterns of interaction.

Adapted from Fewell, R. (1993). Observing play: An appropriate process for learning and assessment. *Infants and Young Children, 5*(4), 35–43. Copyright © 1993 Aspen Publishers, Inc.

dividual children on very specific aspects of target behavior. This approach to assessment is integrated into the planned activities. Activities are designed to meet individualized goals. Teachers employing this approach can document individual progress, select children appropriately for group intervention, and simplify record keeping by using the chart as a combination curricular/assessment tool.

In addition to these curricular approaches, play scales are commercially available for infants, toddlers, and young children throughout the early childhood age span. Teachers can selectively match these to the population of children they serve and to their curriculum. The use of these instruments may assist in program planning and in documentation of child progress. The key in picking these scales is "do they answer the questions you need to ask?" See Chapters Four and Five for a fuller discussion of issues involved in choosing commercial instruments.

⊞ Task analysis

Task analysis is a process in which large goals are broken down into smaller objectives or parts and sequenced for instruction. Task analysis is the process of developing a training sequence by breaking down a task into small steps that a child can master more easily. Tasks, skills, assignments, or jobs in the classroom can be interpreted in various ways.

Task analysis may be done informally. Jorge, a six year old who is having trouble buttoning his shirt, may be unsuccessful, because, you notice informally, that he usually wears tee shirts and sweat shirts. Thus, he lacks experience with buttons. Task analysis may be a more explicit and detailed process that you use with 7-year-old Brenda, who is showing limited writing fluency. The teaching question is: What can you do to facilitate Brenda's writing? To answer, you list all of the steps in writing a story. For example, sitting in a quiet place with writing materials, paper, and some stimulus (picture, discussion, or thought-provoking questions); grasping pen, pencil; applying appropriate pressure to create legible marks on the paper and writing letters together to form words; grouping the words together in sentences; organizing the sentences to convey a story idea, etc. After you list the component parts of the task, you watch Brenda at work. You see what parts of the task she can't do—maybe it's writing letters, maybe it's organizing her thoughts, maybe it's leaving enough space between words to make it possible to figure out what she's trying to say. At any rate, once you have identified the problem, you can decide what to do to help Brenda in your class or you have enough information to refer Brenda for a more specialized assessment.

One way of conducting a task analysis is to examine both the **presentation mode** and the **response mode** of any given task. You know that some children require you to tell directions; some to show directions; some to write directions; and some to tell, show, and write. Even if you habitually use multiple demonstration modes for tasks, skills, assignments, and jobs, you may find that a few children still do not understand what to do. Then, through a task analysis of the presentation mode, you can decide why Joey is not singing at circle time. You may find that he requires more than multiple presentation modes (tell, show, or write). Maybe you have to repeat yourself several times or say it louder, more slowly, or using different words. You may find that Alexandra requires dual methods of presentation—for jumping rope, show her and tell her—but after several weeks of jumping rope with her, the skill becomes automatic. Alexandra can now show and tell Mimi how to be an Olympic jump roper. Task analysis of the presentation mode focuses on why children are not doing what you require, by looking at how you tell them to do it.

When you task analyze the response mode, you look at what you expect Jerome to do, say, write, or show to you. What you see may show that Jerome cannot tell you about the trip to the pumpkin farm but that he can show you what he enjoyed most, may be able to demonstrate how pumpkins are picked, or may be able to draw a picture about the trip. Agatha, by contrast, can't stop talking about the trip. When asked to draw a picture about the trip, she scowls and hastily scrawls a thin orange line around the edges of the paper, then scratches across a few lines to fill in the circle and dumps her work in her cubby. By knowing how Jerome and Agatha are comfortable in responding, letting you know that they have the skill, know the concept, etc., you can set goals that will be appropriate for each of them. That is, you can let Jerome demonstrate what he knows by showing you, while working with him to learn to describe verbally his experiences, knowledge, and attitudes. Thus, Jerome feels successful while moving forward in your program. Agatha can dictate a long tape to you to describe her experiences. You may sit beside her while she draws; she may need just the tiny bit of reassurance that her pumpkins can be interpretations of pumpkins rather than the true representation of the pumpkin of her mind's eye.

In addition to these informal uses, task analysis is a technique for determining the steps in accomplishing a goal on a child's IEP or IFSP. Noonan and McCormick (1993) describe the process of forward chaining or backward chaining through a task in naturalistic early childhood settings. Chaining through a task means starting with an activity that a child has failed. Think about what happens before or what should happen afterward to determine where the failure occurs. Consider the following analogy. Mr. College Freshman is always getting overdraft notices from the bank. He must review the steps of checking account operation to ascertain the key to the task failure. Does he enter all the checks he writes in the ledger? Does he enter bank charges? Does he add and subtract regularly? Does he write numbers clearly? Does he follow the steps that the bank outlines for balancing? Once he has identified the break in the chain of steps to successful bank account management, he can make a plan to avoid overdrafts.

In early childhood settings, teachers focus task analysis on activities necessary to successful participation in the setting. For example, in many early childhood centers, children must brush their teeth after lunch. Selected steps for teeth brushing include the following:

1. Locate the toothbrush, tooth paste, and water source (these may be 3 steps, if necessary).
2. Apply the paste to the brush.
3. Brush the teeth in sequential order: front, sides, backs, etc. (Again these may be listed as more steps, if necessary).
4. Rinse the mouth.
5. Rinse the toothbrush.
6. Dry mouth and hands.
7. Return the materials to storage.

When Josh fails to brush his teeth correctly, you examine the sequence to see where he is missing a step and you teach it to him.

Cegelka & Berdine (1995) describe four ways to develop the particular steps for a task analysis. These include watch a master, self-monitoring, brainstorming, and goal analysis. Early childhood teachers can use each of these approaches to identify and record the incremental steps.

- Watch a master: To know how to help children walk the balance beam, watch someone who is doing this task well.

- Self-monitoring: To know how to help children make a papier-mâché turkey, review the steps that you follow in accomplishing the task.

- Brainstorming: To know how to help children plant a garden in a school plot, ask all the children to give you ideas.

- Goal analysis: To know how to help children develop conflict resolution strategies, review the observable and nonobservable aspects of this task and identify ways to see how it is accomplished.

All approaches to task analysis link assessment to instruction and involve step by step breaking down of tasks into teachable increments.

If a task analysis was successful with one child, it may well apply to another (Wolery, 1989). Hence, teachers should compile a task analysis *bank.* Over time, teachers may find that their task analyses fall into certain patterns related to the children they typically teach or the particular curriculum they are using. When teachers are aware of these task-analysis patterns, writing new task analyses is accomplished much more readily.

Not only does the teacher need to analyze the task; the child who is to learn the task also has to be analyzed in terms of what she can and cannot do. The number of steps in a task analysis depends upon the functioning level of the child as well as the nature of the task. There are a number of questions to be answered about the child which enable the teacher to determine the functioning level (Lerner, Mardell-Czudnowski, & Goldenberg, 1987). How does the child receive, store, and retrieve information? Which avenue of learning does the child seem to prefer: visual, auditory, or tactile? Does the child avoid certain pathways of learning? Does the child do better if more than one pathway is used simultaneously in the teaching process? Is intrusion necessary? How much assistance does the child require to master the step? Answers to these questions will enable the teacher to blend the task analysis of the skill or behavior to be mastered to the current capabilities of the target child.

Dynamic assessment

Dynamic assessment is an approach that combines formal testing and teaching. It is conducted in a one-to-one interview situation with an individual child. In this approach, the teacher uses available assessment information and tries to teach a specific skill. The available test data serve as the foundation of a task analysis for the skill or competency. The approach is derived from the theoretical work of Vygotsky (1978, 1986) and Feuerstein (1979). It is an approach that has been used quite often by speech and language therapists in their work with children who have communication disabilities (cf Wiig & Semmel, 1984). What is required of the therapist or teacher in dynamic assessment is the use of intuitive reasoning as well as conventional thinking in ferreting out why the young child is not successful with a particular skill or competency. The teacher observes as the teaching occurs and modifies the task in the process, so that the child can be successful.

How does a teacher proceed with this technique? First, give—or acquire test information—about the skill or competency in question. Next, try to teach the child the missing pieces, according to the task analysis (or test data), observing and modifying during the teaching process. Finally, retest to document progress. This process of teaching is called the mediated learning experience (Lidz, 1991). The **mediated learning experience** is the teacher using questions, suggestions, and cues to prompt the child to think more consciously about the task at hand and to expand learner expertise.

For example, you wish to encourage Morgan to elaborate her concept of stories. The available data shows that Morgan knows that stories have beginnings and endings. Your objective is for Morgan to know that stories have action that moves the story from the beginning to the end and that by changing these actions the story changes. At a quiet time, you sit with Morgan and read a short, unfamiliar story to Morgan. Then, through a process of questions and answers you help Morgan "see" what you mean about action as part of the story concept. At a later time, you assess whether Morgan has maintained the skill or whether she needs reteaching.

This avenue of assessment is promising for teachers who wish to link instruction to learner outcomes for early childhood settings. The approach links test results to task analysis to teaching to individualization of instruction. It is an opportunity for making the learning process apparent to those children who may need special assistance in linking thinking to academic requirements, whether these requirements are preschool or primary.

Functional assessment

Functional assessment is a focused observational method that links individual assessment to curricular intervention for one student. The method is most appropriate to use when you are concerned about a young child with a serious problem that interferes with successful experiences in the regular classroom. "This model does not focus on typical sequential development but rather on age-appropriate expectations for functioning as independently as possible in specific environments. A functional model of assessment requires that both the individual's skill and the environment be evaluated. Because people function in several environments, each one must be evaluated" (Hoy and Gregg, 1994, p. 240).

It is a method that requires careful observation of small pieces of behavioral interludes. The observation sequence is divided into an ABC order—antecedent, behavior, consequence. Thus, you observe the problem behavior (B) and then look more carefully to see what precipitates the event, the antecedent (A), and note the consequence (C). Before the careful observation, usually you have noticed either the problem behavior or the naturally occurring consequence. As a teacher, you seek to intervene or change the behavior by manipulating the antecedent or the consequence that, in turn, diminishes or extinguishes the target, inappropriate behavior. The method comes from the behavioral analysis tradition of assessment and intervention (cf Cegelka and Berdine, 1995). Although the method has historically been used in situations where children show many problem behaviors that prohibit or limit their participation in mainstream or inclusion settings, the method has broader applicability. It is potentially quite useful as a tool to use in situations that require intervention, such as kicking, screaming, pinching, biting, cursing, or other behaviors that present group management and social acceptance concerns.

For example, suppose that when Martha, a three year old, approaches the children in your class, they run away from her. You do not understand why this is occurring. You are concerned that it may be because Martha doesn't talk, because she walks with an uneven gait, or because she frequently arrives at school with her hair in a mess. Your tentative conclusion is that the children are fearful of Martha because they have limited experience with nonverbal children, that perhaps they are intolerant of her physical limitations, or that they are judging her on her messy appearance. You want to help the children in your class to be accepting of differences. You want to assure them that even though Martha doesn't talk, she is a worthy playmate. You plan a time to observe, so that you can learn what will help Martha approach children confidently and/or what will help the children in your group include Martha in their play.

You watch Martha. You see that she approaches Everett, gets very close to him, then puts her hand palm down on his cheek and pats it. Everett looks at her warily, but continues to mold with play dough while Martha leaves the area. Why, you ask yourself, did Everett look at Martha warily? Why do the children sometimes run and scream when Martha pats their cheeks? If you stop the assessment at this point, you may never know, or you may conclude that it is Martha's appearance or some other historical experience that the children have with Martha that creates this reaction on the part of her classmates. In fact, you may talk to Everett and say, "Martha is your friend. She wants to use the play dough. You, Everett, should invite her to join you." However, you continue your assessment before planning an intervention.

You continue to watch Martha. She approaches Kenneth, moving close with her open palm to his cheek. All of a sudden, instead of patting his cheek, Martha reaches with her nails and scratches a deep gouge in Kenneth's cheek. He screams in rage; Martha tries to pat his cheek; he runs away. You handle the crisis and later plan an intervention to stop the inappropriate social behavior of cheek scratching. An intervention strategy will not be easy to develop, since Martha sometimes pats and sometimes scratches. It is also difficult to develop an intervention that will be meaningful to Martha. Martha is "coping" (cf Zeitlin & Williamson, 1994); she is showing behavior to affect her environment. The fact that the behavior is not perceived as effective by her teachers and peers is not apparent to her. She is doing the best she can, even though it seems erratic to others. She is not learning from the typical techniques of modeling, rule reminding, etc. You, her teacher, must intervene so that she no longer harms the children in her class and so that she may develop a more adaptive behavior style that will serve her in inclusive environments.

To use this approach, you must observe carefully to see what happens first—the *antecedent*; what she does next—the *behavior*; and then develop a suitable intervention—the *consequence*. In Martha's case, the *antecedent* is an open palm to the cheek of a classmate; the *behavior* is a pat or a scratch; and the *consequence* is currently that children stare warily, run away, or scream.

You wish to improve Martha's functioning in class, so you must develop an intervention to change the consequence and extinguish the patting and scratching behavior. You must stop Martha from touching children's cheeks. With your colleagues you plan an intervention strategy, keep records about how the strategy works, and continue through a process until you find a strategy that stops Martha from patting or scratching the cheeks of classmates. You may need to be by her side for several weeks to prevent this behavior. You may choose to reinforce keeping her hand at her side with a positive consequence. Or you may choose a negative reinforcer when she sticks her hand toward a child. You may also help the other children learn cues to steer Martha on a more appropriate path, e.g., "NO, Martha, you can't touch me. You can play here." The key here is that all the children use a consistent phrase.

Bailey and Wolery (1992) discuss this assessment/intervention approach in the context of form and function. "Form refers to the behaviors of children, and function refers to the effects of those behaviors. For example, walking is a form and the effect is to get from one place to another; patting a peer on the leg is a form, and the effect may be to start an interaction; saying 'more' is the form and the effect is that the child receives additional juice" (p. 133). This analytic approach to assessment and instruction is quite useful when teachers cannot always easily judge what the behavior, form, is trying to effect. That is, what is the young child trying to do? What does he want? For example, Kevin, an eight year old whose speech is difficult to understand, says in an agitated and excited fashion, "mumble, mumble, mumble, mumble" (to your ears) at Show and Tell. You respond, "That's nice," since you are reluctant to embarrass him in front of the group. He says, "NO, THEY STOLE!" You adjust your teaching strategy (in private) so that Kevin comes to show and tell with shorter sentences, pictures, pantomime. As his speech becomes more articulate, you encourage him to use longer sentences.

Howard, a six year old, goes to the chalkboard at play time. He picks up an eraser and runs the eraser up and down the chalk tray. He does this every day for the whole play period. What does this behavior mean to Howard? What can you do to change it so that he plays with other children, so that he uses toys? It will not be easy to intervene. Howard doesn't talk and he screams if you try to take away the eraser. You must plan an intervention that will expand Howard's repertoire, but it must be done in small steps.

When using this assessment approach, teachers must consider not only the child and his behavior, but also the environment, schedule, the routines, the rules, the personal interactions, the materials—the "baseline of the program" (Berry & Mindes, 1993). You examine the antecedents to see whether some aspect of the baseline of your program can change to support the behavior that you want to increase. For example, suppose your routine is that everyone must sit on a circle for large group time. Katie, a three year old in your class, does not want to sit on the circle. She resists being held by the teacher assistant. She gets up and runs away. She doesn't participate. What if you change the routine—Katie can come to the circle when she wants to and when she is ready. If she does not come to circle, she must play quietly with her doll or play dough or whatever. You have prevented a disruption to circle. Katie can come to circle when she feels comfortable.

Or suppose Marc, a seven year old, cannot sit for one half hour in the discussion period. You change the rule that desks must be clear for discussion. Marc pays attention to discussion while drawing pictures.

What you have done in these situations is manipulated or changed the baseline so that problem behaviors of children do not interfere with their social experiences (function) in the classroom. These changes are not always straightforward. Think about a dieter who knows that chocolate donuts should not be in the house (antecedent). The ingredients for brownies are in the cupboard. The dieter makes the brownies and eats them. The diet suffers! The dieter must develop other strategies for overcoming the weight gains by examining all of the variables that impact eating patterns, and choose behaviors and consequences accordingly. In the case of young children, the teacher or parent must choose the behavior to change so that the young child can function as well as possible in inclusive situations.

Noonan and McCormick (1993) describe the use of this integrated assessment/intervention approach in naturalistic settings for infants and toddlers. The comprehensive approach they describe applies the principles of behavioral analysis to the environments where the infants and toddlers are served, including the home. Goals developed by the multidisciplinary team may include attention toward self-help skills and play patterns with siblings. The intervention specialist focuses an observation on a finite form (behavior)—putting on a tee shirt—and suggests ways for parents to support the development of this skill.

In summary, this assessment technique should be considered for situations where individual children show annoying behavior, yet conventional methods of observation and intervention have not been effective. It is important to remember that this assessment technique is designed to be used for troublesome social behaviors that interfere with a young child's ability to cope or *function* in the classroom. To be effective, this technique must be applied to particular situations for particular children. It is a precision teaching tool to assess, intervene, and reassess. It is a tool applied to behaviors that are hard to figure out, initially. By using this system of microscopic observation and personalized intervention, children can adapt more effectively to inclusive situations.

Assessment of multiple intelligences

A controversy has been raging for many years over the use of intelligence tests in American schools. According to Gardner (1983), "the problem lies less in the technology of testing than in the ways we customarily think about the intellect and in our ingrained views of intelligence. Only if we expand and reformulate our view of what counts as human intellect will we be able to devise more appropriate ways of assessing it and more effective ways of educating it" (p. 4).

Gardner has attempted to do just that by developing a comprehensive framework based on his theory of **multiple intelligences** (MI). He posits that there are seven areas of intellectual competence (intelligences) that are relatively independent of each other. The seven intelligences are linguistic intelligence, logical-mathematical intelligence, spatial intelligence, bodily-kinesthetic intelligence, musical intelligence, interpersonal intelligence, and intrapersonal intelligence (Gardner, 1983). It is possible to provide classroom learning centers for each of the different abilities (language center, math and science center, music center, movement center, art center, working together center, personal work center) that would help children learn subject matter content while utilizing their own relative strengths.

There are a number of projects that have sprung up across the United States that are based on Gardner's MI theory. One of the first was Project Spectrum, a preschool program that began in 1984 at Harvard and Tuft Universities. In addition to assessing the more traditional areas of linguistic and mathematical abilities, the Project Spectrum assessment battery examines bodily, spatial, mechanical, musical, social, and scientific abilities (Krechevsky, 1991). Figure 6.2 shows the areas of cognitive ability examined in Project Spectrum.

According to Krechevsky (1991), Project Spectrum offers a developmentally appropriate alternative to extending formal instruction downward and embracing a narrow view of academic readiness. Project Spectrum is based on the assumption that every child has the potential to develop strength in one or several content areas and that it is the responsibility of the educational system to discover and nurture these tendencies. The Project Spectrum approach is centered on a wide range of rich activities; assessment comes about as an integral part of the child's involvement over time in these activities. As Figure 6.6 shows, Project Spectrum measures range from relatively structured and targeted tasks (for example, in the number and music domains) to less structured measures and observations (for example, in the science and social domains). The assessment activities are administered throughout the year. Documentation takes a variety of forms, from observation checklists to scoresheets to portfolios and tape recordings.

Distinctive features of the Project Spectrum assessment system include

1. blurring the line between curriculum and assessment by gathering information over time in the child's own environment.
2. embedding assessment in meaningful, real-world activities.
3. using measures that are "intelligence-fair."
4. emphasizing children's strengths.
5. attending to the stylistic dimensions of performance (see Figure 6.3) (Krechevsky, 1991).

Other projects have seen it useful in identifying the gifted, especially gifted children from culturally and linguistically diverse populations. This is particularly significant since the U.S. population has changed dramatically in the past ten years from a predominance of persons of European ancestry to a multicultural mix of immigrants from Latin America and Asia (Maker, Nielson, & Rogers, 1994). According to the 1990 Census, the total number of persons born outside the United States increased 40% between

FIGURE 6.2 Areas of cognitive ability examined in Project Spectrum

Numbers

Dinosaur Game: Measures a child's understanding of number concepts, counting skills, ability to adhere to rules, and use of strategy.

Bus Game: Assess a child's ability to create a useful notation system, perform mental calculations, and organize number information for one or more variables.

Science

Assembly Activity: Measures a child's mechanical ability. Successful completion of the activity depends on fine motor skills and visual-spatial, observational, and problem-solving abilities.

Treasure Hunt Game: Assesses a child's ability to make logical inferences. The child is asked to organize information to discover the rule governing the placement of various treasures.

Water Activity: Assesses a child's ability to generate hypotheses based on his or her observations and to conduct simple experiments.

Discovery Area: Includes year-round activities that elicit a child's observations, appreciation, and understanding of natural phenomena.

Music

Music Production Activity: Measures a child's ability to maintain accurate pitch and rhythm while singing and his or her ability to recall a song's musical properties.

Music Perception Activity: Assesses a child's ability to discriminate pitch. The activity consists of song recognition, error recognition, and pitch discrimination.

Language

Storyboard Activity: Measures a range of language skills including complexity of vocabulary and sentence structure, use of connectors, use of descriptive language and dialogue, and ability to pursue a storyline.

Reporting Activity: Assesses a child's ability to describe an event he or she has experienced with regard to the following criteria: ability to report content accurately, level of detail, sentence structure, and vocabulary.

Visual Arts

Art Portfolios: The contents of a child's art portfolio are reviewed twice a year and assessed on criteria that include use of lines and shapes, color, space, detail, and representation and design. Children also participate in three structured drawing activities. The drawings are assessed on criteria similar to those used in the portfolio assessment.

Movement

Creative Movement: The ongoing movement curriculum focuses on children's abilities in five areas of dance and creative movement: sensitivity to rhythm, expressiveness, body control, generation of movement ideas, and responsiveness to music.

Athletic Movement: An obstacle course focuses on the types of skills found in many different sports such as coordination, timing, balance, and power.

FIGURE 6.2 (continued)

Social

Classroom Model Activity: Assesses a child's ability to observe and analyze social events and experiences in his or her classroom.

Peer Interaction Checklist: A behavioral checklist is used to assess the behaviors in which children engage when interacting with peers. Different patterns of behavior yield distinctive social roles such as facilitator and leader.

Krechevsky, M. (1991). Project spectrum: An innovative assessment alternative. *Educational Leadership, 48*(5), 43–48.

1980 and 1990. A related fact is that 14% of the current school population does not speak English at home (Waggoner, 1993).

Maker et al. (1994) have added two important components to the MI theory to enhance its usefulness for both gifted children and those from culturally and linguistically diverse populations. First, they define a gifted person as a problem-solver, one who enjoys the challenge of complexity and persists until the problem is solved in a satisfying way. This problem-solving ability may be demonstrated within each of the intelligences, and it is demonstrated by some children across all intelligences. Secondly, researchers in creativity and problem solving have developed a matrix of problem types for Gardner's MI theory (Table 6.2) (Maker, 1992; Schiever, 1991).

Using this matrix, Maker et al. (1994) have designed a process called DISCOVER for assessing problem solving in multiple intelligences. Use of this process results in identification of equitable percentages of students from various ethnic, cultural, linguistic, and economic groups (Nielson, 1993). As with Project Spectrum, the DISCOVER assessment takes place in the regular classroom setting. Table 6.3 displays the problem types, activities, and intelligences that are measured in grades K–2, in four of the seven intelligences.

During the assessment of the spatial activity, children are directed to build certain constructions (a rainbow, an animal, or mountains) and then to make anything they want to make. The difficulty of the tasks varies with the age of the child: younger children may make an animal while older children may make a machine. For the mathematical-spatial and mathematical activity, the children begin by making a geometric shape, i.e., a square, a triangle, or a parallelogram, using as many of the tangram pieces from a 21-piece set. Next, the children solve a set of six increasingly complex puzzles. Observers record the time needed to complete puzzles, the

---

FIGURE 6.3 Stylistic features examined in Project Spectrum

Child is
- easily engaged/reluctant to engage in activity
- confident/tentative
- playful/serious
- focused/distractible
- persistent/frustrated by task
- reflective about own work/impulsive
- apt to work slowly/apt to work quickly

Child
- responds to visual/auditory/kinesthetic cues
- demonstrates planful approach
- brings personal agenda/strength to task
- finds humor in content area
- uses materials in unexpected ways
- shows pride in accomplishment
- shows attention to detail/is observant
- is curious about materials
- shows concern over "correct" answer
- focuses on interaction with adult
- transforms task/material

Krechevsky, M. (1991). Project spectrum: An innovative assessment alternative. *Educational Leadership, 48*(5), 43–48.

---

number completed, and the problem-solving strategies used. Finally, for the linguistic activity, the children are given a bag of toys. After a short play period, they talk about some of the toys and tell a story involving any or all of them. An adult transcribes the story verbatim and encourages each child to tell the story in his or her native or dominant language. Older students may tape record their stories, write them, or tell them to an adult (Maker et al., 1994).

Two more activities are conducted after the observers leave the classroom: a math worksheet, which includes computation and open-ended problem solving, and a writing task in which the children write about a topic of their choice. After observing the children, scoring their math worksheets, and analyzing their responses to the open-ended writing exercise, all information of observable behaviors is entered on checklists. A profile of the children's strengths across five intelligences (spatial, logical-mathematical, linguistic, interpersonal, and intrapersonal) is developed. Maker et al. (1993) plan to eventually include musical and bodily-kinesthetic problem-solving in the assessment process (Maker et al., 1994).

TABLE 6.2 Matrix of problem types for Gardner's seven intelligences

	Type I Clearly defined. Use method. Solve correctly.	Type II Clearly defined. Select method. Solve correctly.	Type III Clearly defined. Choose from range of methods. Range of answers.	Type IV Clearly defined. Discover method. Create solution.	Type V Lacks definition. Define problem. Discover method. Create solution.
Linguistic					
Logical-Mathematical					
Spatial					
Musical					
Bodily-Kinesthetic					
Interpersonal					
Intrapersonal					

From "Giftedness, Diversity, and Problem-Solving" by Maker, J., Nielson, A., Rogers, J., *Teaching Exceptional Children, Fall,* 1994, pp. 4–19. Copyright 1994 by The Council for Exceptional Children. Reprinted with permission.

Although assessment of multiple intelligences is in its infancy, early childhood educators can still employ its tenets, not only for potentially gifted children, but also culturally and linguistically diverse learners in their classrooms. This theory has the possibility of benefiting every child.

Summary

This chapter describes the most common alternative assessment strategies in use today. Their use depends on a number of variables such as the age of the child, the amount of time the teacher can invest in the assessment, and the particular skill or skills being assessed. Five alternative assessment strategies were discussed in detail: play-based assessment, task analysis, dynamic assessment, functional assessment, and assessment of multiple intelligences.

TABLE 6.3 DISCOVER process problem types, activities, and intelligences grades K-2

Activities and Intelligences	Problem Type				
	Type I	Type II	Type III	Type IV	Type V
Spatial	Find a piece shaped like a ☐. (Teacher shows a shape.)	Find pieces that look like a rainbow. (Observer shows pictures.)	Find pieces and make mountains. (Observer shows pictures.)	Make any animal with as many pieces as you need. Tell about your animal if you want. (Observer provides connectors.)	Make anything you want to make. Tell about it if you wish.
Mathematical-Spatial	Complete simple tangram puzzles with a one-to-one correspondence between the tangram pieces and the puzzles.	Complete simple tangram puzzles with more than one solution that works.	Complete complex tangram puzzles with multiple solutions.	Make a square with as many tangram pieces as you can.	Make a design or a pattern with the pieces.
Mathematical	Complete one- and two-digit addition and subtraction problems.	Complete magic squares using addition and subtraction.	Write correct number sentences using numbers given (in any order).	Write as many correct number problems as you can with an answer of 10.	None
Linguistic	Provide a label for toys given.	Make groups of toys and tell how items in the group are alike. (Some are obvious.)	Make different groups of toys and tell how items in each group are alike. (Encourage going beyond the obvious.)	Tell a story that includes all your toys.	Write a story about a personal experience, something you made up, or anything you wish.

From "Giftedness, Diversity, and Problem-Solving" by Maker, J., Nielson, A., Rogers, J., *Teaching Exceptional Children, Fall,* 1994, pp. 4–19. Copyright 1994 by The Council for Exceptional Children. Reprinted with permission.

⊞ CHAPTER 6 Suggested further readings

Armstrong, T. (1994). *Multiple intelligences in the classroom.* Alexandria: Association for Supervision and Curriculum Development.

Gardner, H. (1993). *Multiple intelligences: The theory in practice.* New York: Basic Books.

ACTIVITIES

1. With a partner, go to a local park or playground. Between the two of you, see if you can find examples of solitary play, parallel play, group play-associative play, cooperative play, functional play, constructive play, dramatic play, games with rules, unoccupied behavior, and onlooker behavior as defined in Figure 6.1. Discuss your findings with each other to see if you can reach total agreement.

2. Select a long-term objective that you think would be worthwhile teaching to a young child.

Genishi, C. (Ed.). (1992). *Ways of assessing children and curriculum.* NY: Teacher's College Press.

Lidz, C. (1991). *Practitioner's guide to dynamic assessment.* New York: Guilford.

Linder, T. (1993). *Transdisciplinary play-based assessment: A functional approach to working with young children* (rev. ed.). Baltimore: Brookes.

McAfee, O., & Leong, D. (1994). *Assessing and guiding young children's development and learning.* Boston: Allyn & Bacon.

CHAPTER 6 Study questions

1. List four reasons why teachers should know about alternative assessment strategies.

2. Why has play assessment become such a popular assessment strategy? Provide a rationale for its use.

3. When doing a formal task analysis, what are the two ways in which the teaching steps can be sequenced? Describe each way, giving a developmentally appropriate early childhood example.

4. What does dynamic assessment add to the task analysis process?

5. Explain in your own words the characteristics of a mediated learning experience (MLE).

6. Define functional assessment. For what type of problems is this strategy most often used?

7. Explain the relationship of antecedents, behaviors, and consequences in functional assessment.

References

Bailey, D. B., & Wolery, M. (1992). *Teaching infants and preschoolers with disabilities* (2nd ed.). New York: Merrill.

Berry, C., & Mindes, G. (1993). *Planning a theme-based curriculum.* Glenview, IL: Good Year Books.

Bricker, D., & Cripe J. (1992). *An activity-based approach to early intervention.* Baltimore: Paul H. Brookes.

Cegelka, P. T., & Berdine, W. H. (1995). *Effective instruction for students with learning problems.* Boston: Allyn & Bacon.

Feuerstein, R. (1979). *The dynamic assessment of retarded performers: The learning potential assessment device, theory, instruments, and techniques.* Baltimore: University Park Press.

Fewell R. (1991). *Play assessment scale.* Miami, FL: University of Miami.

Gardner, H. (1983). *Frames of mind: The theory of multiple intelligences.* New York: Basic Books.

Garvey, C. (1993). Special topic: New directions in studying pretend play. *Human Development, 35*(4), 235–240.

Hirsch, E. S. (Ed.). (1984). *The block book* (rev. ed.). Washington, DC: National Association for the Education of Young Children.

Hoy, C., & Gregg, N. (1994). *Assessment: The special educator's role.* Pacific Grove, CA: Brooks/Cole.

Johnson, J., Christie, J., & Yawkey, T. (1987). *Play and early childhood development.* Glenview, IL: Scott, Foresman.

Krechevsky, M. (1991). Project spectrum: An innovative assessment alternative. *Educational Leadership, 48*(5), 43–48.

Lerner, J., Mardell-Czudnowski, C., & Goldenberg, D. (1987). *Special education for the early childhood years* (2nd ed.). Englewood Cliffs, NJ: Prentice-Hall.

Lidz, C. (1991). *Practitioner's guide to dynamic assessment.* New York: Guilford.

Linder, T. (1993). *Transdisciplinary play-based assessment: A functional approach to working with young children* (rev. ed.). Baltimore: Brookes.

Maker, J. (1992). Intelligence and creativity in multiple intelligences: Identification and development. *Educating Able Learners, 17*(4), 12–19.

Maker, J., Nielson, A., & Rogers, J. (1994). Giftedness, diversity, and problem-solving. *Teaching Exceptional Children, Fall,* 4–19.

Mindes, G. (1982). Social and cognitive aspects of play in young handicapped children. *Topics of Early Childhood Special Education, 2,* 14.

Noonan, M. J., & McCormick, L. (1993). *Early intervention in natural environments.* Pacific Grove, CA: Brooks/Cole.

Schiever, S. (1991). *A comprehensive approach to teaching thinking.* Boston: Allyn & Bacon.

Van Hoorn, J., Nourot, P., Scales, B., & Alward, K. (1993). *Play at the center of the curriculum.* New York: Macmillan.

Vygotsky, L. (1978). *Mind in society: The development of higher psychological processes* (M. Cole, V. John-Steiner, S. Scribner, & E. Souberman, Eds.). Cambridge, MA: Harvard University Press.

Vygotsky, L. (1986). *Thought and language* (A. Kozulin, Trans.). Cambridge, MA: MIT Press.

Waggoner, D. (1993). 1990 census shows dramatic change in the foreign-born population in the U.S. *NABE News, 16*(7), 1, 18–19.

Weber, C., Behl, D., & Summers, M. (1994). Watch them play; watch them learn. *Teaching Exceptional Children, Fall*, 30–35.

Westby C. (1991). A scale for assessing children's pretend play. In C. Schaefer, K. Gitlin, & A. Sandgrund (Eds.), *Play assessment and diagnosis*. New York: Wiley.

Wiig, E., & Semmel, E. M. (1984). *Language assessment and intervention for the learning disabled*. Columbus, OH: Merrill.

Wolery, M. (1989). Using assessment information to plan instructional programs. In D. Bailey & M. Wolery (Eds.), *Assessing infants and preschoolers with handicaps*. Columbus, OH: Merrill.

Wolery, M., & Bailey, D. (1989). Assessing play skills. In D. Bailey & M. Wolery (Eds.), *Assessing infants and preschoolers with handicaps*. Columbus, OH: Merrill.

Zeitlin, S., & Williamson, G. G. (1994). *Coping in young children: Early intervention practices to enhance adaptive behavior and resilience*. Baltimore: Paul H. Brookes.

CHAPTER 7

Recording and Reporting to Parents and Others

Terms to Know
- confidentiality
- report card
- multidisciplinary staffing
- stakeholders
- accountability

CHAPTER OVERVIEW This chapter discusses the recording and reporting issues for all stakeholders in the assessment system for young children. The importance and role of routine parent/teacher conferences as part of a comprehensive assessment system are highlighted. The chapter begins with issues and suggestions surrounding recording, storing, and maintaining child files. The topics of parent permission and parent participation in the assessment process are included. Special procedures for partnerships with parents as clients are delineated. Examples and issues related to report cards and portfolio assessment reporting procedures are included. The teacher's role and responsibility in multidisciplinary staffing are described. Finally, there is a section on issues and suggested report procedures regarding the other stakeholders in the assessment system—administrators, boards, legislators, and the public.

Topics Discussed
- Recording and reporting in the assessment system
- Maintaining confidentiality of assessment information
- Involving parents in assessment

- Conferencing with parents
- Preparing report cards
- When families are clients
- Multidisciplinary staffing
- Reporting to other stakeholders

Recording and reporting in the assessment system

As discussed in Chapter Two, collaboration and communication between parents and teachers begins at enrollment. If parents view the entrance of their child to the care and education system positively, then subsequent contacts at conference and report card times will start favorably. Parents will enter the conference with the expectation of respect, cooperation, and mutual discussion of the best interests of their child.

Conference and report card periods are the summative opportunities for parent-teacher communication. It is a time when all parties in the assessment system—parent, child, teacher and other professionals—share information from their diverse perspectives. It is a time to reflect on the past and to prepare appropriate intervention, teaching, and learning goals for the future.

In preparation for these times, teachers must formally reflect about each child in the program, collect records, and prepare for the conference or translate the material to child-study or report-card format. These efforts must match the philosophy, curriculum and parent program.

Maintaining confidentiality of assessment information

As teachers prepare written records for these conference intervals, careful attention is required for the ethical and legal responsibilities for confidential child progress records. Teachers maintain **confidentiality** by treating assessment and other child records as private documents that must be recorded, shared, and stored so that only authorized school or agency officials and the child's parents know the contents of these materials. Official school or agency records should be stored in only one place (PL 93-380, the Family Educational and Privacy Rights Act). This includes demographic information, family and social history, academic history, attendance records, medical data, test scores, anecdotal notes, and report cards (narrative or checklist). These records must be housed in a locked file. Authorized school personnel (principal, teacher, specialists) may view the records and are charged with the maintenance of them. Parents may see the records by appointment within 45 days of the parent initiated request.

In the classroom, before records become *official,* teachers must safeguard notes, scores, and drafts of reports. Teachers must also choose with care the words that they use in recording notes and progress. Behavior should be described specifically. Judgments, opinions, and hypotheses should be clearly labeled as such. Broad sweeping generalizations and value judgments should be avoided. Teachers and other professionals may only write about observations and experiences that they have the credentials to assess. For example, teachers are not qualified to judge mental health and intelligence. Teachers may appropriately discuss observable concerns and problems in performance. In Box 7.1 illustrations of appropriate and inappropriate practices are shown.

BOX 7.1

Inappropriate

■ Garfield has caused me a lot of concern.

   Very hyperactive and immature. He needs a medical exam and perhaps something to calm him down!

Appropriate Practice

■ Ms. Taylor collects notes and checklists that she developed for use with the kindergarten. At report time, Ms. Taylor notices as she reviews her notes that Garfield spends an average of five minutes on drawing, painting, puzzle activities. He spends an average of about 10 minutes in the block corner. At the circle times, Garfield wiggles, but listens attentively to the stories. In writing, Ms. Taylor can report the facts of her observations and notes. She may then interpret the facts with a sentence or two: Garfield prefers block play. This activity seems to hold his interest more than other available areas in our room. He seems to enjoy story time. He follows the story line well. Whether Ms. Taylor initiates a discussion about unusual activity level will depend on additional information available: family has new baby, Garfield responds to structure and limits offered. Garfield is probably functioning within typical limits for 4 1/2 year olds.

Inppropriate

■ Patty is lazy and shirks responsibility for getting work done. She must be prodded to do neater work.

Appropriate Practice

■ Patty is a third grader in Mr. Merrill's class. Mr. Merrill assigns work at the beginning of the week. Each third grader is responsible for personal time management. Assignments include: small group project work, individual work sheets for math, reading books by interest and level. Science, art, music, drama, and physical education are separate subjects taught by subject area specialists. Students who do not finish assignments at school must taken them home. Mr. Merrill notices near the end of the quarter that Patty has many worksheets that are incomplete. He notices that the ones that require

BOX 7.1 (continued)

writing are written in a haphazard fashion. Stories prepared by Patty are short: one or two sentences. Mr. Merrill reflects that this behavior is new for Patty. In second grade, she completed assignments and seemed enthusiastic about school. Mr. Merrill plans an open-ended parent conference, rather than a narrative report summarizing his findings. He plans to ask Patty's mother, Ms. Jones, questions about school from Patty's perspective and from Ms. Jones' perspective. Then he will ask Ms. Jones if there are unusual stresses at home. Following this discussion, Mr. Merrill will make a teaching plan to assist Patty.

If required to write a narrative report for the quarter, Mr. Merrill can state the following: Patty has not finished assigned work at school. She has written very short essays. This approach to school work is very different than her approach in second grade. Ms. Jones, let's meet to discuss how we can assist Patty in becoming a successful third-grade learner.

Inppropriate

- Alan doesn't copy from other children anymore, but he lacks original ideas. Goes home for lunch and forgets to come back from the playground.

Appropriate Practice

- Alan, a first grader, seems to like to work with friends. He thrives on their stimulation. He likes active play. Lunchtime is his favorite time of the day. He needs some assistance in remembering to return to the room after lunch. We are developing a plan with Alan.

These notes were prepared by teachers prior to parent conference time. The notes represent the reflections of the teachers. Parents can be similarly involved.

Involving parents in assessment

Before parents come to school to hear the report of the school or at the conference, teachers can suggest real assessment partnerships for parents:

1. Ask parents for their goals for their children. This will provide an opportunity for you to talk with parents about the curriculum and their child.

> Ms. Berkeley the parent of a kindergartner, believes that her son Seth is gifted. She bases her assessment on Seth's early talking. Ms. Berkeley wants Seth to read at the end of the first quarter of kindergarten.

Ms. Myers, the kindergarten teacher, explains the developmental stages of literacy to Ms. Berkeley. She shows Ms. Berkeley evidence of Seth's progress and invites Ms. Berkeley to keep a log of stories and other literacy activities that occur at home over the first quarter of the year.

2. Ask parents for their opinion about homework assignments.

Ms. Donohue asks children in her third-grade class to interview a senior citizen, relative, or friend. Children must be prepared to summarize their interviews in a paragraph. M/M Robin have moved from out of town and know no one in the neighborhood. Their daughter Sylvia is distraught that she will fail the assignment. Sylvia has attended a developmentally inappropriate third grade. Ms. Donohue learns of Sylvia's distress through the return of the parent questionnaire about homework and can reassure Sylvia before the problem becomes cast into a concrete mountain. Ms. Donohue suggests, for example, that Sylvia can interview Ms. Donohue's mother, who is a school volunteer, the chief engineer, the security guard, or other friendly adults around the school.

3. Provide checklist or open-ended question sheets for parents to record their own experiences with their childrens' progress in a subject area.

Mr. Lester, the science teacher, suggests several take-home science experiments for young children attending Bowman Early Childhood Center that serves children birth to age eight. Parents and children are encouraged to try the experiments at home. Parents, with their child's help, record experiment results. They are encouraged to keep a notebook of experiments, results, any problems, and a record of concepts. At conference time, parents share with teachers the observations and solicit suggestions for associated readings. Teachers can comment on the observations from school. The partnership is solidified.

4. Use the written parent comments at conference time. "My child . . .
    a. understands more of what he/she reads
    b. enjoys being read to by family members
    c. finds quiet time at home to read
    d. sometimes guesses at words but they usually make sense
    e. can provide summaries of stories read
    f. has a good attitude about reading
    g. enjoys reading to family members
    h. would like to get more books from the library
    i. chooses to write about stories read
    j. is able to complete homework assignments"
    (Fredericks & Rasinski, 1990)

Similar questionnaires can be developed for any subject or developmental area. These items serve as suggested activities for parents as well as involving parents in the assessment process. Ms. Jewel can develop a list of questions for parents of the three year olds in her program about favorite play activities:

- enjoys pretend play with dolls and small figures, cars, spaceships
- enjoys water play at bath time or in kitchen sink with parent or responsible older sibling
- likes to go to the park to run and chase friends
- loves to act out favorite stories
- sings songs from school

All of these procedures provide meaningful, personalized opportunities to involve parents in the regular child care and educational lives of their children. Sometimes the results of these regular contacts, or initial contacts, will require specialized assessment to develop appropriate planning for children with special needs. In those cases parent involvement is not only recommended but required as a formality.

Parent permission is required for any specialized assessment of children. This includes any measure beyond the usual and customary actions of teachers and care givers—for example, a speech therapist screening Lori for a lisp, an in-depth assessment by a school psychologist on Bartholomew, or a physical-therapist review of Daniel. Permission is best obtained as an outgrowth of a routine or special conference with parents.

Conferencing with parents

Preparing parents for the experience

Preparing parents is an important teacher role. Many approaches to communication of expectations are needed due to the diverse needs of parents. Parents themselves may have ideas about good preparation strategies. The parent community may be especially helpful in those situations where cultural and linguistic differences between teachers and parents affect basic communication. So, in preparation for conferences, teachers continue their parent communication through various formats.

Teachers create a welcoming environment by being available to parents before and after school. During these informal chats, a comfort level is established. Teachers can set times to be available by phone. They communicate with parents by notes and in newsletters. At conference time, teachers may make suggestions in the newsletter of effective conference participation. Regular—weekly, monthly—newsletters (cf Berger, 1995) to parents often contain information about class activities, wishes for volunteers and recyclable material, as well as parent-education pieces such as Box 7.2.

Pre-conference survey to parents

Child-care programs and public schools may wish to develop a survey to send to parents. This may be particularly useful when parents are entering a program. These entrance procedures are discussed in Chapter Two. A survey gives parents time to clarify their goals for their children and also an opportunity to solidify their knowledge. It may serve to prepare them for the world of child care or school. This also may help a teacher guide the discussion. Parents should feel empowered because they have had an opportunity to prepare for their first encounter with the school.

Primary teachers may survey parents about past experiences with school through the use of open-ended questions.

- When you think about it, what excited Willard most about second grade? Were there assignments or activities that he seemed excited to do and couldn't wait to go to school that day?
- Which projects seemed most difficult for Willard?
- Did Willard enjoy cooperative assignments with classmates?
- Were there some children that Willard had difficulty working with?

BOX 7.2

Newsletter Suggestions to Parents

- Think about your child before meeting with the teacher. What do you know about the school schedule, routine, and curriculum? What do you want to know more about? Jot down a couple of notes. Identify any particular developmental issues that you think the teacher may have suggestions for.

- Think about what your child tells you about school. If your child is old enough, ask what the child expects to happen at the conference. Ask if there are any problems with the curriculum or peers.

- Come prepared to learn about ways to help your child at home. Besides supervising any homework, find out what you can do to further the school objectives. Listen to suggestions about ways to volunteer at the school. If you are not free during school hours, find out what you might do in the evening or on weekends. Remember that parents who participate in school show their children that school is important. Their children respond by achieving.

■ How do you describe Willard as a learner, worker?

■ What are the most important learning goals for third graders from your perspective?

Teachers will want to develop the questions so that they are focused and related to their school goals. Writing style and language should be suited to the school community.

The Ohio Department of Education (1990) published a guide for school districts and parents called *Study Skills Begin at Home.* The developmental guidelines include suggestions for health and nutrition, including television management and sleep routines. Suggestions are given for appropriate parent/child television viewing. Skills included in the manuals are locating information, organizing information, recalling information, adjusting reading rate, formalizing study methods, using graphic aids, and following directions. Age-appropriate expectations are listed and illustrated for preschool and primary ages. The materials serve to help parents invest in the partnership with the school. Progress on home activities can be shared with teachers and assist teachers in responsive programming for individual children and families. Such materials also serve to empower parents as experts in the lives of their children. This may be particularly important in situations where parents are uncertain or insecure about their own levels of educational attainment.

Staging effective conferences

The seating and room arrangement will influence the success of a conference. If possible, choose a small conference room for the conferences so that quiet may be preserved. If not possible, be sure that your classroom has enough adult-sized chairs so that parents and teachers can be treated equally. Be sure everyone can see each other at the conference and that there is appropriate space. Too much open space may be intimidating. Constant brushing against participants may also be disconcerting.

Greet parents at the door and introduce yourself by first and last name or by following the conventions of the community for formality. It is inappropriate to call parents by their first names and to call yourself Ms. Teacher. Some parents prefer the formality of being addressed as Mr. and Mrs. Parent and are comfortable if you introduce yourself as Ms. Teacher.

Observe appropriate time-keeping customs for the community in scheduling and holding conferences. Conferences should be held when parents can come to school conveniently. Child care should be provided, if necessary. If parents view starting time as a target time to arrive at the meeting, then allow appropriate latitude in keeping with the cultural community perspective.

Provide opportunities for parents to participate in decision making about their child's educational plan. Some parents will come with questions and suggestions. Others will have limited information about school. Some will remember with horror their own negative experiences. Others will be intimidated by the structure of the meeting. That is, the number of professionals may intimidate parents who are insecure with their own development or educational attainment.

Bell (1989) makes the following suggestions for parent-teacher conferences:

- Notify (or invite) parents about the purpose, place, date, and length of time.
- Identify any parent concerns.
- Help children understand that conferences are routine.
- Collect relevant materials.
- Listen carefully and be tactful in presenting information that parents may regard as threatening or with distress. For example, Mrs. Lawyer may not be delighted to hear that her daughter has failed the second grade math test.
- Make notes of relevant information after the conference is over or secure parent permission to make notes.
- With the parents' assistance, summarize the conference. If the conference is one where a written report, test scores, and grades are discussed, share a copy of these materials.
- Plan follow-up activities, interventions, and conferences with parents.

These suggestions apply to preparation for conferences with all parents.

In addition, teachers must be sensitive to individual needs of parents. For example, a sit-down conference may be difficult for a young mother who has a new baby and a preschooler in your program. She may prefer to visit by phone. She may invite you to her home. Teachers must be sensitive to parent preference in regard to the location of the conference. Some parents may prefer not to have the privacy of their home invaded by the school. Others may feel that it is their responsibility and appropriate for the parent to go to the school. It is a demonstration of their perception of the *good* parent. For example, Mrs. Cobb, the mother of 10 children and without a car, categorically refused to have her youngest child's teacher come to the home. This is in spite of the one-hour bus trip necessary for Mrs. Cobb to arrive at the school. She cared for her children and going to school was a demonstration of care.

Suggested procedures for further individualization of conferences can be obtained by surveying parents to determine their preferred level of participation.

■ How much time do you spend at night discussing your child's day at school? (de Bettencourt, 1987 p. 26)

■ How many hours a day do you work? (de Bettencourt, 1987 p. 26)

■ Do you find it stressful to help your child at home with school-assigned tasks?

■ What do you do with your child that is fun?

Using portfolios effectively at conferences

Prior to the first set of parent conferences, think about how portfolios are used in your program. Define for yourself or in consultation with others the purpose of portfolio assessment. Is this the only information collected? What other sources of information are available? How are students and parents involved in deciding what stays in the portfolio?

Hill, Kamber, and Norwick (1994) suggest that portfolios be shared with parents biweekly. Children look through the collection of their own work. Then they write a letter to their parents about what they have studied. Younger children might choose samples of work to go home. In Hill's suggested format, parents review the work over the weekend. Then, they send comments to their child and teacher about their impressions. Donovan (1995) developed a two-way form for The Chicago Public Schools Project of Erikson Institute, as shown in Figure 7.1.

Preparing report cards

The form of a report card must match the philosophy and educational approach of the school or program. That is, in developmentally appropriate preschool and primary settings, parent conferences, narrative reports, and checklists are appropriate. Letter grades and arbitrary rankings are not appropriate for young children. As school districts move toward the philosophy of holistic instruction and performance assessment, new report processes are developed. **Report cards** are formal, written documents that form a legal academic history for each child in your program. They are sent home to parents at regular intervals.

Teachers and schools must be clear about the criteria and choose criteria according to the evidence available for report cards. Kovas (1993) describes three categories.

FIGURE 7.1 Parent response form.

Parent Response Form		Teacher Reply Needed?	
Date Initials	Comments From Teacher	Yes	No
	Comments From Parent		

Donovan, (1995).

1. **Product criteria:** What can the child produce at a particular point in time? Does the product match expected developmental or academic progress?
2. **Process criteria:** How does the child function as a learner? Is his progress appropriate for age, stage, or grade?
3. **Progress criteria:** What gain has the child made in relation to his previous performance at a point in time? Individual evaluation is key. Comparison to the group is not a part of this approach.

Many districts use a combined method. The combination yields a fuller picture and provides opportunities for a description of special needs and social context in relation to the criteria.

Claridge and Whitaker (1994) describe the procedure used by Tucson Unified School District. Teachers in Tucson use a rubric description of student progress. General categories include:

Learner Qualities

- self-directed learner
- collaborative worker
- problem solver
- responsible citizen
- quality producer

Content Areas

- reading
- writing

- listening and speaking
- mathematics
- social studies
- science
- health
- fine arts (p. 7)

Operational descriptions derived for each of these categories reflect district philosophy and the Arizona State Essential Skills. Teachers can write additional comments after either the learner characteristics or the content areas. In addition, teachers describe how decisions were made for the choice of the functioning level. The process is still being refined.

Ann Arbor schools (Sperling, 1994) prepare performance outcomes for each grade (K–2) in math, reading, and writing. Tasks and criteria establish benchmarks. Outcomes can be assessed as not yet, developing, achieving, and extending. Teachers use record keeping for the benchmarks as direct input for the report card. Examples of outcomes and report card entries are shown in Box 7.3.

Aurora Colorado Public Schools (Kenney & Perry, 1994) involved parents and children in the process of developing new report cards. First, the district developed rubrics (definitions) for comparing student perfor-

---

BOX 7.3

Kindergarten outcome: Counts to 20

- **Not yet**
  counts 1 to 5
  counts to 10, but skips one or more numbers
  may be able to count along with someone else

- **Developing**
  counts from 1 to 10 but cannot count from 11 to 19 without errors
  counts to 20 but skips one or more numbers
  when asked for the next number, may need to start counting from 1

- **Achieving**
  counts orally from 1 to 20 without any errors
  automatically knows the next number

- **Extending**
  counts beyond 20
  counts by 2s, 5s, and/or 10s
  counts backward (p. 11)

mance to established outcomes. District personnel developed a brochure to describe the new report card. After sending it home, they invited parents to comment by completing a questionnaire. Children were thoroughly oriented to the new card. Through this process, the district developed proficiency ratings for both content outcomes and for learner behavior. Teachers keep notebooks with a page for each proficiency. On the page they record procedures children use to develop and sample products. Immediate effects of the approach include greater student and parent satisfaction with the communication between school and home. Everyone understands the goals, the measures and the rubric describing progress.

Report cards are powerful communicators with parents. They are familiar, most parents received them when they were students. However, they have sometimes served to stifle self-esteem and promote child/parent/teacher conflict due to the ambiguity or inappropriate yard stick measure applied.

- Suzy was an A student in all subjects—reading, science, math, and social studies—when she was eight years old. But no matter how hard she tried, she could not produce uniformly round, slanted, looped handwriting as required by the teacher. The teacher gave her an F in handwriting. Thirty years later, as her child enters third grade, she shudders about this nightmare.

- Leroy remembers being whipped for low marks in "effort." At seven, he could read and compute well. He did not choose to do all the worksheets required by the teacher. The worksheets seemed boring to him.

- Mrs. Stewart comes to school at the end of the year for a final conference. She wonders why her son, Everett, received a D in math. The teacher, Mrs. Packard, had sent home papers with shiny faces and stars all year. At the mid-year conference, Mrs. Packard assured Mrs. Stewart that Everett performed in math in accordance with expectations. The fact that Mrs. Packard thought Everett was "a bit slow" never entered the conversation.

Today, educators have a chance to communicate in fairer ways with parents. Wiggins (1994) suggests that report should clearly indicate

- how a child's performance compares to local and national norms.
- child progress toward learner outcomes.
- child progress compared to previous achievement level.
- progression of learner goals from grades K–3 so parents have a perspective of the big picture.

- enough subdivisions of learner outcomes so that parents can clearly see the scoring or evaluation criteria.
- descriptions of learner development that include quality of work, comparisons to expectations for long-term goals.

Whenever teachers report to parents in conferences, in report cards, or casually at drop-off/pick up time, goals for the report should be clear. The frame of reference should be kept in mind. Parents want to know the following:

- What is my child's present achievement level?
- Is my child functioning at average, above average, or below average level for his developmental age or grade level?
- How do my child's work samples compare to his previous work and to those of other children?
- What can I do as a parent to help my child be a better student?
- Are you his teacher doing everything you can to assist, challenge, encourage my child?
- Does my child get along with friends and peers in the setting?
- Is my child making progress, i.e., does my child have weaknesses? What strengths does my child have?

In addition at report time, parents may be invited to critique their own efforts and to seek suggestions for ways that they can meaningfully provide help to their child.

As teachers prepare for reports to parents, reflective questions include: "Are you confident about the reliability of the data that you plan to report to the parent?" "Did you use an appropriate method to gather the data?" "Is the material stated in objective or appropriately qualified terms?" "Is the information appropriate for the problem?" "Is there evidence to support the interpretation of the data?" "Do the data provide new information?" "Do the data fairly represent the child as a learner or as an achiever in a content area?" "Are there any circumstances that would cast doubt on the accuracy of the information?" Guerin and Maier (1983, p. 139).

Common errors

Teachers should also check that their reports do not make the *common types of errors*—computation or recording errors and overlooking important developmental information and situational factors (Guerin & Maier, 1983, 142). For example, Victor, a two year old, has difficulty holding a crayon. He was a premature baby who is small, but making good progress in language and other cognitive and social/emotional areas. He should be allowed developmental latitude in acquiring fine motor skills. Also, Aretha, a five year old, is the only survivor of a house fire. She doesn't talk to the teacher and begins to suck her thumb. It is not an appropriate time to interpret this behavior as socially immature.

When families are clients

Sometimes parents seek early intervention or education experiences that involve the whole family. These situations include the times when there is an at risk birth of an infant, when parents are concerned about the development of their child, and when others recommend to parents that an educational experience may assist the family. When the family is the client, the family must be involved in assessing priorities and planning interventions (cf Turnbull, 1986). Sometimes it may useful to involve the family in record keeping. The family record-keeping involvement offers the potential to educate parents as well as involve and inform them about the progress in the program.

Popp (1992) describes a method for family literacy projects. The procedure is to collect portfolio material that reflects parent and child growth. Examples of the portfolio contents include a page of the storybook that the parent and child are writing; photo of holiday activities, such as stuffing a a turkey, and written paragraph about it; drawings illustrating a parent reading a story; songs written by parents and child; photos of activities that parent and child enjoy; and videos and audiotapes of activities. Parents and the teacher can review these items to develop plans for future program participation.

To the extent possible, in situations where the teacher is part of a team working with a multi-problem family, the parent should be part of the assessment process. Sometimes, parents may be involved with a social worker or psychologist to assist with parenting or personal issues. Part of that process will include parent self-assessment. Teachers will be responsible for communicating and eliciting appropriate cooperation in the assessment of children involved at the level of readiness that the parents possess.

In the Women's Treatment Center, Chicago, a State Pre-School program involves parent participation in the classroom. Women in the program are concentrating on rehabilitation of their lives dominated by substance abuse. Some of the women have a history of child abuse and neglect. Teachers work carefully with the therapeutic staff to pick a good time for moms to participate in the classroom. The assessment aspect involves teachers pointing out to mom the appropriate play of the young child. As time goes by, mom can recognize appropriate limits and play activities. She can then be involved more concretely in the assessment of her child.

In this scenario, parents are involved in assessment of themselves as well as their children. This can demystify the assessment process for them and provide positive empowering opportunities that can counter any previous negative experience that they may have.

⊞ Multidisciplinary staffing

Staffing conferences are potentially stressful times for parents. Parents are thrust into the school or agency turf, frequently outnumbered by the array of experts who have evaluated their child and who have begun to make preliminary plans for services for the child. The most stressful times are those when the parents have just completed an initial evaluation. Each of the professionals who participate in this meeting must prepare to report assessment results in a way that will honestly describe the scores and impressions, but each must sensitively recognize the parents' perspective. This requires judgment of the social, educational, emotional, and economic context of the family. It requires empathy.

Teacher role

Reporting screening results

Teachers are responsible for knowing the technical characteristics of the measures that they are administering. They must then explain the process and the results of the assessment to parents. Teachers must understand the process of typical child development and variations due to social, cultural, and economic conditions.

Mrs. Jenkins is a member of the Child Find Team in Local School District, New York. Local uses the DIAL–R to screen children in the spring and in the fall. Mrs. Bond brought Carrie to the spring screening. Carrie is two. She is the third child in the Bond family, her siblings are 10 and 6. Mrs. Bond is concerned that Carrie doesn't talk very much at home.

Mrs. Jenkins reviews the procedures and limitations of the DIAL–R. Mrs. Bond was an observer and participant in the process, so this review is by way of a refresher. Then, Mrs. Jenkins interprets the results of the screening.

Carrie's performance is within developmental limits. Mrs. Jenkins and Mrs. Bond examine opportunities for Carrie to talk. Maybe older siblings are talking for her. Mrs. Jenkins tells Mrs. Bond about a weekend program for parents and tots. They agree to meet in three months or sooner if Mrs. Bond is still worried.

Initial conference or referral conference

At an initial or referral conference, early childhood teachers appropriately listen to evaluation results presented by professionals who have assessed the child. Teachers also listen to parent perceptions and concerns. In addition, teachers must be prepared to describe their program. Each must identify modifications that can be easily incorporated for an optimum inclusion experience. Teachers are responsible for identifying necessary support services for the program.

Ms. Seefeldt has 25 kindergartners in a developmentally appropriate play-based kindergarten class in Baltimore. She needs to be able to describe her program. What are the routines, schedule? How are the plan made?

What modifications does she make for the three children with special needs in her room now? For example, Betty has a diagnosis of spina bifida with some cognitive delays. What assistance will Ms. Seefeldt need to provide so that Betty receives a developmentally appropriate program, yet allows Ms. Seefeldt to continue her fine work with the 24 other kindergartners? Ms. Seefeldt may appropriately request a teacher assistant to care for Betty's medical needs. She will be able to describe the justification for this request.

Ms. Seefeldt will listen to the psychologist's suggestions about appropriate cognitive intervention. The speech therapist will schedule regular visits to the classroom. Ms. Seefeldt will implement suggestions for follow-through into her regular curriculum.

Ms. Seefeldt will express a welcoming attitude toward Betty's parents. She will assure Mr. and Mrs. Columbus that Betty will be treated fairly and kindly by the kindergartners. She will invite them to visit the room before enrollment and during the first weeks of school.

Annual individual education plan conference

At annual individual education plan conferences, teachers are responsible for reporting progress on the annual goals that are derived for every child with special needs. This conference is a **multidisciplinary staffing** that includes all of the professionals and parents of children with special needs. They must state and justify deviations from the plan that have occurred through the year at the classroom level. Teachers must report progress in all the ways that they have gathered the information. Progress data may include observations, checklists, screening results, achievement scores, curriculum progress, and diagnostic assessment test scores. Teachers must listen to the concerns and issues raised by parents and other professionals at this conference. In addition, they must have thought through the next steps for the children in their care. What are appropriate educational goals? How will these goals be implemented in the normalized environment and routine? What additional assessment information is needed to plan an effective program?

Baby Stacie, the firstborn daughter of Mr. and Mrs. Hewlett, is 18 months old. She and Mrs. Hewlett have regularly attended the infant-stimulation program for children with cognitive delays and Down syndrome. The facilitator-teacher of the program is Mrs. Meadows. The program meets weekly for one hour. During the hour program, Mrs. Mead plans gross motor activities, songs, and exploration of infant toys. Parents assist their own children throughout the morning. Mrs. Mead, her assistant, the physical therapist, the occupational therapist, and the speech therapist join in the play as individual demand dictates.

At the multidisciplinary conference, Mrs. Meadows reports that Mrs. Hewlett and Stacie have attended regularly. Mrs. Hewlett has learned the songs. Stacie smiles and laughs when the familiar songs are sung. Stacie is following along with the circle activities, happily ensconced in Mrs. Bond's lap. Preferred toys for Stacie are foam blocks and water toys.

Mrs. Meadows suggests that Stacie seems to be making fine motor progress—her grasp is improving. She is prepared to state that Stacie should participate another year in the program. She will listen to suggestions from the physical therapist, occupational therapist, and language therapist. Otherwise, she has no strong recommendations for a program change.

Kevin, a three year old in the Mother Goose Child-Care Center, has finished his first year of inclusion placement. Mrs. Gardner, the head teacher for the three and four year olds, presents his progress. The multidisciplinary staffing is attended by Kevin's mother, Ms. Wood, who is 18 and enrolled in a work-study program, the district mainstream coordinator, and the child-care center director.

Goals for Kevin for the year included:

1. Following the center's routines with support.
2. Beginning to use words to express needs.
3. With support, using words to solve disputes.

Mrs. Gardner reports with the results of checklists and anecdotal notes that Kevin does not follow the center's routines. He wanders from the group at circle time and from the playground. Kevin does not speak in intelligible language to the staff. Kevin continues to take toys away from peers and hits children when they will not give them up.

Mrs. Gardner reports that Ms. Wood has regularly volunteered with the program. She has taken a leadership role in identifying speakers and parent needs.

Mrs. Gardner likes Kevin. He is warm and affectionate in her one-on-one contacts with him. She wants to keep him at Mother Goose, but she is worried that other children and parents are beginning to complain about his combative behavior. Mrs. Gardner asks whether the Mainstream Coordinator can give more specific suggestions for modifying the structure for Kevin. She asks whether there are ways that Ms. Wood and she can work together to maintain Kevin's enrollment in Mother Goose Center.

Jose, a second grader with a learning disability, lives in a school district that plans to move from self-contained special education to inclusion. Mr. Decker is Jose's second grade teacher. The resource LD teacher, the inclusion administrator, the school psychologist, the speech therapist, and Mr. and Mrs. Castillo, Jose's parents, attend a multidisciplinary staffing conference.

Mr. Decker reports that Jose is cooperative and well-liked by his peers. He seems to pay attention in small group activities. When working with a partner, Jose completes written assignments quite well. In large group discussions, Jose frequently stares out the window, fidgets, looks into his desk, and sometimes rolls the pencil on the desk. Mr. Decker and the children have learned to ignore this distractible behavior. Mr. Decker prepares written notes for Jose when necessary. Jose pays close attention when he knows something about the subject at hand.

Plans are made for third grade. Goals for developing and enhancing note taking and other supports for large group discussions are planned. Mr. Decker knows that Jose will be fine in Ms. Heather's third grade. He will talk with her about the cuing and mediation strategies that he has developed with Jose.

Mr. and Mrs. Castillo will help Jose with organizational skills in the summer, including color coding notebooks, folders, and a planning calendar for third grade. They will send him to an art program for part of the summer. Part of the program will help Jose enhance fine motor skills and develop his interest and skill in art.

The preceding discussion is directed toward the teacher's role in the assessment system with children and parents. Another important role for teachers is reporting to additional stakeholders in the educational lives of children and families. These include administrators, boards, school councils, legislators, and the public at large.

Reporting to other stakeholders

The importance of reporting to other **stakeholders** has acquired new urgency as teachers seek to preserve the child's best interests in the face of greater demands for high-stakes performance results. The high-stakes issues are discussed in Chapter Five and Chapter Eleven. Teachers must assume responsibility for reflecting, recording, and reporting group assessment results according to their holistic philosophical beliefs regarding developmentally appropriate practice. Otherwise, the progress of young children may continue to be measured according to test scores and reports alone.

One method for reporting results to these other stakeholders is to use illustrations of the progress of individual children to validate the method of teaching that you are using. For example, if your goal for first grade is to show that the children in your program can write a simple story, review individual child reports and tally how many children can write a story. Then, use samples from the reports on individual children to illustrate the different levels of sophistication of stories written by the children in your program. Thus, you have shown that children are reading and writing and that they have achieved these skills without the use of workbooks.

Another method for demonstrating child accomplishment through the use of assessment information is to use displays of work samples. Show the graphs that children are making. Display the write-ups of scientific experiments conducted by children. Show the solutions generated for performance-based tasks in social studies.

The most comprehensive way to demonstrate child and class accomplishment to other stakeholders through assessment information is to be able to describe the assessment system. You should be able to thoughtfully address the following issues in nontechnical language:

- philosophy of the program
- program goals
- teaching methods
- ways that child progress is monitored
- how adjustments are made to accomplish child goals
- ways to see the precursors of reading, writing, math and other learnings

These are, after all, the questions that you answer in collaboration with parents. The difference in the two reports—parents/others—is the emphasis shift from an individual and particular child to a group of children. The process for preparations of an **accountability** report is the same as illustrated in Figure 7.2. Recording and reporting assessment results to parents and others is one of the integral roles of the teacher.

Summary

Reporting assessment and progress to parents and other stakeholders is a key part of the educational process. The technique for reporting must match the purpose. Each teacher must have a repertoire of methods. At the beginning of programs, teachers describe the philosophy and curriculum to parents. Teachers report casually to parents in daily chats or telephone visits. Teachers report at regularly scheduled times through conferences and report cards. Teachers report when problems arise. On each of these occasions, the teacher must be sensitive to the emotional and social context of the child and his family. Teachers must respect parent individuality. Teachers must be prepared to articulate clearly and concisely in writing and orally. Finally, teachers must understand the role and limitations of the diverse assessment methods that are included in

FIGURE 7.2 Accountability through reflection on goals and practices resulting in changes.

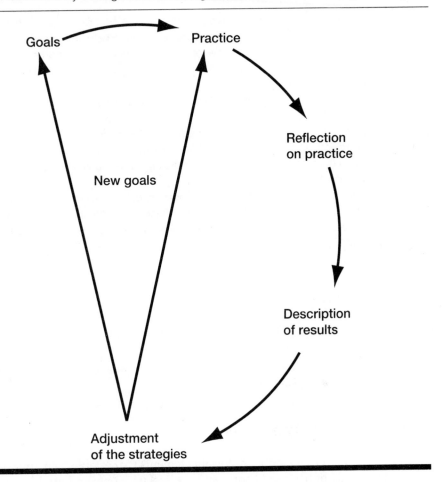

their program. Assessment procedures and reporting must match the philosophy and the curriculum.

⊞ CHAPTER 7 Suggested further readings

Azwell, T., & Schmar, E. (1995). *Report card on report cards: Alternatives to consider.* Portsmouth, NH: Heinemann.

Hart, D. (1994). *Authentic assessment: A handbook for educators.* Menlo Park, CA: Addison Wesley.

ACTIVITIES

1. Collect sample report cards from the communities in your area. Examine the criteria that teachers must address. Develop an assessment plan to help you answer the questions.
2. For a grade level of your choice, develop a performance task to address one of the required reporting areas. If possible, try the task on a child. Report and discuss your results with colleagues.
3. With permission, interview parents about their experiences in receiving information from child-care centers and schools. Discuss your experiences with colleagues. Were there any improvements that you might suggest?
4. With permission, sit in on a parent conference. After the conference discuss your observations with the teacher who conducted it. Ask any questions that may have concerned you about the proceedings.
5. With a classmate, visit a school board or local school council meeting. Observe the proceedings. Pay particular attention to issues of accountability that arise in the meeting. With your classmate, plan how you might address the requests for information that might arise if you were teaching in the school.

McLoughlin, J. A., & Lewis, R. B. (1990). *Assessing special students* (3rd ed.). Columbus, OH: Merrill.

Perrone, V. (Ed.). (1991). *Expanding student assessment.* Alexandria, VA: Association for Supervision and Curriculum Development.

Wiggins, G. P. (1993). *Assessing student performance: Exploring the purpose and limits of testing.* San Francisco: Jossey Bass.

CHAPTER 7 Study questions

1. What are the important elements that establish an atmosphere of trust and cooperation between parents and teachers, as well as preserving confidentiality and collaboration in the interests of young children?
2. How does an early childhood teacher prepare for conferences with parents that include assessment discussions? What are issues that effect the success of the conference?
3. How does an early childhood teacher prepare for report cards? How does this preparation link to curricular and assessment plans?
4. Describe ways that report cards can be responsive to district and statewide learner outcome goals. Where does assessment fit in this picture?

5. What is the early childhood teacher role in the multidisciplinary staffing? How is assessment information used in these meetings? What must early childhood teachers understand about the assessments of other professionals so that best practice for young children is assured?

6. How can early childhood teachers participate in the accountability stakes with regard to assessment of young children? As advocates for best practice, what must teachers understand about assessment and reporting so that legislators and others fairly interpret assessment activities, reports, and results?

References

Bell, G. E. (1989). Making the most of parent-teacher conferences: Tips for teachers. *Focus on Early Childhood, 2,* 2.

Berger, E. H. (1995). *Parents as partners in education: The school and home working together* (5th ed.). Columbus, OH: Merrill.

Claridge, P. B., & Whitaker, E. M. (1994). Implementing a new elementary progress report. *Educational Leadership, 52,* 7–9.

deBettencourt, L. U. (1987). How to develop parent partnerships. *Teaching Exceptional Children, 19,* 26–27.

Donovan, M. (1995). *Parent response form for Chicago Public Schools Project.* Chicago: Erikson Institute on Early Education.

Fredericks, A. D., & Rasinski, T. V. (1990). Involving parents in the assessment process. *Reading Teacher, 44,* 346–349.

Guerin, G. R., & Maier, A. S. (1983). *Informal assessment in education.* Palo Alto: Mayfield.

Hartshorne, T., & Boomer, L. W. (1993). Privacy of school records: What every special education teacher should know. *Teaching Exceptional Children, 25,* 32–35.

Hill, B. C., Kamber, P., & Norwick, L. (1994). Six ways to make student portfolios more meaningful and manageable: Involving students, peers, and parents in portfolio assessment. *Instructor, 104,* 118–120.

Ireton, H. (1994). *The child development review.* Minneapolis: Behavior Science Systems.

Kenney, E., & Perry, S. (1994). Talking with parents about performance-based report cards. *Educational Leadership, 52,* 24–27.

Kovas, M. A. (1993). Making your grading motivating: Keys to performance-based evaluation. *Quill and Scroll, 68,* 10–11.

Ohio Department of Education. (1990). *Study skills begin at home: Book 1: Preschool.* Columbus, OH.

Ohio Department of Education. (1990). *Study skills begin at home: Book 2: Kindergarten–Grade 3.* Columbus, OH.

Popp, R. J. (1992). *Family portfolios: Documenting change in parent-child relationships.* Louisville, KY: National Center for Family Literacy, occasional paper.

Sperling, D. H. (1994). Assessment and reporting: a natural pair. *Educational Leadership, 52,* 10–13.

Turnbull, A. P., & Turnbull, H. R. (1986). *Families, professional and exceptionality: A special partnership.* Columbus, OH: Merrill.

Wiggins, G. (1994). Toward better report cards. *Educational Leadership, 52,* 28–37.

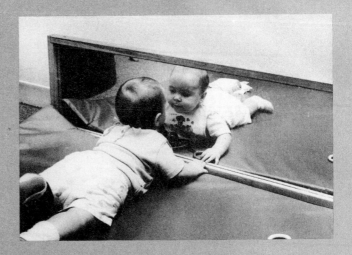

CHAPTER 8

Building a Child Study

Terms to Know

- child study
- primary responsibility
- child find team
- diagnostic evaluation

- referral question
- psychoeducational evaluation
- typical and atypical development

CHAPTER OVERVIEW   This chapter shows how a child study serves as a summary point in a comprehensive assessment system. Purposes of child studies are identified. Elements of child studies are delineated. Suggestions for writing child studies are made. Examples of child studies are shown with analyses and issues to ponder.

Topics Discussed

- Child studies in the assessment system
- Purposes of child studies
- Elements of a child study
- Conducting a child study to determine teaching or intervention strategies
- Examples of child studies

Child studies in the assessment system

A **child study** is an in-depth look at a particular child at a specific point in time. A study summarizes the information available from all sources:

child, parent, teacher, and specialist. In addition, questions are answered and raised through the process of gathering the material for the report of the child study. Some studies are brief and geared to one developmental or teaching issue. Other studies are complex and include formal assessment.

Purposes of child studies

Child studies serve diverse purposes. A study summarizes available knowledge about a child at a point in time. In early childhood, different professionals may assume **primary responsibility** for the preparation of this summary report, depending on the age of the child and the questions raised about development.

- *At birth,* Sheila who shows a low Apgar score will have a case study summarizing available medical and social history information. Plans derived from the known information delineate proposed medical intervention. Diagnostic tests are planned. If necessary, further family history is gathered and social service intervention is planned.

- *At preschool,* the **child find team** summarizes screening results on Oswald. Oswald shows no difficulties. The child study ends there.

- Robert displays speech and language problems. Screening results are summarized. Robert and his family are referred to a speech therapist for **diagnostic evaluation.** The child study evolves. First, the child find team assumes primary responsibility for summarizing available history and screening results. Then, the speech therapist adds diagnostic assessment results and any questions that may occur during the assessment process. If the speech therapist questions Robert's intellectual capacity, then a referral to a psychologist occurs. The evolution of the study continues. At any point in the process, the available information can be summarized and results discussed with Robert's parents so that permission for diagnostic assessment is obtained and so that plans for Robert can be made.

- Ms. Hayes who teaches at Merry Mack Preschool meets twice a year with parents. She collects observational material and samples of each child's work and writes a narrative report to share with parents. There is a child study of progress at Merry Mack for each child in the program.

- Mr. Anastasiow worries about Albert, a second grader. Albert seems sad. He has no friends at school. He watches everything and seems to know answers when called upon, but doesn't complete any projects or write in his journal. Mr. Anastasiow gathers any available achievement test scores and his own observations and contacts Albert's parents to share his concerns. He summarizes the material. A case study evolves.

In each of these examples, the reasons for developing the child study are different. The procedures are the same: summarizing and organizing information for effective screening, assessment, and intervention planning for children.

⊞ Elements of a child study

Items to consider in answering questions about a child's development include those listed in the following section. Whichever professional is initiating the study or whoever is the child manager should comment on known information in these areas. When information is unknown or when there are different perceptions about available facts, these can be summarized and questions identified. What are the **referral questions?** A child study is a dynamic process. The process begins with basic demographic information that is pertinent to the questions at the time. As available and for the purpose of serving the child and family, items to consider include the following:

1. identifying information: name, age, sex, birth date
2. description of the child: appearance, general physical characteristics, personality, position in the family
3. questions, concerns, problems
4. family background: siblings, family's social-economic status, known family problems, concerns, family crises or tragedies, parental attitudes, separation issues, home, neighborhood
5. medical history: circumstances of child's birth
6. early developmental milestones
7. current functioning: self-help and daily living skills, handling of body functions; body movement and use of body (motility, energy); facial expressions; speech and language; emotional reactions (expression and control of emotion and feelings; imagination and fantasy; self-concept; self-management skills); reaction to other children; reaction with adults; play or school activities; thinking and reasoning; problem-solving skills; health; developmental progress for social; emotional; cognitive; physical skills, communication skills; school adjustment (attendance and arrival, reaction to routines, following directions, taking turns, response to support and individualization)

When a child study is prepared because there is an educational or group care issue or concern, or a summary is prepared, the child study may include items and descriptions related to a child's adjustment to this group setting. In addition, an observer may record, suggest, or include any ideas about any changes that may assist teachers in preparing a more suitable environment.

Conducting a child study to determine teaching or intervention strategies

When a child study is prepared because there is a question about learning or socializing in a child care or educational setting, the following factors should be considered.

- physical environment of the group setting
- snack, lunch, naps, toileting, routines
- scheduling and planning
- individualization
- activities
- record keeping
- teacher style and interactions
- parent communication and activities

Once all the material for a child study is gathered, a summary report must be written. The first step before writing the report is becoming familiar with the information available. Next, organize it to address the purpose of the study—report, referral, or summarization of a year. A checklist for preparing the report follows in Box 8.1.

Examples of child studies

In the following sections, child studies are included as examples. Notes about the progress and limitations of the studies follow.

Case study 1: Tomas, a creative wonder

This summary is based on observations over time in a home-care situation. Children in the home are Tomas, the three year old and an infant, Martha, one year old. The report reflects impressions of Tomas' function-

BOX 8.1

Writing Reports

- ▌ check accuracy of information for all the details
- ▌ sequence the events correctly
- ▌ outline the information
- ▌ prepare neatly and proofread
- ▌ check clarity of expression
- ▌ check to see that there is specific and descriptive information
- ▌ differentiate fact from impression
- ▌ Give test scores
  - ▌ include as available
  - ▌ interpret according to directions and limitations
  - ▌ watch technical aspects of the test—validity and reliability
  - ▌ watch age of child at administration—infant scores should be used and interpreted in preschool children only when these are a part of a trend.

ing based on available anecdotal data. Tomas is bilingual. He speaks to me in English. To his parents and other native Spanish speakers, he converses easily in Spanish.

Tomas is a creative and outgoing three-year-old boy who loves to be around people. He is quite a conversationalist. He is kind, full of love, and just completely adorable. His big, brown eyes and spiked black hair are only part of his charm. He is most known for his vivid, descriptive creativity.

Tomas is an imaginative and engaging playmate. He loves to talk about his past adventures and comes up with wonderful ideas for make-believe. This outgoing style is his strongest trait. He has many different hats available to him on a low hanging coat rack in his room. He also has many other props that he uses to full capacity. He has a full slate of characters that he can become at any moment.

What surprised me the most is the way he shares everything. He likes to make sure that I have some toys to play with and that we take turns if that is what the game called for. He really made me feel like I was a part of what we were doing, not just sitting in on his games. Tomas likes to get other people involved in his play and seems happiest when playing with others.

October 26   Brief notes

12:45   What do you want to play? T very eager. Swordfights with shields. Tells rules.

1:05   Hats. Firefighter, cowboy, Seems bored. What to play?

1:15   Armies. Takes most of the grays. Always wins. I'm clueless.

Immediate reflections

We played armies for about 20 minutes. This is hardest time I've had taking notes. He moves as much as Martha the one year old, but requires more interaction. He really likes to win. He seemed pretty fair in the swordfight, but in playing armies he seemed to keep the upper hand. I really had no clue how to play since I never played armies before. He was very helpful when playing with the hats. He helped "outline my character." He seemed really sad when I left.

Reflection

Tomas puts much emotional energy into the people with whom he plays and the results could work against him. He enjoys my company so much that at times he occasionally began to exhibit a slight stutter. This is not a developmental trait for concern, but a typical developmental variation.

Characteristically for a three year old, Tomas only wants to play games he can win and will stop in the middle of a game if the opponent is doing too well.

If challenged by a question that he does not know the answer, e.g. Why do flies walk on the ceiling? he says that he doesn't know or rejects the question altogether by asking to skip it.

A new baby entered Tomas's family during the past year. Tomas seems to accept this baby well. He continues his progress with self-help and likes to play with the baby.

Tomas seems to handle transitions with ease. However, transitions that left him without a playmate, (i.e., from playtime to lunch) seem to affect him the most.

Overall, Tomas seems a joy to be around and seems to enjoy being around others. After spending time with him, I can see why his parents feel he will be in a people-oriented occupation when he grows up. As for now, he wants to be a teacher. As for the future, he can be anything. (Case study used with permission of Talaga, 1991)

Notes on the process of the study of Tomas

Readers can easily see that the observer likes this little boy very much. She describes him in glowing terms. The question she raises about "emotional energy" as a potential for "working against him" is unclear, a value judgment, and not substantiated.

The writer reassures the reader that Tomas' stutter is developmentally appropriate, a dysfluency of excitement. Although the writer assures the reader that Tomas handles the new baby well, one wonders if this is true. He seems to demand attention, e.g., transition to no playmate affects him the most.

Teachers receiving Tomas with this report will have the information that he is energetic, likeable, and without obvious concerns for speech, language, cognition, and physical concerns.

Parents reading the report will know that Tomas is adored by the observer, a shared venture.

Case study 2: Sam from the nanny perspective

Sam is a healthy three-year-old boy. He is the oldest of two children (brother Zach 1½). Sam's family is very well off. They live in an upper-middle class neighborhood and their house is huge with plenty of space for the children and then some. Sam's mom is 35 years old and his dad is 37. Mom is a registered nurse who is now a full-time homemaker at the present. Dad is a business executive. They seem to be very laid-back people. I might even call them permissive parents to some extent. It seems that the kids get whatever they want most of the time. As they grow older this might become a problem because they will not have learned the value of saving for something that they really want and they will not realize that they cannot have everything they want. Their parenting style may also change as the boys get older as well, which will help. I cannot see them ever being authoritarian, but I can see them being more authoritative by always listening to what a child has to say about a certain situation.

In the past year and a half, I have had the opportunity to see Sam four to five times a month and to see him almost every Sunday at the Health Club nursery where I work. Thus, I have observed him in two different settings. He is a very energetic boy, who is always smiling and joking around. He is outgoing. Although most of my observations are anecdotal, I have also done some Piagetian tests with him, naturalistic observations where I have watched for a length of time, casual or incidental observation when I just happened to hear him say something or see him do something without consciously observing him, and listening to what he says. I have asked open-ended questions, and observed art and play.

Through observation, I notice that Sam plays by himself or in parallel play. He does, however, sometimes play with other children, especially if they are building something or playing with miniature cars. He loves to build things with Legos and he also loves to put together race tracks or train tracks. He is very interested in playing with particular things like trains and tools. He has his own tool set but would much rather use his father's tools.

According to the stage of play, Sam should be beginning to play cooperatively with peers, which he is not really doing but I have not observed him at preschool. He does some dramatic play such as acting like he is a super hero. He has developed greater facility with sensorimotor play. He loves to play with balls and he is beginning to show some interest in constructive play. He is starting to get interested in art activities and is really interested in small blocks, clay, and puzzles.

In Piagetian terms, Sam should be at the pre-operational level of development. Sam has achieved object permanence. He knows that just because something is changed does not mean it still is not the same thing or if something is hidden he knows that it is not gone. He has also achieved "functional dependency." He has proven this repeatedly when playing with cars or balls. He knows that if he pushes the car harder it will go faster and if he throws the ball harder it will go farther. He still is egocentric. Whenever I try to give him a different way of looking at something, he always says, "No let's just do it my way" or "How about we just do it the way I said." I have tried to test him to see if he has achieved number constancy. I tried this by giving him red and yellow crayons to see if he realizes that if there are four red crayons and two yellow crayons that there are more crayons total rather than more red ones or yellow ones. But every time I do this, he does not pay attention. This tells me that he has not achieved this milestone yet, but I do not think he should quite yet, either.

Sam's sleeping habits are very poor. When I first met him he slept pretty well, but in the past five months he has had very poor sleeping habits. He usually does not even go to bed anymore while I am there unless his parents are going to be really late. The latest he has stayed up with me is 11:00 p.m. He does not sleep in his room anymore. He sleeps in the extra bedroom with his father most of the time. He does not get the recommended 10 hours of sleep a night. He does, however, take a two-to-four-hour nap during the day. He does not seem to be preoccupied with any worries, but he really likes to sleep with his dad right now. The thing that bothers me is that they give in to him almost all the time (at least when I am there they do). I think maybe they should lay with him until he falls asleep or read a story to him to relax him, but I do not think he should be sleeping in the extra bedroom with his father as much as he does. The only reason I can think of, maybe for this happening, is that his aunt died in August. I have talked to him about it. Actually, he brought it up because there is a picture of her out. He told me that his aunt was dead. I asked him how that made him feel and he said sad. He told me that she died, but was not as clear about how. I got the feeling from that conversation that he understood that death was final, so I do not think that he is afraid to go to sleep, but maybe he is, or maybe it is just a stage. Maybe talking to him more will enlighten me.

Sam is basically toilet trained. Sometimes at night he has accidents, but during the day he never does. He is very relaxed about going to the bathroom; it never is a big deal at all. He likes to have me go with him sometimes, if he is wearing something that is hard to get off.

He eats fairly well. Sometimes he eats better than other times. He loves to talk to me and his brother while he is eating. He makes a lot of silly jokes and is very enjoyable.

He has a very good relationship with both of his parents. I get the impression that he idolizes his father because he is not around as much. He tells me about going to the store with his father or cutting the grass with his father. They have a riding mower and Sam loves to cut the grass with his father during the summer. He also is always there helping his father fix things. He is really into tools. On one occasion when I was there, he had his father's tools and was fixing his father's jeep. He did this for well over an hour. He would tell me what he thought was wrong with it and then pretend to fix it.

Overall, I feel that Sam is a happy, well-adjusted child. He seems to enjoy life and loves his family very much. My concern, however, is his sleep pattern. Regarding his sleep, I think I should talk to him more about sleeping and maybe that will give me some insight into his problem. I might also want to talk more about his aunt's death. I think what might help is if his bedtime is more structured. If he goes to bed at a certain time and does certain things before going to bed, it will become more structured and may be easier for him to go to sleep.

I was just having a casual conversation with Sam when he went over to a picture on the table, picked it up and said Aunt Sue died. He wanted to tell me that his aunt was roller skating and she died. (Actually what happened was that she was roller blading and collapsed when she got home with roller blades still on and was in a coma for a month. She had a brain aneurism.) He told me that he was sad that she died. Wow, what a scary thing for a child to understand. (Case study used with permission of Polachek, 1991)

Notes on the process of the study of Sam

In this study, the reader gets a snapshot of home life for a three year old. The writer notes that the parents are indulgent, a value judgment. She does not establish observational grounds for the assertion that the children "get everything they want." She also infers that getting things is equivalent to not appreciating value. This is not substantiated by the report.

The observer's expectation for play at the cooperative level seems high. Three year olds are just beginning to socialize in this way. Solitary play may be just as important at this stage. Sam certainly demonstrated constructive play competence, as reported by the observer.

The writer substantiates typical cognitive development through the discussion of performance on Piagetian tasks and for that matter through the discussion of constructive play activities.

The writer concludes that Sam idolizes his father . . . and attributes this to the father's absence . . . but this is a typical stage of identity formation.

The conclusions that the observer reports are (1) typical child, and (2) sleep disturbances. Further evidence is required. Three year olds frequently have nightmares and sleep disturbances. An added variable to consider is the death of a close relative. What is the family reaction to this death? The younger brother and jealousy may also be factors.

A teacher receiving Sam may expect a typical three year old with no known problems.

Parents receiving this report may wish to think about the sleep disturbance and decide whether this is a problem for the family. Otherwise, they may be reassured that development is in line for Sam.

Case study 3: Baby Ralph

Ralph is a 12-month-old boy who receives monthly early intervention sessions to monitor his development in all areas. He lives with his mother, father, and seven-year-old sister, Tracey. Services were initiated following the death of his three-year-old brother, Michael, in a home accident. Michael was involved in a preschool special education program before his death. Tracey had been scheduled to be screened by the school district to determine if she had special education needs before Michael's death and her own injuries in the home accident.

Ralph's mother, Connie, is 21 years old. She received special education services for the mildly mentally retarded from elementary school through the beginning of high school. She quit high school in her first year due to an unplanned pregnancy. Connie is quiet, often looks depressed, and holds her head down when spoken to. She has little eye contact. She says that Ralph is smarter than Michael was and she is not sure why Ralph needs this program, yet she comes each month and calls if she has to miss. She loves her children. She does have eye contact with them and provides them with food and clothing. She does not talk to them very much.

Ralph's father, Arthur, age 29, has a high school diploma and works seasonal jobs. Ralph's parents do not view him as having any special needs. Child assessment revealed that Ralph is approximately 6 months delayed in personal, social, and communication development. Qualitative concerns exist with fine- and gross-motor development.

Ralph receives health care through the County Hospital Medicaid Program. Extended family members assist with financial needs. Tracey receives treatments for her burns in a large Los Angeles hospital 35 miles from home. Prior to Michael's death, Connie received birth control services and counseling from a California Public Health Program, but services were discontinued due to funding cuts. Connie pursued her GED but discontinued the program due to learning difficulties. Homemaker services were also being investigated but were discontinued at the parent's request. Connie has expressed an interest in obtaining a job.

Parent requests: a job for mother; second grade program for Tracey

Providers' assessment of need: parenting skills; parent-child interactions; homemaker skills; financial planning assistance; special education screening for Tracey; tutoring for GED courses, vocational assessment, and assistance in placement; health care management.

Notes on the study of Ralph

The writer is an early intervention specialist who has summarized notes of an initial conference with Connie, Ralph's mother. She has identified the problems that the family presents, both from the record and from the interview. She has made notes of what the family wants in further early intervention service. In addition, she has prepared her own list of suggested services. At a multidisciplinary staffing, she will choose which of the suggestions to share immediately and relate those to parent goals. The effectiveness of future collaboration will depend on the sensitivity of the specialist in weaving the different agendas—parent and early intervention—together.

Case study 4: Ted

Ted, a twenty-one-month-old boy, and his mother, Mrs. Morgan, had been referred for assessment by a physician who, along with Mr. and Mrs. Morgan, was concerned about a possible language delay and the quality of Ted's walking. The doctor's report stated that Ted had been suffering from upper respiratory problems and ear infections since one month of age. Ted's mother filled out a family form which stated that the oldest sibling, now ten years old, was an apnea baby. The five-year-old sibling has no hearing in one ear, and the three-year-old sibling is in an early intervention program due to a developmental speech delay. Mrs. Morgan drives the three year old to therapy appointments three times per week.

Developmental history

The Shaker Heights Child Find program was responsible for screening Ted a day after his first birthday. At that time, the Denver Developmental Screening Test results indicated a slight language delay. All other areas were scored within normal limits. However, during this time frame Ted had eye surgery due to one eye turning inward. He is to wear prescription lenses with bifocals. Mrs. Morgan reported that she has been busy with her other children and cannot buy the glasses until next month.

The Battelle Development Inventory was used to determine if Ted was eligible for services six months ago when he was fifteen months old. At that time, Ted performed well in the cognitive domain and passed in the area of gross-motor skills. He passed, even though he could walk only two feet before falling down, as reported by the nurse. The occupational therapist explained that the quality of the walking is not a consideration with this test. Ted scored at eleven months in expressive communication and at nine months in receptive communication. Once again a discrepancy seemed to exist since Ted used no speech imitations, no word sounds, and could not follow any directions. However, at the same time, Mrs. Morgan reported that Ted said a few words. The developmental specialist who did the testing was confused by the results and recommended an arena assessment, so that other specialists might contribute insights.

Mrs. Morgan scheduled an appointment within a month but did not keep the appointment. Mrs. Morgan reported that her mother was ill and that she had assumed care of her. This care included having her mother move to the family home. For the next five months, all attempts to reach her were unsuccessful. Finally, Mrs. Morgan initiated contact with the center and reported that in the interim her husband had walked out on her, the four children, and her mother. At this point she had contacted a lawyer to file for maintenance support.

Arena assessment

Ted, on the day of the arena assessment, was wearing his shoes on the wrong feet to correct a "toeing in" problem. Mrs. Morgan also had not bought the corrective shoes that were prescribed months ago.

Ted held up well throughout the one-hour session. The occupational therapist used a fine motor adaptive checklist that combined items from the Bayley Scales of Infant Development, the Revised Gesell Developmental Schedules, and the Denver Developmental Screening Tests–R. At 21 months, Ted vocalizes but does not talk. He does a lot of 'mouthing' of objects. He enjoys putting objects into and out of a container. He turned his head to sounds made behind and to each side of him but he did not seem to comprehend the words. Sometimes he responded to gestures or demonstration. He did not respond to a loud, firm "no" from the therapist who tried to get him to stop an activity. There was no eye contact made and Ted appeared to have difficulty focusing on objects.

The physical therapist concluded that Ted is unstable when walking, has difficulty getting into and out of a chair, trips himself when attempting to run, cannot step on an object on the floor, cannot shift the weight of his feet, and cannot climb stairs. According to the physical therapist, Ted's problem seems to be solely in his feet. "His hips are in place and structurally he looks good."

The speech therapist seemed to feel that the inside of Ted's mouth looked intact, but she could not continue her assessment because Ted was ready for a nap and began to cry.

Discussion

The members of the team met for an hour after the assessment session. They completed a checklist and summarized as follows: Ted was content throughout the session. Although unaware of the situation, he was friendly and cooperative and moderately active. He adapted to the tasks required. He was tolerant of handling. Socially, Ted showed poor responses to interaction and initiated no interaction. He was not distracted by visual or auditory stimuli. Even though he did not understand the tasks presented, he was not easily frustrated. The reliability of the test results were judged to be "average."

Notes on the process of the study of Ted

This team is just beginning to work with the family. They have identified a number of problems through observation during the arena assessment. In addition to the developmental problem, they have a record of the family emotional problems, based on the interview with Mrs. Morgan. They have a history of the Morgans' previous involvement with the agency. The next step will be the development of a plan that addresses the mother's emotional needs as well as Ted's early intervention needs. They have the basis of referral for social services and interagency collaboration.

Case Study 5: Marie in first grade, an example from a student

A child study is a very useful and interesting way to learn about a child. I chose Marie, age 6, to observe in a school setting. I wanted to know about her physical abilities, social emotional traits, and intellectual capabilities. My plans included observations of her reactions and behavior in relation to materials, activities, and regular routines. I wanted to summarize my personal interactions with Marie, as well. Other details I expect to learn about Marie include her response to structured and unstructured time; her choice of activities; her response to rules, reactions, and interactions with peers; and attention span as it relates to the schedule. I used anecdotal notes, interest questionnaires, and a review of Marie's journal and reflections about my conversations and interactions with Marie to prepare this report.

The report contains a review of developmental progress from my perspective as a student teacher. The concluding section suggests further questions and possible curricular changes.

Physical characteristics

Marie has bangs and long blond hair that is usually tied back into a ponytail, or she will often wear a brightly colored barrette or other fancy hair decoration. Marie has very fair skin and sparkling olive green eyes. Some other physical traits include a very slender body build. In comparing Marie's height with the rest of the children in the first grade, I find her to be about average.

Marie usually wears casual, comfortable looking and pretty clothes, but nothing too fancy. She wears cotton knit pants and coordinating shirts, sweatsuit outfits, or jeans and colorful sweaters. Depending on the outfit, Marie wears her white and pastel colored gym shoes or her shiny black patent leather shoes. When she wears her black shoes, she likes to hang her feet out of her shoes when she is working at her desk during the day. Marie also proudly wears a complete Brownie uniform once a week that consists of a dress, white short sleeve blouse, white tights, and a sash decorated with several colorful patches and pins that she earned.

Physical abilities

The information that I have about gross motor skills comes from the day the first graders completed a simple stretching routine and a stand-up, sit-down story. During the stretching routine, Marie used her hands and placed them on different parts of her body. For example, stretching her hands above her head, putting her hands on her tummy, and standing on one foot. Marie completed all these tasks with ease.

In the many observations of fine motor and eye-hand coordination, Marie displays good skills. She uses small muscles of her hands and fingers during journal and story writing and art projects, while doing fingerplays and when using the chalkboards for writing words and math problems. Marie consistently uses her right hand to hold the chalk, pencil, crayons, markers, or scissors. By looking at samples of Marie's writing you can see that her letters are smoothly written and her drawings are carefully drawn and colored. This is evidence of her fine motor control. Also, when doing a finger play such as Five Fat Turkeys, Marie finds it easy to follow the actions and put up one finger at a time.

I observed Marie's eye-hand coordination when she played one of her favorite games, the memory game. She uses her eyes carefully to choose which card she wants to turn over and then very quickly carries out this action.

During an art project with scissors, Marie correctly holds scissors with her thumb in one hole and her second finger in the other. She cuts very rapidly along only the outside edges of the "Little Red Hen" paper.

Marie seems to enjoy activities and materials with eye-hand coordination. She often chooses these works.

Social characteristics

Marie is very comfortable in the classroom when interacting with me or the first grade teacher and with the other children in the first grade. Marie easily adjusts to the weekly volunteer visits by her mother. When Marie's mom comes into the classroom to listen to children read, Marie grins and quickly says, "Hi, Mom" and then goes back and continues her project.

During large group discussions, Marie is always paying attention and is very focused on what is going on, but she does not always actively participate in the discussions. Marie does not always raise her hand, but when she is called on she can answer a question and she knows what is going on. Marie is always really involved and interested in listening. Frequently she is sucking on her two middle fingers, seemingly quite absorbed in the large group activity.

Marie usually follows the rules that are set. She makes sure that others are following as well. During free-reading time or when she is working in a small group, Marie gladly and willingly shares her materials, and sometimes offers to help others, if needed. Marie also likes to "take charge" of the small group she is working with. Marie is very open about expressing her needs and wants, thoughts, and ideas to her friends, her teacher, and me. Marie does not seem to have a particular friend in the class. She is flexible and plays with a variety of children. I saw her display friendliness toward many children.

With adults, she seems to enjoy reading and talking. She seems very comfortable about asking either the teacher or me when she needs something. Marie seems to feel that she is an important part of the group and she seems very satisfied with the social interaction and atmosphere.

Emotional characteristics

Marie is very confident. She is extremely sensitive. She is sensitive to other children's and adults' expectations, needs, and wants. I feel that Marie is an easy-going child who is not easily upset by the slightest change: she accepts and adapts to changes. She seems very self-assured. She is enthusiastic about school and learning. She makes things fun for herself. She is very eager and willing to try new activities and experiences. Marie has an outgoing personality in comparison to other children in the class. Marie seems to require only a minimum of praise to keep her on tasks. This seems a demonstration of self-confidence. Other children in the class are constantly seeking praise for their accomplishments. For example, one day Marie made a wire sculpture. Carol, the child sitting next to Marie during this project, saw Joseph bring me his sculpture and I commented on the unique aspects of Carol's and Joseph's sculptures. Carol then returned to her desk and told Marie about my comments. Marie replied: "She likes everyone's sculpture."

I did observe several times a combination of slight frustration and a low level of anger. For example, Marie was reading a big book to me, the story of *The Little Red Hen*. Two friends, Alicia and Ruth, wandered over to listen. Marie is an excellent reader, but occasionally she encountered a word that took extra time to decode. Alicia or Ruth prompted her. Marie seemed very bothered when this happened. She quickly turned around and gave the two girls an angry look and said: "Alicia, I'm reading! Ruth, I'm reading!" Marie isn't bothered when other children stand by her as long as they are listening and not helping her.

In a more recent observation, I watched Marie playing the memory game with Josh and Steve. Both Marie and Steve are familiar with the rules. The rules according to Marie are to pick up the bunny card, turn it over, but leave the card on the table so that everyone can see the word on each card. Then, if two cards do not match, turn the cards back in their same place on the table.

Marie was upset because Josh did not follow the rule. Josh picked up the first card and held it in his hand while attempting to find the other matching bunny card. Marie reacted with an angry look and loud comments to Josh about the correct way to play the game. She called Josh's name loudly, pointing out to Steve that Josh was not playing correctly. Marie showed her frustration with Josh by taking the cards out of his hand and placing them on the table. Josh did not seem to mind, but he didn't change the way he played the game.

This demonstration of frustration is not very common for Marie. Usually she displays excitement, contentment, satisfaction, curiosity, and happiness.

Intellectual characteristics

Marie is very good at expressing her ideas and getting her point across to whomever she is speaking to, other children or adults. Marie's speech is clear and understandable. Her voice and speaking pattern are well controlled, unless she is upset with another child; then she talks too much.

Clearly she feels comfortable speaking. She is willing to read aloud to the class any books she brings from home. Marie likes to share her experiences with the class and talk about items she brings from home.

When required to report on a current events article from the newspaper, Marie writes a summary of the article and reads this to the class. She rarely adds spontaneous comments to this article.

Marie loves to talk about her journal. Marie possesses good letter and number recognition skills. She can hear and write letter sounds. She is an excellent reader and always seems willing to try to do something new. She recognizes and identifies many familiar words in the classroom environment and attempts to try reading new words she encounters.

Marie's writing, with the use of inventive spelling, reveals much information about her level of understanding. Marie can easily read the words she writes and she will gladly read them to any adult who is interested. Often when she is really concentrating, Marie has her tongue hanging out of her mouth. She is deeply involved, focused, and really enjoying what she is working on at these times.

Marie is at the stage of play where she is concerned about the rules of games. She relates to her peers and she enjoys playing with them. She seems to enjoy competition and has a strong moral interest in fair play.

My observations lead me to the conclusion that Marie enjoys school and is learning. She has a strong chance of doing well in school because she is interested in school activities and learning. She possesses an easygoing personality and ability to cope and accept change with equanimity. Marie might enjoy tutoring her peers and working with cooperative learning activities. She seems ready for a variety of small group activities and partner activities. She seems ready for further academic challenges.

A concern to address is Marie's reaction to peers who try to help her. To help with this problem, I will encourage her to talk with friends in a more pleasant tone of voice. We might develop alternate remarks for her to use on these occasions. For example, "Today, I don't want you to help me. . . . I like it when I can read all the words to Miss Hamm."

The entire first grade might discuss helping one another and how to learn from others. This is a class that does not have much experience with cooperative learning or conflict resolution, so Marie's reaction to stress is not drastically different than her peers, but the strident response does not serve her well. (Case study used with permission of Hamm, 1991)

Notes on the process of the study of Marie

Physical characteristics
In this section, the reader develops a picture of Marie, Marie as a person, and Marie's interest in Brownies.

Physical abilities
Marie is right-handed. Fine motor skills seem well developed. Only one observation of gross motor skill is reported; therefore, results may be tentative. However, no gross motor problems are reported either.

Social characteristics
Marie and her mom appropriately separate when mom visits the class. In large group settings, Marie is an observer rather than a dynamic participant. Thus within normal limits, she knows what is going on, but does not choose to "volunteer." Marie generally conforms to school rules. She leads in small group situations, sometimes to the point of bossiness. Marie relates easily to adults.

Emotional characteristics
The author has not really separated social and emotional characteristics in this study. She describes Marie as confident, self-assured, and somewhat bossy.

Intellectual characteristics
Speech and language skills are well developed. A social/emotional issue is reported in this section, as well—Marie's tendency to talk too much when frustrated. Marie is interested in writing and reading; no academic problems are evident.

The author reports Marie's interest in games with rules. Marie thrives on competition with peers, a social/emotional dimension of her behavior.

Summary
The author finds Marie well-adjusted, developing typically. The author recommends some conflict resolution and cooperative learning activities for the class and for Marie, in particular. For the reader, the question remains, . . . "Does Marie need this special help?" Is there a different expectation for the author than practiced in the social environment of this school? Readers of this study have a snapshot of Marie in time. Details of intellectual progress are limited in this discussion. Does this mean that Marie is on target, cognitively—probably. The author most likely would report particular intellectual difficulties, but readers do not know for sure. No particular problems exist in the mind of the observer. A change in cur-

riculum is suggested. This change should enhance social-emotional adjustment, independence, and conflict resolution.

A teacher receiving this report will expect Marie to function well in the second grade. The new teacher might wish for test scores and details of the curriculum recorded in some way, so that a curriculum could be planned in Marie's best interests.

Parents receiving the report will most likely be pleased that the observer reports no problems. They may worry about the tendency toward bossiness. On the other hand, they may feel that this is a healthy expression of confidence.

Psychoeducational evaluation

In this section, readers have the opportunity to view a professionally developed report. This report is complete and demonstrates a comprehensive portrait of the assessment process. It is a **psychoeducational evaluation** that incorporates developmental psychological and educational tasks.

Name: **Jackie S.**   *Date:* **1–21–94**
Birth date: **July 11, 1986 (C.A.=7–6)**
Grade: **PDLC**

I. Presenting problem
Jackie was referred for evaluation by her parents. Jackie has had medical and educational problems in the past and her parents wanted an independent evaluation conducted outside the school system to determine if her problems might be categorized as a learning disability.

II. Background information
Jackie was first identified as a child in need of special services in the fall of 1989 when she was three years old. She was placed in the preschool special education program on a diagnostic basis as formalized test results were inconsistent. In addition, she was to receive occupational therapy services beginning March, 1990, on a weekly basis to integrate primitive postural reflexes, improve balance and equilibrium, and improve tactile processing and body position sense. Eventually she was diagnosed as having a developmental delay in most areas: gross motor; fine motor; and conceptual, receptive, and expressive language. She continued to receive services, including speech and language therapy, in the preschool special education program until she was reevaluated prior to her sixth birthday.

Home environment

Jackie lives at home with both parents and a younger sister, Stephanie (DOB: 5–31–91). Both parents work outside the home so Jackie goes to a baby-sitter before and after school. English is spoken at home. In the past, Mrs. S. has expressed concern regarding Jackie's frequent stubborn responses and passive resistance to parental direction. Jackie is described as having adequate self-help skills and preferring solitary activities. She enjoys reading books, coloring, and other quiet activities at home.

Medical history

Jackie is under the care of specialists at a metropolitan university hospital for a medical condition described as an "inborn error in metabolism." The symptoms of uncontrolled vomiting began after the age of two and required about 20 hospitalizations between 1989–91. The situation has abated somewhat since the age of five. She is on a maintenance dosage of antibiotic to prevent the recurrence of ear infections which may trigger the vomiting episodes. In addition, in February of 1991, Jackie had bacterial meningitis.

A recent physical therapy evaluation (10–93) indicates physical causes for her gross motor delays. Her gait pattern deviation is attributable to femoral retroversion in both femurs and decreased mobility in both ankle joints. Jackie seems to control her posture primarily by visual input, but she is not able to overcome her gross motor skill delays. Direct physical therapy service was recommended to improve postural control, increase weight shifting during transfers, and improve the quality of her gait pattern.

According to her classroom teacher, Ms. Petit, the last school check for auditory screening noted a possible mild hearing loss in her left ear. This should be rechecked as it could be attributed to one of Jackie's frequent ear infections. On the other hand, if confirmed, this could have direct bearing on the development of language, both receptively and expressively.

Educational history

A complete psychological assessment was conducted in early 1992 to determine the best placement for Jackie following her preschool special education program. Results from a number of different instruments were consistent in concluding that Jackie was functioning at that time around the borderline range with apparent deficits in motor skills, language functioning, concept formation, and adaptive behavior. However, a great deal of inconsistency was noted in her daily classroom performance making it difficult to determine if her learning problems were related to emotional factors, learning disability problems, health problems, limited learning potential, or a combination of factors. Due to Jackie's apparent lack of readiness for a standard academic kindergarten curriculum, she was placed in a primary developmental learning class (PDLC) with additional speech and language and occupational therapy. Jackie has now been in this program for eighteen months.

The teacher's report (11/93) indicates progress in all areas but continued problems as well.

III. *Current assessment*

The following battery of tests was attempted on 1/21/94:

Kaufman Assessment Battery for Children (K–ABC)

Goodenough-Harris Drawing Test

Test of Early Language Development (TELD)

Auditory Discrimination Test (ADT)

Developmental Test of Visual-Motor Integration (VMI)

Motor-free Visual Motor Test

Peabody Picture Vocabulary Test-Revised (PPVT–R)

Behavior Rating Profile

Kaufman Assessment Battery for Children

The Kaufman Assessment Battery for Children (K–ABC) is a standardized test of mental processing (intelligence or aptitude) and achievement for children between the ages of 2.6 and 12.6 years. It yields a number of different scores:

- Sequential Processing (emphasis on the serial or temporal order), Jackie's score: 100 (+ or −9)
- Simultaneous Processing (emphasis on the integration of stimuli), Jackie's score: 71 (+ or −7)
- Mental Processing Composite: 79 (+ or −7)
- Achievement: 80 (+ or −4)

A significant difference (.01) was noted between sequential and simultaneous processing and between sequential processing and achievement, with sequential processing being higher in both comparisons. This suggests that Jackie performs significantly higher on tasks that require the ordering of information than the integration of information and that this particular strength is much higher than where she is currently functioning on school-related tasks. The sub-tests that contributed to this significant difference were Number Recall and Word Order, two tasks that required short term auditory memory while not requiring perceptual organization, spatial memory, or visual motor coordination. A third sub-test on which Jackie scored within the normal range was Gestalt Closure. Even though on two items her impulsivity to respond rapidly interfered, she self-corrected and was given credit for these responses. All other sub-tests of mental processing were below the range where two of every three children would score (85–115).

On the achievement sub-tests, Jackie scored in the normal range on Faces and Places, indicating average general factual knowledge. However, the other four achievement scores were all more than one standard deviation below the national mean, and grade equivalents for Arithmetic and Reading/Decoding would place her below a beginning first grade level.

Goodenough-Harris Drawing Test

The Goodenough-Harris Drawing Test is a measure of intellectual maturity (the ability to form concepts of increasingly abstract character). Drawing a person involves the abilities to perceive, to abstract, and to generalize. Jackie's drawing of a man consisted of a head with eyes, nose, smiling mouth, ears, a scribble for hair, and two feet. There was no trunk or arms. This earned her seven points for a scaled score of 64, indicating a much lower level of maturity than mental processing or achievement.

Test of Early Language Development

The results of the Test of Early Language Development (TELD) also indicated that Jackie has a strength in short term auditory processing, but this does not compensate for her weakness to comprehend questions. For example, when told the story "Billy was tired. He hadn't taken a nap. What do you think he said to his mother?" Jackie replied, "I don't want to take a nap." When asked "Who is in your family?" Jackie replied, "Catherine, Adam, Grandma, Mom, Dad, and Jessica." Three of these responses are not appropriate. Other instances of inappropriate responses related to her age (nine), father's name, sister's name, address, phone number, and the name of her school.

Auditory Discrimination Test

The Auditory Discrimination Test (ADT) results place Jackie in the below average range of discrimination ability in comparison with other seven year olds. This test requires the examiner to stand in back of the child and say two words. The child merely indicates whether they are the same or different. Jackie understood the task (as she did with all tests), but I definitely felt that she said anything, just to get done with the task (40 pairs of words). There were no indications during the three hour session that she had difficulty hearing me or distinguishing between words that sound similar.

Developmental Test of Visual-Motor Integration (VMI)

The Developmental Test of Visual-Motor Integration (VMI) requires the child to coordinate what is seen with what is drawn. Jackie successfully copied ten drawings which yields a scaled score of 5 (M=10; S.D.=3) and an age equivalent of 5–7. This is considerably below her chronological age.

Motor-free Visual Perception Test

In order to separate whether this low score is due to a visual perception problem or a visual-motor problem, the Motor-free Visual Perception Test was administered. Unfortunately, the results are invalid as Jackie was no longer willing to cooperate with me.

Peabody Picture Vocabulary Test–Revised

The Peabody Picture Vocabulary Test–Revised (PPVT–R) was also attempted, but Jackie was not willing to attempt this test either.

Behavior Rating Profile

The Behavior Rating Profile was completed by Jackie's primary teacher, Ms. Petit, and both parents. Although the section to be completed by the student was completed, the questions were asked in such a way that Jackie responded in an impulsive manner, invalidating any score.

Both Jackie's teacher and mother scored Jackie's behavior within the normal range for a child her age while her father's scores indicate that he perceives her behavior as less mature than the average seven year old. However, Jackie's teacher is comparing her with other children within a special class so that, too, must be taken into consideration. Behaviors which are of concern to Jackie's teacher include her inability to concentrate in class, nervous habits, and social imperceptions regarding her peers. Jackie's parents perceive Jackie's behavior similarly on two-thirds of the test items; areas of primary concern appear to be Jackie's controlling behavior in the home. She is unwilling to take orders or follow parental rules and demands immediate gratification.

Behavior during testing

Jackie had no difficulty separating from her father and exhibited no anxiety during the three-hour session. Fortunately, the K–ABC was administered first, while Jackie was able to attend. However, from the beginning there were obvious signs of impulsivity. I imposed limits and that helped Jackie control her behavior somewhat. She often answered an oral question before I had finished asking it, sometimes correctly even without having all of the necessary information. However, this behavior also interfered with sub-tests requiring a motoric response.

Although all the mental processing sub-tests of the K–ABC allow the examiner to teach the task if the child does not understand the directions, this was never necessary. Jackie always understood the task and received credit for the beginning items. She even understood the directions on the complicated sub-test of Word Order and this is one of the tasks where she scored well in the average range.

One humorous exchange occurred on Faces and Places. When shown a picture of George Washington and asked to identify him, Jackie answered "Martin Luther King." She correctly identified Abraham Lincoln, but also said that Muhammad Ali was Martin Luther King. Finally, when shown a picture of Martin Luther King, she responded correctly. This should be scored in light of the fact that today was two days after the King holiday, but even if I deduct for this correct response, her score on this subtest is still well within the normal range.

Jackie exhibited very controlling behavior. Once she made up her mind that she did not want to do a particular task, that was the end of the discussion. She did not want to comply with my tasks, even when she was bored and had nothing else to do. When given the opportunity to control the situation, Jackie displayed an active imagination and enjoyed pretending that she was healing a sick stuffed turtle by putting scotch tape on him.

On the other hand, Jackie exhibited somewhat independent behavior for a child her age. When she took a bathroom break, she told me it was not necessary to wait for her, that she would meet me at my office, which she did. Since the surroundings were completely foreign to her, this indicated an ability to function realistically in new surroundings. Jackie also indicated when she was ready to have a snack. There were many canteens from which to choose, but she quickly decided on a sweet roll and chocolate milk and never wavered from her decision.

IV. Summary

Jackie S. is a pleasant, 7½ year old youngster who was seen for a complete **psychoeducational evaluation.** Results from the battery of tests and input from her parents and her current teacher indicate that Jackie is currently functioning primarily in the low average range, although a few scores are within the average range and a few scores in the retarded range. A significant difference between sequential and simultaneous processing of information on the K-ABC suggests that Jackie can process serial or temporal information much better than information which requires the integration of stimuli. This should be of assistance in school-related activities, since most school tasks rely heavily on ordering of information. Jackie also scored within the normal range on Faces and Places, a sub-test which requires long-term memory retention, but did not show the same strengths on other achievement sub-tests where she consistently scored between one and two standard deviations below the mean on the K-ABC.

Jackie scored in the low average or retarded range on the Goodenough-Harris Drawing Test, the Test of Early Language Development, and the Developmental Test of Visual-Motor Integration, all of which required her to integrate information, one verbally and two nonverbally. Some of the more informal questions asked of Jackie were more revealing that the actual test questions, such as where she lives and who is in her family. The answers to these questions leads me to confirm that Jackie has severe learning disabilities. Although she scored below average on the Auditory Discrimination Test as well, there were no indications that Jackie had any difficulty in distinguishing between words that sound similar.

An area of concern, to both her parents and her teacher, is Jackie's behavior patterns. She shows classic signs of learning disabilities: distractibility, impulsivity, and social imperceptions. Jackie's controlling behavior may be her way to make sense out of her environment. When she doesn't understand what to do or how, by resisting the task, she avoids the situation. Unfortunately, it also does not add to her body of knowledge and keeps her on a plateau. Jackie needs to be given the opportunity to be in charge at times when she complies with requests, not just when she resists requests.

Although Jackie has many problems—cognitively, motorically, behaviorally, and socially—her overriding problem appears to fall into the category of learning disabilities, and she should be treated accordingly. In addition, it would be most helpful for Jackie's parents to learn strategies for dealing more effectively with Jackie's behaviors in the home.

Respectfully submitted,

CM-C

Registered psychologist

Notes on the process of the study of Jackie

This is an example of a study that a teacher may expect to receive when a child with special needs is placed in a classroom or is receiving service in a program. It is very complete, detailed, and well-organized and contains suggestions for the child, family, and the teacher.

Summary

Each of these examples of child studies shows a summary point in the assessment process. Teachers and others conduct child studies so that all the information on a particular child is gathered in one place. Usually this summarization occurs when there are developmental or educational questions to be answered. Then, a team of parents, teachers, and other professionals will review the available material and plan next steps in the process.

In each of these vignettes, the reader is allowed to see the dynamic process of child-study development. The observers report progress from their vantage points. Available history and school progress are included.

A diverse group of studies is presented—children in various settings, of various ages, ranging in **typical** to **atypical development,** and in the sophistication of the reports—to help guide you in preparing your own reports and in reading those of others.

The notes following the child studies raise questions for your further consideration and elaboration of the issues and concerns. The teaching-assessment-reteaching process continues.

CHAPTER 8 Suggested further readings

Almy, M., & Genishi, C. (1979). *Ways of studying children.* New York: Teachers College.

Bergen, D. (1988). *Play: As a medium for learning and development.* Portsmouth, NH: Heinemann.

Genishi, C. (Ed.). (1992). *Ways of assessing children and curriculum: Stories of early childhood practice.* New York: Teachers College.

McWilliams, P. J., & Bailey, D. B. (1993). *Working together with children and families: Case studies in early intervention.* Baltimore: Paul H. Brookes.

CHAPTER 8 Study questions

1. What are elements of child studies? When, how, and who conducts child studies? Where do child studies fit in the assessment system? For which child study does the early childhood teacher assume primary responsibility?

2. What is a child find team? How does the team plan, implement, and interpret assessment of young children? What is the early childhood teacher responsibility for the team?

3. Why must early childhood teachers ground their child studies in their knowledge of typical and atypical child development? What are the risks to parents and young children of faulty knowledge and interpretation?

4. Examine the sample child studies. Compare the studies to the criteria of important elements for child studies. Develop a plan to gather the missing information. Identify appropriate assessment strategies.

ACTIVITIES

1. Pick one of these child studies for further consideration. Plan the next steps in assessment, intervention, or teaching. Compare your notes with a colleague.
2. Observe a child in school or child care. Summarize your information in a child study in as much detail as available. Outline your next teaching, intervention, or assessment steps.
3. With permission, review a child study for a child in a center or school. Outline the next steps in teaching, intervention, or assessment.
4. Plan a parent interview for a child you are studying. What additional information will assist in the teaching, intervention, or assessment of the child? Compare your notes with colleagues.

References

Almy, M., & Genishi, C. (1979). *Ways of studying children.* New York: Teachers College.

Hamm, C. (1991). "A case study of Marie," submitted in partial fulfillment of Education 245, Observation of Young Children. Chicago: Roosevelt University.

Papalia and Olds. (1990). *A child's world: Infancy through adolescence.* New York: McGraw Hill.

Polachek, L. (1991). "A case study of Sam," submitted in partial fulfillment of Education 245, Observation of Young Children. Chicago: Roosevelt University.

Talaga, M. (1991). "A case study of Tomas," submitted in partial fulfillment of Education 245, Observation of Young Children. Chicago: Roosevelt University.

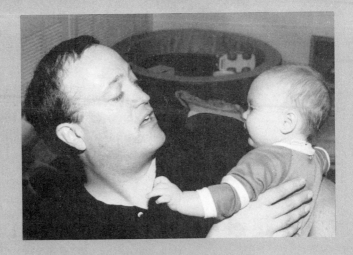

CHAPTER 9

Special Issues in Infant and Toddler Assessment

Terms to Know

- case finding
- screening
- diagnosis
- Apgar Rating Scale
- prenatal testing
- amniocentesis
- ultrasound
- chorionic villus biopsy (CVS)
- gestational age
- established risk
- biological risk

- environmental risk
- P.L. 99–457
- individualized family service plans (IFSP)
- family involvement
- drug-exposed babies
- fetal alcohol syndrome (FAS)
- multidisciplinary team
- interdisciplinary team
- transdisciplinary team
- arena approach to assessment

CHAPTER OVERVIEW This chapter covers the special issues in infant and toddler assessment, the aspects of assessment that are different from birth (or even prior to birth) to age three than assessment of preschool and primary children. In order to identify problems in the development of infants and toddlers, you need to understand the meaning of development, recognize developmental milestones, and grasp the factors that affect developmental change in the first three years of life.

Topics Discussed

▮ The total assessment process of infants and toddlers
▮ The importance of assessment in the first three years
▮ Current assessment issues and trends
▮ Ecologically and developmentally relevant assessment strategies
▮ The integration of assessment information into programming

⊞ The total assessment process of infants and toddlers

Interest in the prompt and accurate identification of infants and toddlers with developmental disabilities or potential learning problems has increased significantly in the last ten years or so. Data-based studies examining early intervention services which report encouraging findings and legislative initiatives have provided the incentive for this interest. Moreover, cost/benefit analyses indicate that for every $1.00 invested in early intervention services, there is a $3.00 reduction in long term, public special education costs (Berrueter-Clement, Schweinhart, Barnett, Epstein, & Weikart, 1984). Where does assessment come into the picture with infants and toddlers?

The assessment of infants and toddlers is complicated by the rapid growth and early non-verbal nature of children, our dependence on talking as a measure of understanding developmental progress, the inadequacy and/or inaccuracy of many standard measures, and inextricably linked family and cultural factors that influence development. To determine infant and toddler competencies fairly and for best services to infants and toddlers in their diverse learning environments, the assessment process must be based on an integrated developmental model and involve multiple sources of information and multiple components. An assessment should follow the following sequence:

1. Establish an alliance of trust with parents. Listen to their views of the baby's strengths and challenges.
2. Realize that parents may not share all of the baby's developmental history at once. They will share more as they trust.
3. Initial observation should occur in a familiar or naturalistic setting with parents or care givers present.
4. Later observations and assessments by clinicians should offer parental opportunity for participation.
5. Utilize standard measures and tests sparingly to answer a specific question that can be answered no other way.

6.   Interpret all of the gathered material from observations, interviews, and formal assessments in a developmental framework that incorporates knowledge of child development in a social/cultural context. (Zero to Three Work Group, 1994)

These ideas have guided the preparation of *Diagnostic Classification: 0–3*,(Zero to Three, 1995). This manual should serve as a reference for all who serve the birth to three population so that the assessment of infants and toddlers can be systematic, comprehensive, and inclusive of diverse settings with various care givers. The measure of humans begins at birth or before and continues lifelong. How, then, is assessment focused in infancy? The sections that follow elaborate.

The importance of assessment in the first three years

Not too long ago, when a baby was born, the primary questions asked, after determining the sex of the baby, were "How much does the baby weigh?" and "How long is the baby?" Nowadays, it is far more common to ask, "What was the Apgar score?" The **Apgar Rating Scale** (Apgar, 1953) is used routinely in most hospitals across the United States to screen newborn infants. The test is given one minute after delivery and then repeated

at five minutes (and sometimes ten minutes) after delivery. Five easily observed signs—heart rate, respiratory effort, muscle tone, reflex response, and color—are scored on a scale from 0 (poor) to 2 (good). Total scores in the 0 to 3 range suggest extremely poor physical condition, are very serious, and indicate an emergency concerning the infant's survival. A fair condition is indicated by a score of 4 to 6 and a score of 7 to 10 implies a good condition. Color is the least dependable of the signs, since not all babies can be judged on pink and blue tones. All babies can be assessed by a darkening glow as oxygen flows through the baby (Berk, 1993). The purpose of this screening is to determine the developmental status of the baby at birth and to identify, as early as possible, infants who may be at risk for serious developmental problems. According to Knutson, Biro, and Padgett (1987), many children with special needs can be identified at or shortly after birth. Most babies, that is 97 percent, are born without major birth defects (American College of Obstetricians and Gynecologists, 1994). Nonetheless, for the other 3 percent, early identification, screening, and assessment are integral parts of early intervention services.

Prenatal testing

However, the Apgar Rating Scale may not be the first instrument used for determining the developmental status of a baby. Many parents opt for **prenatal testing** such as **amniocentesis** in which a slender needle is inserted through the mother's abdomen into the embryonic sac surrounding the fetus in the womb. A small amount of amniotic fluid is withdrawn for biochemical analysis (American College of Obstetricians and Gynecologists, 1994). The fluid contains fetal cells that can be analyzed to determine fetal maturity, chromosomal and metabolic abnormalities such as phenylketonuria (PKU) and congenital hypothyroidism, or 250 other genetic abnormalities such as Down syndrome, Tay-Sachs disease, and spina bifida. This diagnostic procedure is usually performed during the fourteenth to eighteenth week of pregnancy but can be performed as early as 12 weeks. In addition to looking for abnormalities, amniocentesis can also determine the sex of the fetus.

Ultrasound (sonography) is another, less intrusive, screening method in which sound waves enable the technician to determine the fetus's development. Also usually performed during the fourteenth to sixteenth week of pregnancy, this monitoring provides a picture (really an outline) of the placenta and fetus without the use of X rays or the puncturing of a fetal part.

Another method of prenatal testing that may eventually replace amniocentesis is **chorionic villus biopsy** (CVS) (Batshaw & Perret, 1986; American College of Obstetricians and Gynecologists, 1991). This procedure is performed earlier than amniocentesis or ultrasound, usually in the first trimester (9th to 12th week of pregnancy), before the mother feels any movement of the fetus. The main advantage of this earlier screening is that a decision to terminate a pregnancy is usually emotionally easier and medically safer at this earlier stage. In this procedure, an instrument is inserted through the vagina into the uterus. Guided by ultrasound, some chorionic tissue, which is the fetal component of the developing placenta, is removed by suction and examined under a microscope. Since fetal cells exist in relatively large numbers in the chorion, they can be analyzed directly, unlike the process in amniocentesis that requires 2–3 weeks for the fetal cells to grow in a culture medium. CVS has been used successfully to detect certain chromosomal abnormalities, measure the activity of specific enzymes, and determine the sex of the fetus.

A fourth prenatal test is accomplished by drawing blood (Batshaw & Perret, 1986; American College of Obstetricians and Gynecologists, 1994). In this least intrusive and least expensive method, blood is analyzed for alpha-fetoprotein (AFP) levels. A small amount of blood is drawn from a vein in the woman's arm during the first 15–18 weeks of pregnancy. This test can detect fetuses with spina bifida, other open fetal defects (higher levels than normal of AFP), or Down syndrome (lower levels than normal of AFP). Unfortunately, this procedure may miss as many as 10 percent of Down syndrome fetuses because it is only a screening test. It can only assess a woman's risk of having a baby with a certain birth defect, whereas a diagnostic test can usually show whether a baby has the birth defect or not. Adding certain tests to the AFP test can give more information about the risk of having a baby with Down syndrome than the AFP test alone (American College of Obstetricians and Gynecologists, 1994). These are called multiple marker screening (MMS) tests, but the best combination of tests is not yet known. By measuring other substances in the woman's blood, usually with the same blood sample used for the AFP test, the accuracy of the screening may be increased.

All four methods are utilized, not only to satisfy the parents' curiosity, but to relieve parental concern and anxiety over possible difficulties and to identify any deviations prior to birth that might cause the parents to elect aborting a fetus with serious, maybe even fatal, defects. Such procedures carry with them many ethical issues that eventually must be resolved.

Assessment at birth

A common measure that describes the infant's status at birth is the determination of **gestational age.** Weight alone is not a sufficient indicator of age because an infant can be larger than average for gestational age or smaller than average for gestational age (O'Donnell & Oehler, 1989).

Knowing the infant's weight in relation to gestational age is a measure of maturity which distinguishes between prematurity and growth retardation in the small for gestational age (SGA) infant as well as identifying the large for gestational age (LGA) infant who may need medical care and follow-up procedures.

Another scale that is frequently used shortly after birth, although not as often as the Apgar, is the *Neonatal Behavior Assessment Scale* (NBAS) (Brazelton, 1984). This is a more detailed examination designed to identify abnormalities in the central nervous system and sensory abilities, but it goes beyond a focus on neurological reflexes. It can describe the quality and level of the infant's behavior, detect changes in the infant's behavior, assess the impact of treatment interventions, and predict future development and function. According to Bergen and Wright (1994), it is a better predictor of later developmental outcome than the Apgar score. In 30 minutes, this 28-item behavioral evaluation also measures the infant's responses to the environment. When the evaluation is done in the presence of the parent(s), it enables the primary caregiver(s) to see all the sights and sounds their newborns are capable of responding to and the unique way in which they do so. Positive research findings by Field, Dempsey, Hallock, and Shuman (1978) suggested that the administration of the NBAS helped the mother to "become more sensitized to the unique abilities of her infant, more interested in observing his or her development, and more active in promoting and providing stimulation to facilitate their development." In fact, at least one hospital program uses the NBAS as a way to discuss parental perceptions of their infant's capabilities rather than teach about infant behavior (Cardone & Gilkerson, 1989). The rationale for using the NBAS in this manner is the evolving literature on the helping process indicating that people are more likely to engage with professionals in helping relationships if they feel that they themselves are producing results rather than being taught (Dunst & Trivette, 1988). Widerstrom, et al. (1991) concur that this knowledge of child development gleaned from the NBAS and their baby's specific competence can facilitate improvement in parenting skills.

A screening that is mandated in most states before the infant leaves the hospital is obtained by a blood sample taken with a heel stick. The blood is analyzed for metabolic diseases which may result in retarded growth and development. Among these diseases are phenylketonuria (PKU) and congenital hypothyroidism.

Principles of child development

No two babies, not even identical twins, are exactly alike. Each will develop somewhat differently based on genetic and environmental factors. Furthermore, there is no single theory of child development that all experts accept (Meisels & Provence, 1989). However, there are a few general observations about very young children that are commonly accepted:

1. Development is determined by multiple factors.
2. Developmental change is supported, facilitated, or impeded by environmental influences.
3. Societal and cultural influences on the child are mediated by parental figures.
4. The family plays a unique role and makes vital contributions to the child's development.
5. Parenthood is a developmental and adaptive process.
   (Meisels & Provence, 1989)

When working with infants and toddlers, it is important to recognize the early childhood milestones. Teachers can find examples of milestones in the *NAEYC Position Statement on Developmentally Appropriate Practice in Early Childhood Programs* (Bredekamp, 1987). In addition, caregivers should consult milestone lists that are embedded in a theoretical discussion of issues such as attachment, perception, emotions, language, etc. (cf Gonzalez-Mena & Eyer, 1993). By being aware of these milestones, an early childhood educator can often allay unwarranted concerns of parents. Even though the rate of development has little predictive value in general, severe delays in skill development or unusual milestone patterns may indicate a problem (Friedman, 1989). Answers to the following questions may help determine if the child should be referred in the first year. Are the child's skills consistently delayed in a *number* of areas such as motor, language, and self-help? Has the one-year-old child started to *understand* some words? Are there any doubts about the child's hearing? Is the child's motor development significantly delayed in a *variety* of tasks, such as sitting, crawling, standing, and walking?

Risk factors

While most infants and toddlers develop without developmental problems, there are several different factors that put infants at risk (Blackman, 1986; National Center for Clinical Infant Programs, 1986). These factors, which can be divided into three categories, are not mutually exclusive; thus, an infant may be at risk due to one or more of the following:

1. **Established risk:** infants in this category possess a gene abnormality; a malformation or structural problem with the brain or central nervous system; or received alcohol or illegal drugs in utero. These factors are known to contribute to challenges in development.
2. **Biological risk:** infants in this category have a prenatal, perinatal, or neonatal difficulty, including low birth weight, respiratory distress at

birth, central nervous system infection, or difficult birth process. These difficulties are associated with challenges to development.

3. **Environmental risk:** infants in this category may be affected by family or social stress. Factors that contribute to challenges in development include malnutrition during pregnancy or in the period immediately following birth. Additional difficulties include patterns of care by the primary care giver that may be inadequate. Overall family poverty contributes risk to this category.

Socioeconomic status has been shown to have a greater effect on the development and subsequent school functioning of a child than the biologic risk factors with the exception of the very low birth weight (less than 1500 grams or 3.3 pounds) infant (Cohen, 1983).

The relationship between these three categories of risk, the 10–12% of children who have some degree of disability when they enter school, and the total number of children in the population is complicated as illustrated in Figure 9.1. A full discussion of the interactions of environmental and biological risk factors can be found in *The Handbook of Early Childhood Intervention* (Meisels & Shonkoff, 1990). In brief, poverty heightens the likelihood of established risk. Child abuse, malnutrition, and accidents also heighten the development of special needs that will be identified before school entrance. Disability can range from visual and hearing impairment to complex mental and physical handicaps. Other children will be identified during the school years as having learning disabilities and/or socioemotional problems.

As an early childhood educator working with infants and toddlers, what warning signals would you be aware of? Here are some of the criteria that would suggest that a child is at risk (Blackman, 1986). The more of these signals that are attributable to any one child, the more likely that the child will have a problem. Table 9.1 lists these warning signals under eight categories.

However, we need to realize the near impossibility of predicting the prospects for any child's development, whether of extremely low birth weight or typical birth weight, whether disabled or not, and whether at risk or not (Ensher & Clark, 1994). Many children with risk factors later develop health or developmental problems, especially those with more than one category of risk (Bennett, 1984). Nevertheless, some children with none of these risk factors later develop the same problems. There are also many children with these risk factors who grow and develop normally (Knutson et al., 1987). In other words, longitudinal developmental predictions based upon constitutional factors alone are weak and inaccurate (Kochanek, 1988). Many assessment instruments used with infants, babies, and toddlers do not have predictive validity. Still, they remain useful as tools with concurrent validity for describing current development. To

---

TABLE 9.1 Warning signals: basic criteria for tracking at-risk infant and toddlers

---

1. **Parental and psychosocial factors:**
   ▮ no prenatal care
   ▮ maternal age of less than 15 years
   ▮ maternal phenylketonuria (PKU)
   ▮ maternal acquired immune deficiency syndrome (AIDS)
   ▮ parental sensory impairment (deafness or blindness)
   ▮ maternal use of certain therapeutic drugs (e.g., anticonvulsants, antineoplastics, anticoagulants)
   ▮ parental substance abuse
   ▮ parental mental retardation
   ▮ parental psychiatric disorder
   ▮ inability to provide basic parenting functions due to impairment in psychological or interpersonal functioning
   ▮ lack of permanent housing

2. **Newborn**
   ▮ low birth weight
   ▮ respiratory distress
   ▮ intracranial hemorrhage
   ▮ neonatal seizures
   ▮ clinical evidence of central nervous system abnormality
   ▮ microcephaly or macrocephaly (head circumference less than 3rd percentile or greater than 97th percentile)
   ▮ central nervous system infection
   ▮ hyperbilirubinemia greater than 20 mg/dl
   ▮ hypoglycemia (serum glucose less than 2 mg/dl)
   ▮ suspected hearing impairment
   ▮ suspected visual impairment
   ▮ major congenital anomalies

3. **Issues regarding health maintenance**
   ▮ absence of regular professional health supervision
   ▮ inadequate caregiving and protection

4. **Newly diagnosed familial disorder with developmental implications**
   ▮ tuberous sclerosis, familial retardation syndromes, (e.g., fragile x syndrome), and metabolic disorders

5. **Evidence of growth deficiency/nutritional problems/anemia**
   ▮ excessive deceleration in growth in weight, height and/or head circumference (failure to thrive)

TABLE 9.1 (continued)

6. **Known central nervous system insult**
   ∎ infection—meningitis, encephalitis, etc.
   ∎ trauma
   ∎ toxin
   ∎ metabolic
   ∎ asphyxia
   ∎ malignancy of the brain or spinal cord

7. **Severe chronic illness**
   ∎ respiratory (e.g., bronchopulmonary dysplasia [BPD])
   ∎ cardiac
   ∎ renal disease
   ∎ chronic otitis media
   ∎ seizure disorder
   ∎ malignancy

8. **Atypical or delayed cognitive socioemotional, motor, sensory, or behavioral development**
   ∎ failure on a standardized developmental/sensory screening test
   ∎ significant concern of parent, regular caregiver, or health provider regarding child's competence or emotional well-being
   ∎ evidence of reactive attachment disorder of infancy and early childhood
   ∎ evidence of delay or abnormality in achieving expected emotional milestones such as pleasurable interest in the human world; ability to communicate emotional needs clearly and intentionally; and increasingly complex, organized, and integrated behavioral and emotional patterns

---

Blackman, J. (1986). *Warning signals: Basic criteria for tracking at-risk infants and toddlers.* Washington, DC: National Center for Clinical Infant Programs.

---

overcome the low predictive validity, periodic checks are recommended for infants and toddlers with one or more risk factors. All children and families should be examined on multiple occasions between birth and three years of age due to significant variation in child developmental pathways as well as ongoing changes in family status (Kochanek, 1988). It has been suggested that these examinations occur three to four times during the first year, twice during the second year, and once every year thereafter, preferably until the child completes second grade. Additionally, we need to incorporate environmental factors (Nichols & Chen, 1981) and parent/child interaction (Cohen & Beckwith, 1979) into a model with

FIGURE 9.1 Relationship between risk factors that can be identified at birth and disability present by the age of school entry

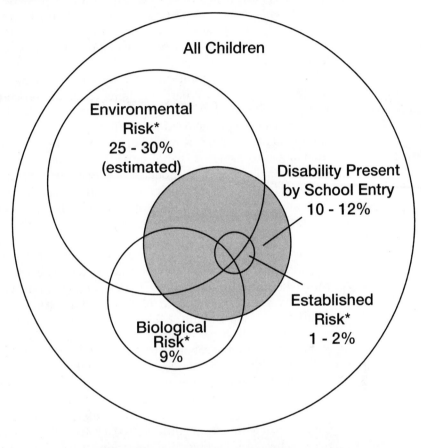

All Children

Environmental Risk*
25 - 30%
(estimated)

Disability Present by School Entry
10 - 12%

Established Risk*
1 - 2%

Biological Risk*
9%

*Factors that can be identified at birth

From Knutson, M., Biro, P., & Padgett D. (1990). Tracking infants at risk: Washington state's high priority infant tracking system. *Journal of Pediatric Health Care, 1*, p.181.

measures of child performance because adding these elements gives more power in predicting the occurrence of cognitive, language, and motor deficiencies in school-aged children (Kochanek, 1988). Such a model for identifying handicapped infants and young children is found in Figure 9.2. This multivariate, interactional risk model indicates the complexity of the problem of prediction and the need for sources of data beyond those presented by the child alone. The caregiver's response and adaptation to the developing child is just as important as assessing the newborn and developmental status (Kochanek, 1988). Furthermore, it is just as important to identify vulnerable, low-resource families within which children are at a substantial risk for subsequent school failure (environmental risk) as it is to identify children with developmental deviations (established and biological risk).

Another way of defining the children we are seeking to assist is by calling them those who are hard to parent, teach, or befriend (Barnett, Macmann, & Carey, 1992). This description shifts the emphasis from the child's characteristics to problem situations that are embedded within the family, community, and child care or school systems. Although some of these children may be considered "handicapped" or "disabled" by traditional definitions, many others are not. According to Barnett et al., (1992), the rationale for the identification of these children is guided by the need to restore or improve the functioning of the family, classroom, or peers, thus affecting the well-being of all group members.

Why do we want to predict which at-risk infants will indeed have atypical development and identify those who already have problems? One reason is that clinical experience and research suggest that babies who show very poor functioning or substantial gaps in development are unlikely to catch up on their own (McCune, Kalmanson, Fleck, Glazewski, & Sillari, 1990). Many infants, babies, and toddlers come to early childhood programs with histories of one or more risk factors. For instance, each year about 250,000 infants, about 6.5% of all babies born in the United States, are born weighing 5.5 pounds or less and of these, more than 43,000 weigh less than 3.5 pounds (National Center for Clinical Infant Programs, 1986). Modern technology has enabled us, as a society, to save the lives of these premature infants, as early as 24 weeks in utero, who previously would not have been able to live. In addition, 100,000 to 150,000 infants (3 to 5%) are born each year with congenital deviations that lead to mental retardation (National Center for Clinical Infant Programs, 1986). The likelihood of having a low-birth-weight infant or one with congenital deviations in your day-care program, thus, is quite high. Systematic identification and follow-up will enable such babies to receive treatment and intervention services needed at an early age to prevent serious and unnecessary disability (Knutson et al., 1990).

Many premature babies, under good environmental circumstances, eventually do *catch up*, developmentally speaking, but the amount of their prematurity should be taken into account, at least during their first two years, when determining their developmental status. The outcomes for these children can be significantly improved with early, comprehensive

FIGURE 9.2 Identifying handicapped infants and young children: a multivariate, interactional risk model

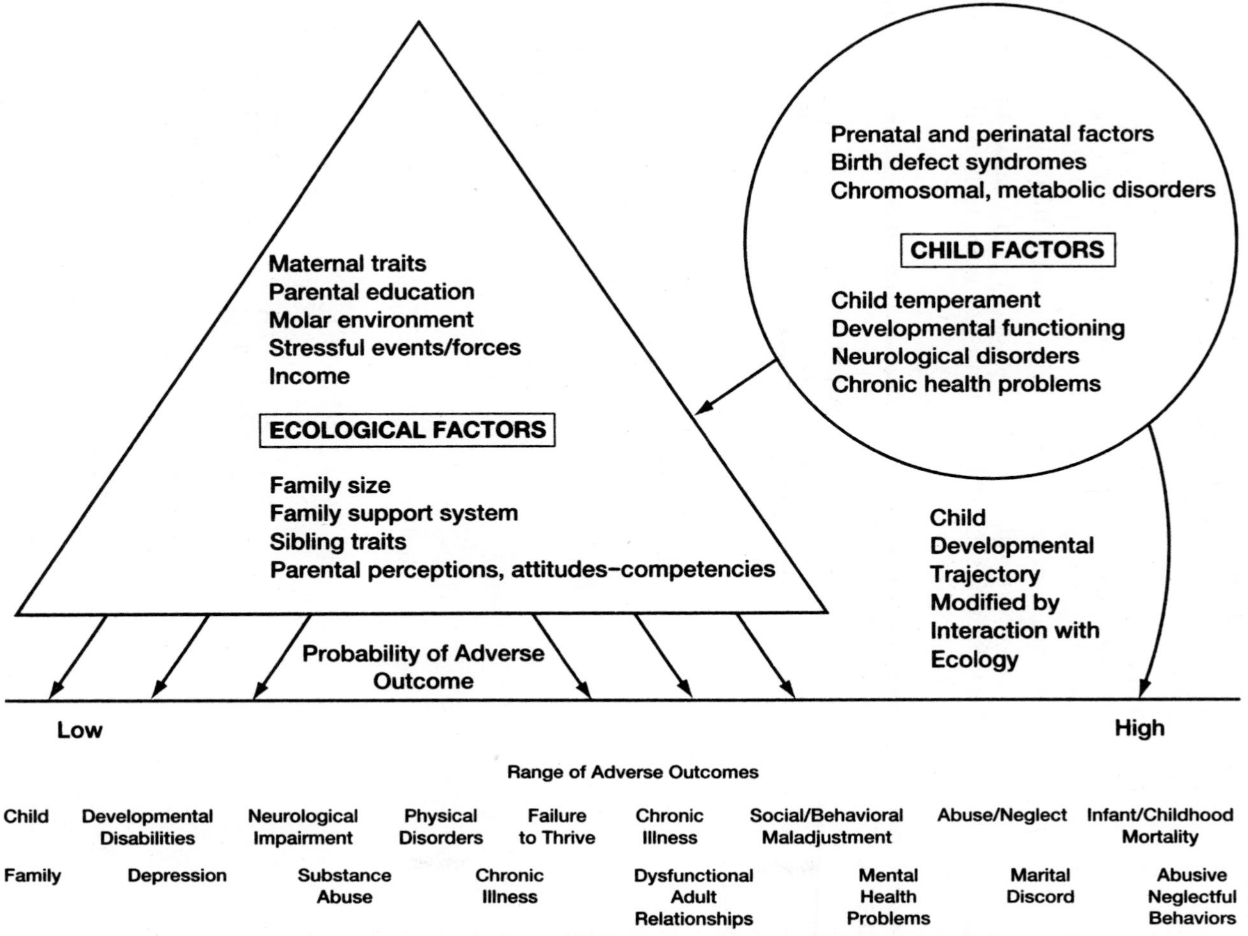

CHILD FACTORS

Prenatal and perinatal factors
Birth defect syndromes
Chromosomal, metabolic disorders

Child temperament
Developmental functioning
Neurological disorders
Chronic health problems

Child Developmental Trajectory Modified by Interaction with Ecology

ECOLOGICAL FACTORS

Maternal traits
Parental education
Molar environment
Stressful events/forces
Income

Family size
Family support system
Sibling traits
Parental perceptions, attitudes–competencies

Probability of Adverse Outcome

Low — High

Range of Adverse Outcomes

Child	Developmental Disabilities	Neurological Impairment	Physical Disorders	Failure to Thrive	Chronic Illness	Social/Behavioral Maladjustment	Abuse/Neglect	Infant/Childhood Mortality
Family	Depression	Substance Abuse	Chronic Illness		Dysfunctional Adult Relationships	Mental Health Problems	Marital Discord	Abusive Neglectful Behaviors

From Kochanek T. (1988). Point of view: Conceptualizing screening models for developmentally disabled and high-risk children and their families. *Zero to Three, IX*(2), p. 17.

intervention (The Infant Health and Development Program, 1990). This intervention can take place in high-quality group day care. The task for early childhood educators is to figure out how to take advantage of early infant developmental processes to make positive outcomes more likely (Anastasiow, 1990). The early childhood educator needs to determine how the protective factors within the child or the environment can moderate the adverse developmental impact. Identifying and facilitating such protective factors should be our central mission (Shonkoff & Marshall, 1990).

There are a number of screening instruments that may be utilized by medical, psychological, and/or educational staff during the first three years. Table 9.2 lists some of the common screening tests for this age range.

TABLE 9.2 Common screening instruments for 0–3 age range*

Name of test	Age range	Areas screened
Battelle Developmental Inventory Screening Test	0–8 yrs.	personal-social, adaptive, motor, communication, cognitive
Denver Developmental Screening Test-Revised	2 wks.–6 yrs.	personal-social, fine-motor-adaptive, language, gross motor
Developmental Profile II	birth–9yrs.	physical, self-help, social. cognitive, communication
Developmental Indicators for the Assessment of Learning	2–6 yrs.	motor, concepts, language, social-emotional
Early Language Milestone Scale	0–3 yrs.	language development
Home Screening Questionnaire	birth–3 yrs.	child's home environment
Minnesota Child Development Inventory	6 mo.–6 yrs.	general development, gross motor, fine motor, expressive language, self-help, personal-social, comprehension-conceptual, situation comprehension
Preschool Language Scale	1.5–7 yrs.	auditory comprehension, verbal ability
Receptive Expressive Language Scale	1 mo.–3 yrs.	receptive, expressive, & inner language

*More information about these screening instruments can be found in Appendix A, including name of the publisher.

The guidelines listed in Chapter Four regarding test evaluation need to be considered in the selection of a screening test.

Current assessment issues and trends

What makes assessment of infants and toddlers different from assessment of preschool and primary age children? Some of the unique characteristics of infants and toddlers include the following.

- They lack expressive skills.
- They are struggling with separation issues.
- They demonstrate a limited attention span.
- They are uninfluenced by extrinsic motivation.
- They adapt slowly to new surroundings.
- They fatigue easily and need naps.
- They refuse to cooperate.
- They exhibit a wide range of normal behaviors.
- They demonstrate highly variable hour-to-hour behavior, although behavior and personality are globally stable over years.
- They tend to put the testing materials in their mouths (McCollum et al., 1989).

Another important difference is that although the term *development* implies a high degree of continuity and stability in behavioral change across time, in general the first few years are characterized by lack of permanence in development and lack of smoothness in behavioral change (Dunst & Rheingrover, 1982). This means that the infant or toddler may demonstrate a developmental milestone one day and never perform it again for days, weeks, or months. Or the baby progresses on a regular basis and then reaches a plateau and stays at that point of development for a long time.

There are a number of issues and trends that need to be understood by the early childhood educator in order to see the overall picture of infant and toddler assessment. The following will be discussed: P.L. 99–457; principles that guide infant and toddler assessment; family involvement; and special at-risk populations.

P.L. 99–457

At the beginning of this chapter, it was stated that legislative initiatives were partly responsible for the recent interest in the prompt and accurate identification of infants and toddlers with developmental disabilities or potential learning problems. The most significant legislation affecting children with special needs since the passage of P.L. 94–142, the Education for All Handicapped Children Act in 1975, was the passage of **P.L. 99–457,** the Education of the Handicapped Act Amendments in 1986. While P.L. 94–142 mandated a free, appropriate education in the least restrictive environment for every school-aged child with a special need, it did not mandate the provision of educational programs for non-school-age children. This was corrected by the 1986 amendments, one of which (Part H) provides for handicapped infants and toddlers. This law recognizes both the central role of families in the lives of their children and the tremendous potential of early intervention to enhance the development of infants and toddlers with special needs. Handicapped infants and toddlers are defined as individuals from birth through age two who require early intervention services because they:

(a) are experiencing developmental delays as measured by appropriate diagnostic instruments and procedures in one or more of the following areas: cognitive development, physical development, language and speech development, psychomotor development, or self-help skills or

(b) have a diagnosed physical or mental condition that has a high probability of resulting in developmental delay. Such terms may also include, at a state's discretion, individuals from birth to age 2, inclusive, who are at risk of having substantial developmental delays if early intervention services are not provided. (Statute Sec. 672)

P.L. 99–457 requires that each state define the criteria for developmental delays and for risk. Therefore, the populations eligible for services will vary from state to state. The legislation also requires the "performance of a timely, comprehensive, and multidisciplinary evaluation of the functioning of each handicapped infant and toddler, and the needs of the families to appropriately assist in the (child's) development." According to the mandate, delays may occur in one or more of the following areas: cognitive development; physical development, including vision and hearing; language and speech development; psychosocial development; and self-help skills. Ongoing procedures are expected to identify (a) the child's unique needs (b) the family's strengths and needs related to the development of the child and (c) the nature and extent of early intervention services that are needed by the child and the child's family to meet these needs. Implementing such statements requires sensitivity in order to avoid premature labeling, particularly of minority children. Fortunately the mandate also has procedural safeguards which includes frequent parent and professional review of **individualized family service plans** (IFSPs), as well as the right to appeal, the right to confidentiality of information, the right to prior notice to parents in their native language, the assignment of surrogate parents, and the establishment of procedures to ensure that services are provided while complaints are being resolved.

Principles that guide infant and toddler assessment

Once it is determined that an infant or toddler should be referred, there are a number of principles that guide the assessment approaches with very young children. First of all, assessment is seen as a continuing, evolving process rather than a discrete activity that can be initiated and completed at a single point in time. Thus, assessment must be continuously blended with intervention (Bagnato & Neisworth, 1991).

Since infants display complex patterns of interaction with the world from birth, there has been a continuing movement to document their behaviors and reactions in some formal way. The most striking aspect of the evolution of infant assessment has been the logical shift from measuring what we think of as intelligence (Neisworth & Bagnato, 1992) to assessment of a number of interrelated systems in very young children combined with a move toward interdisciplinary assessment (McCune et al., 1990). As it is not possible to divide the infant's skills and activities along such lines as motor, social, and cognitive domains in the early weeks of life, and even during the first three years such a division remains somewhat artificial, it is necessary to assess the infant's behavior and capacity by considering the underlying internal organization that has been suggested by current developmental theory. This should be accomplished by professionals with training in many diverse fields of study. Thus, assessment of very young children involves the sampling of behavior. A specific task is presented and then analyzed to determine the baby's underlying competencies and ways of organizing the world. For example, if we roll an attractively decorated ball to a baby sitting on the floor and request that it be rolled back, we learn about the baby's interest in the object and ability to roll it back as well as how the baby relates to requests. If we see whether the toddler can lick food from around her mouth, we are really observing sensory awareness, voluntary control of oral structures, and body awareness. If we engage the baby in playing peek-a-boo, we can observe social awareness, turn-taking, role perspective, imitation, body awareness, cooperation, and anticipation or prediction. Identifying the critical functions underlying each task enables the assessment team to use the information for program planning purposes.

To get the most reliable results, assessment should take place in multiple settings (home, child care, or school) and on multiple occasions when the baby is awake and alert and when the parents are not anxious or under stress. This reduces the pressure to finish the assessment on a particular day and reduces the parents' feeling that the child failed any particular task (Bagnato & Neisworth, 1991).

Family involvement

The assessment process should be shaped by family priorities and information needs, as well as by child characteristics and diagnostic concerns (Johnson, McGonigel, and Kaufman, 1989). This necessitates the involvement of the family, the identification of the family's strengths and priorities, and the family's determination of which aspects of their family life are relevant to their child's development. Family values and styles of decision-making must be reflected in the assessment process.

All aspects of infant evaluation should reflect interactions between the child, the family, the professional, and the setting (Ensher & Clark, 1994). Areas that should be included in any infant evaluation are infant endurance and states of alertness, responsiveness to new tasks and unfamiliar situations, spontaneous activity, unstructured discovery, levels of frustration and irritability, and interaction with varied objects and toys in addition to the infant's interaction with caregivers.

When preschool and primary-aged children are assessed, parents may sit and observe or not even be present. However, parents are an integral part in the assessment of infants and toddlers. Why should we involve parents in the assessment? First of all, it acknowledges that parents know their baby best and are their baby's most important teacher. It implies that parents are most likely to get a (typical) response from the baby. **Family involvement** provides a more complete understanding of the child and how the child fits into the family, not only through the assessment process but through interviews. Family involvement provides a basis for planning intervention that fits within everyday routines and coordinates what occurs in the group setting with what occurs at home. Goals need to be established by parents in conjunction with the developmental status of the child. In this way, parental anxiety is reduced and parents learn how professionals plan learning experiences and activities for their baby. Now parents are part of a problem-solving team where all the answers are not known. This increases the parents' involvement and likelihood that they will believe the results and work with the team for the benefit of the child.

Special at-risk populations

One alarming trend in the United States is the growing population of cocaine-exposed newborns (Rist, 1992). There are an estimated one million women of childbearing age who use the drug and 30,000 to 100,000 of these deliver cocaine-exposed babies each year (Cowley, 1991). Although more common among poor, high-minority, urban populations, such infants are found among all socioeconomic and racial groups throughout the country. According to the National Association for Perinatal Addiction Research and Education (NAPARE), early identification of the mother's cocaine abuse and early treatment of the infant are the two keys to success with cocaine-exposed infants. Early identification can be accomplished through urine testing during or after pregnancy but some hospitals still do not conduct substance-abuse assessment. One must realize that the infant is not only at direct risk from the effects of the drug(s) used by the mother during pregnancy but also at indirect risk from the mother's behavior (Weston, Ivins, Zuckerman, Jones, & Lopez, 1989). Many **drug-exposed babies** are being abandoned at hospitals and are being referred to as *boarder babies*.

Crack-exposed infants are usually small and underweight; some have birth defects such as deformed hearts, lungs, digestive systems, or limbs, or some form of neurological damage which is attributed to cocaine exposure in the uterus. Others, however, do not have these problems. In general, crack babies are irritable, tremulous, and difficult to soothe for at least the first three months. They are typically hypersensitive with uncontrollable tremors and crying. They sleep poorly, cry when awake, and avoid eye contact.

Older crack-exposed babies and toddlers exhibit some of the same behaviors as the infants: difficulty in developing human attachments, the inability to deal with many stimuli at once, and the tendency to act overly aggressive or to withdraw completely when overstimulated. They lack the skills and characteristics necessary for free play. Thus, they scatter and throw toys or pick them up and put them down, without any purpose or involvement. They need to be taught how to play and how to concentrate on a toy or a task for more than a few seconds. Such children need lots of attention, structure, and emotional support (Rist, 1992).

Another special population of infants are those who have been exposed to excessive amounts of alcohol during pregnancy. Such infants often develop what has come to be recognized as **fetal alcohol syndrome** (FAS). The United States produces 5,000 to 10,000 children with full-blown fetal alcohol syndrome each year, and ten times that number may suffer the similar but less severe symptoms of fetal alcohol effect (Cowley, 1991). Manifestations of this syndrome are retarded physical and mental development, microcephaly, short eye slits, and possible limb and cardiac deviations. Many alcoholic mothers, just as drug-addicted mothers, are also subject to environmental factors such as low socioeconomic status, poor nutrition, and anxiety which may also place the fetus at risk. Even moderate drinking may be related to central nervous system dysfunction and retardation of growth. Abel, Randall, and Riley (1983) found that babies born to moderate drinkers show the effects of maternal drinking but do not have all of the features associated with fetal alcohol syndrome.

Even nicotine has been linked to lower birth weights in infants. Vorhees and Mollnow (1987) report that "birth weight deficits found in children are dose dependent and average about 200 grams. Perhaps most significantly, the risk of having a low-birth-weight child (less than 2,500 grams) is doubled among women who smoke." Other research suggests that the children of smoking mothers may have deficits in auditory processing (Picone, Allen, Olsen, & Ferris, 1982).

Ecologically and developmentally relevant assessment strategies

Assessment of infants and toddlers is characterized by a blend of testing, informal observation, and parental interviews over an extended period of time. Traditional instruments (norm-referenced and criterion-referenced [see Chapter 4]) often have the goal of quantifying a child's abilities, which means putting a number or score to the responses, but often they fail to address the more qualitative aspects of a child's abilities such as appropriateness of movement patterns, social competence, and attentional abilities (Hauser-Cram & Shonkoff, 1988; Barnett et al., 1992). As a result, there is a definite trend in infant and toddler assessment away from traditional instruments toward more ecologically and developmentally relevant assessment strategies that lead directly to program planning.

The team approach

PL 99–457 also mandates that services to at-risk and handicapped infants, toddlers, and their families be provided by professionals from several disciplines who need to work cooperatively. The purpose of the team is to determine eligibility and develop the IFSP. There are a number of disciplines mentioned in P.L. 99–457 (Part H) which are expected to be involved in the assessment and program development of an infant or toddler. They are a special educator, nurse, speech and language pathologist, audiologist, occupational therapist, physical therapist, psychologist, social worker, and nutritionist. Of course it is unlikely that all of these disciplines would be involved in any given assessment. The exact composition of the team would be determined by the background and issues surrounding the particular child. Besides the parent, others who might be directly involved are the early childhood educator, the building or program administrator, counselor, and the adapted physical education specialist. These individuals make up the early intervention team.

What may best distinguish early intervention teams from one another is neither their composition, since they are all composed of some combination of the above disciplines plus the family, nor the tasks that include assessment and intervention, but rather the structure of interaction among team members. Three service delivery models that structure interaction among team members have been identified and differentiated in the literature: multidisciplinary, interdisciplinary, and transdisciplinary. Each type will be described.

Multidisciplinary team

On the **multidisciplinary team,** the team members from a variety of disciplines review the pertinent child and family history in preparation for the assessment. Each team member conducts a separate assessment, using discipline-specific instruments and resources. Usually, standardized diagnostic evaluation instruments are used. Assessment results are discussed with the family separately by each discipline team member, and each team member develops separate goals and intervention strategies. There is minimal interaction between team members and a perfunctory exchange of information. Separate reports are written and shared with the family. Evaluation of the assessment process is done on an individual basis. The family and the case manager, the one professional from the early intervention team assigned to each family as an advocate and link to community resources, coordinate interventions and serve as a communication link between disciplines (Garland, 1989). Peterson (1987) compared the mode of interaction among members of multidisciplinary teams to parallel play in young children: "side-by-side" but separate. Linder (1983) has noted that interaction among team members in this model does not foster services that reflect the view of the child as an integrated and interactive whole. This can lead to fragmented services for young children and confusing or conflicting reports to parents. The lack of communication between team members places the burden of coordination and case management primarily on the family.

Interdisciplinary team

On the **interdisciplinary team,** the team members work cooperatively to make role assignments according to the particular needs of a child or family. There is a sharing of information. The team discusses the case and helps the family prepare for the assessment process. There are formal channels of communication, such as regular meetings, that encourage team members to share their information, discuss individual results, and develop intervention plans. Team members still do their separate assessments, even if they are in the same room at the same time, which elicits behaviors in specific areas of development, using their own discipline-related instruments and resources. Standardized instruments are difficult to use when the team assesses together. Generally, each specialist is responsible for the part of the service plan related to his or her professional discipline. Assessment results are shared with the family, and the program plan may be developed by all team members at the same meeting. Family members participate as full members of the team in determining assessment results and in developing the program plan. Reports are written separately and compiled for the team and family by one team member who serves as the case manager (Garland, 1989).

Transdisciplinary team

On the **transdisciplinary team,** one team member meets with the family to discuss and decide their possible role in the team assessment and shares pertinent child and family history with team members. A pre-assessment meeting is held to prepare the team members for their assessment roles. The assessment facilitator, coach, and observers are chosen based on the child, family, and team needs. A family member, usually the parent, may choose to be the assessment facilitator. Only the family and/or the facilitator interact with and handle the child during the assessment while the others observe. The team members who are observing record the child's behavior in all domains across disciplinary boundaries. The arena, as the testing area is called, is not appropriate for the use of standardized assessment instruments. Staff and family review the child's strengths and needs and develop a program plan together. The team cooperatively writes a report, integrating all child behavioral domains. The family may choose to participate. The team meets afterward to review and clarify the assessment process (Garland, 1989). Thus, in this approach, there is a sharing of both information and roles for maximal interaction.

An in-depth look at the arena assessment model

The rationale for an **arena approach to assessment** is that it allows for input from multiple team members while simultaneously reducing the number of professionals who must handle the child. It acknowledges that development does not occur in discrete domains so the same activity can be observed by the language therapist, the physical therapist, the early childhood psychologist, and the parent and each will see different aspects of development from their perspective. The arena approach eliminates redundancy for the child and parents, thus saving time and reducing cost. It provides a forum for team members to share with and learn from each other, resulting in more team consensus, immediate diagnostic and treatment data, and immediate results for the parents (McCollum et al., 1989).

Arena assessment is characterized by the following elements:

1. A primary facilitator serves the family.
2. Team members observe, as one conducts an assessment.
3. Parents and team members give information to the facilitator.

4. Team members may assist each other.
5. Parents provide information and may implement the assessment measures.
6. Parents confirm the infant's performance for the team (McCollum et al., 1989)

Each professional member of the arena team must observe parent/child interactions and structured and free play, encourage parent participation, maintain observation notes; compare behavior to available standards, form diagnostic impressions, share information and contribute recommendations to the Individualized Family Service Plan (IFSP), and write a descriptive report (McCollum et al., 1989).

The transdisciplinary arena assessment model maximizes communication, interaction, and cooperation among team members.

The integration of assessment information into programming

Infant assessment is in actuality infant intervention, according to Bagnato and Neisworth (1991). The continuous observation of the infant and toddler along with talking with the parents provides the opportunity to note the child's responses and blend the assessment into the intervention plan. As much as possible, the assessment process simultaneously serves as a guide to individual programming and program planning and evaluation.

The assessment team needs to answer a number of questions in order to plan the most appropriate program for the child and the family (Widerstrom, Mowder, & Sandall, 1991). Not only do teachers and other team members need to know *what* the child can do but *how* the task is performed. In addition to examining the critical functions mentioned earlier in this chapter, team members need to examine the quality of the performance. Then team members need to determine what the infant or toddler needs to learn next, what the baby is unable to do and why, and finally how this particular baby learns best. The answers to all of these questions will enable the assessment team and family to develop the most appropriate program for the infant or toddler, including the daily planning that integrates the goals and objectives of the IFSP into the routines of the early childhood setting. Without a doubt, the most important purpose of assessment is program planning and monitoring of individual and group progress.

Summary

This chapter describes the role that assessment plays in the lives of all infants, often even before they are born. After describing the total assessment process that is used with infants and toddlers and the importance of assessment in the first three years, current assessment issues and trends such as Public Law 99–457, principles that guide infant and toddler assessment, and the significance of family involvement are discussed. Up-to-date facts are given about infants who have been exposed to drugs, alcohol, or nicotine during pregnancy. There are a number of ecologically and developmentally relevant assessment strategies addressed that are currently considered state-of-the-art. These include various types of team approaches, particularly the transdisciplinary team with an emphasis on the arena assessment model. Finally, the chapter ends with a short discussion on the integration of assessment information into programming since the most important purpose of assessment is program planning for individual infants and toddlers.

⊞ CHAPTER 9 **Suggested further readings**

Bailey, D., & Wolery, M. (1989). *Assessing infants and preschoolers with handicaps.* Columbus, OH: Merrill.

Bondurant-Utz, J., & Luciano, L. (1994). *A practical guide to infant and preschool assessment in special education.* Boston: Allyn & Bacon.

Linder, T. (1993). *Transdisciplinary play-based assessment: A functional approach to working with young children* (rev. ed.). Baltimore: Brookes.

Rossetti, L. (1990). *Infant-toddler assessment: An interdisciplinary approach.* Boston: College-Hill.

⊞ CHAPTER 9 **Study questions**

1. What are the five readily observed signs rated on the Apgar Rating Scale?

2. List four prenatal testing measures.

3. Why is it recommended that the Brazelton Neonatal Behavior Assessment Scale (NBAS) be administered in the presence of parents?

4. Knowing that an infant or toddler has one or more risk factors is important. What is even more important for the early childhood educator to know?

5. What are characteristics of infants and toddlers that make assessment with them different than with older children?

6. What are the criteria for developmental delays and for risk as defined by your state under P.L. 99–457?

ACTIVITIES

1. Visit the newborn nursery in your community. Observe the infants through the window. Note difference in size, coloring, movement, etc. Ask the hospital administrator or head nurse if you could observe any screening (e.g., Apgar, Brazelton).
2. Visit an early intervention program in your community. Observe the children to see if you can ascertain the reason they are in the program. Observe the speech therapist and the physical therapist as well as the early interventionist. Inquire if any of the children also spend time in another child-care program in the community.
3. Visit a neonatal intensive care unit (NICU) at a level three hospital. This facility will probably be further from home than the other two programs. Ascertain if any infant is stabilized enough for you to observe. Depending on the facility's policies and the amount of time you have to spend on this activity, there may be other roles for you to play in the NICU.

7. List three principles that guide infant and toddler assessment.
8. What are the benefits of family involvement? The drawbacks?
9. What do crack-exposed infants and toddlers need the most from early childhood professionals?
10. List the professionals who could be involved on an early intervention team according to P.L. 99–457.
11. List advantages of the transdisciplinary team approach over the multidisciplinary and interdisciplinary approaches.
12. What is the most important purpose for assessing infants and toddlers?

References

Abel, E., Randall, C., & Riley, E. (1983). Alcohol consumption and prenatal development. In B. Tabakoff, P. Sutker, & C. Randall (Eds.), *Medical and social aspects of alcohol abuse.* New York: Plenum.

American College of Obstetricians and Gynecologists. (1991). *Pregnancy.* Washington, DC: Author.

American College of Obstetricians and Gynecologists. (1994). *Maternal serum screening for birth defects.* Washington, DC: Author.

American Medical Association. (1958). Apgar score. *Journal of the American Medical Association, 158*(15), 1988.

Anastasiow, N. (1990). Implications of the neurobiological model for early intervention. In S. Meisels & J. Shonkoff (Eds.), *Handbook of early childhood intervention.* New York: Cambridge University Press.

Apgar, V. (1953). Proposal for a new method of evaluating the newborn infant. *Anesthesia and Analgesia, 32,* 260–267.

Bagnato, S.J., & Neisworth, J.T. (1991). *Assessment for early intervention.* New York: Guilford.

Barnett, D., Macmann, G., & Carey, K. (1992). Early intervention and the assessment of developmental skills: Challenges and directions. *Topics in Early Childhood Special Education, 12*(1), 21–43.

Batshaw, M., & Perret, Y. (1986). *Children with handicaps: A medical primer* (2nd ed.). Baltimore: Brookes.

Bennett, F. (1984). Neurodevelopmental outcome of low birth-weight infants. In V. Kelley (Ed.), *Practice of pediatrics* (pp. 1–24). Philadelphia: Harper & Row.

Bergen, D., & Wright, M. (1994). Medical assessment perspectives. In D. Bergen, *Assessment methods for infants and toddlers: Transdisciplinary team approaches* (pp. 40–56). New York: Teachers College.

Berk, L.E. (1993). *Infants, children and adolescents.* Boston: Allyn & Bacon.

Berrueter-Clement, J., Schweinhart, L., Barnett, W., Epstein, A., & Weikart, D. (1984). *Changed lives: The effects of the Perry preschool program on youths through age 19* (Monograph No. 8). Ysilanti, MI: High/Scope Educational Research Foundation.

Blackman, J. (1986). *Warning signals: Basic criteria for tracking at-risk infants and toddlers.* Washington, DC: National Center for Clinical Infant Programs.

Brazelton, T.B. (1984). *Neonatal assessment scale* (2nd ed.) (Clinics in Developmental Medicine, No. 88). Philadelphia: J.B. Lippincott.

Bredekamp, S. (1987). *Developmentally appropriate practice in early childhood programs serving children from birth through age 8.* Washington, DC: National Association for the Education of Young Children.

Cardone, I., & Gilkerson, L. (1989). Family administrated neonatal activities: An innovative component of family-centered care. *Zero to Three, X*(1), 23–28.

Cohen, S. (1983). Low birth weight. In C. C. Brown (Ed.), *Pediatric round table: 9. Childhood learning disabilities and prenatal risk* (pp. 70–78). Shillman, NJ: Johnson and Johnson Baby Products.

Cohen, S., & Beckwith, L. (1979). Preterm infant interaction with the caregiver in the first year of life and competence at age two. *Child Development, 50,* 767–776.

Cowley, G. (1991, Summer). Children in peril [Special edition]. *Newsweek,* pp. 18–21.

Dunst, C., & Rheingrover, R. (1982). Discontinuity and instability in early development: Implications for assessment. In J. Neisworth (Ed.), *Assessment in special education.* Rockville, MD: Aspen.

Dunst, C., & Trivette, C. (1988). Helping, helplessness, and harm. In J. Witt, S. Elliott, & F. Gresham (Eds.), *Handbook of behavior theory in education*, pp. 343–376. New York: Plenum Press.

Ensher, G., & Clark, D. (1994). *Newborns at risk: Medical care and psychoeducational intervention* (2nd ed.). Rockville, MD: Aspen.

Field, T., Dempsey, J., Hallock, N., & Shuman, D. (1978). Mother's assessments of the behavior of their infants. *Infant Behavior and Development, 1,* 156–165.

Friedman, J. (1989, August). First year milestones. *American Baby,* pp. A17–A21.

Garland, C. (1989). Arena assessment: A preconference workshop at the International Early Childhood Conference on Children with Special Needs, Denver, CO.

Gonzalez-Mena, J., & Eyer, D.W. (1993). *Infants, toddlers, and caregivers* (3rd ed.). Mountain View, CA: Mayfield.

Hauser-Cram, P., & Shonkoff, J. (1988). Rethinking the assessment of child focused outcomes. In H. Weiss & F. Jacobs (Eds.), *Evaluating family programs* (pp. 73–94). Hawthorne, NY: Aldine.

Infant Health and Development Program. (1990). Enhancing the outcomes of low-birth-weight, premature infants. *Journal of the American Medical Association, 263*(22), 3035–3042.

Johnson, B., McGonigel, M., & Kaufman, R. (Eds.). (1989). *Guidelines for recommended practices for the Individualized Family Service Plan.* Chapel Hill, NC: NECTAS.

Knutson, M., Biro, P., & Padgett, D. (1987). Tracking infants at risk: Washington state's high priority infant tracking system. *Journal of Pediatric Health Care, 1,* 180–189.

Kochanek, T. (1988). Point of view: Conceptualizing screening models for developmentally disabled and high-risk children and their families. *Zero to Three, IX*(2), 16–20.

Linder, T. (1983). *Early childhood special education: Program development and administration.* Baltimore, MD: Brookes.

McCollum, J., Azar-Mathis, R., Henderson, K., & Kusmierek, A. (1989). Assessment of infants and toddlers: Supporting developmentally and ecologically relevant intervention. *Illinois technical assistance project.* Springfield, IL: Illinois State Board of Education.

McCune, L., Kalmanson, B., Fleck, M., Glazewski, B., & Sillari, J. (1990). An interdisciplinary model of infant assessment. In S. Meisels & J. Shonkoff (Eds.), *Handbook of early childhood intervention.* NY: Cambridge University Press.

Meisels, S.J., & Provence, S. (1989). *Screening and assessment: Guidelines for identifying young disabled and developmentally vulnerable children and their families.* Washington, DC: National Center for Clinical Infant Programs.

Meisels, S.J., & Shonkoff, J.P. (Eds.). (1990). *Handbook of early childhood intervention.* Cambridge: Cambridge.

National Center for Clinical Infant Programs. (1986). *Infants can't wait*. Washington, DC: Author.

Neisworth, J., & Bagnato, S. (1992). The case against intelligence testing in early intervention. *Topics in Early Childhood Special Education, 21*(1), 1–20.

Nichols, P., & Chen, T. (1981). *Minimal brain dysfunction: A prospective study*. Hillsdale, NY: Erlbaum.

O'Donnell, K., & Oehler, J. (1989). Neurobehavioral assessment of the newborn infant. In D. Bailey & M. Wolery (Eds.), *Assessing infants and preschoolers with handicaps*. Columbus, OH: Merrill.

Peterson, N. (1987). *Early intervention for handicapped and at-risk children: An introduction to early childhood-special education*. Denver, CO: Love Publishing.

Picone, T., Allen, L., Olsen, D., & Ferris, M. (1982). Pregnancy outcome in North American women: II, Effects of diet, cigarette smoking, stress, and weight gain on placentas, and on neonatal physical and behavioral characteristics. *American Journal of Clinical Nutrition, 36*, 1214–1224.

Rist, M. (1992). The shadow children: Preparing for the arrival of crack babies in school. *Annual editions, early childhood education, 92/93*. Guilford, CT: Dushkin.

Santrock, J. (1988). *Children*. Dubuque, IA: William C. Brown.

Shonkoff, J., & Marshall, P. (1990). Biological bases of developmental dysfunction. In S. Meisels and J. Shonkoff (Eds.), *Handbook of early childhood intervention*. New York: Cambridge University Press.

U.S. House of Representatives. (1986). *Education of the handicapped act amendments of 1986* (Report 99–860). Washington, DC: U.S. Congress.

Vorhees, C., & Mollnow, E. (1987). Behavioral teratogenesis: Long-term influences on behavior from early exposure to environmental agents. In J. Osofsky (Ed.), *Handbook of infant development* (2nd ed.). New York: John Wiley & Sons.

Weston, D., Ivins, B., Zuckerman, B., Jones, C., & Lopez, R. (1989). Drug-exposed babies: Research and clinical issues. *Zero to Three, IX*(5), 1–7.

Widerstrom, A., Mowder, B., & Sandall, S. (1991). *At-risk and handicapped newborns and infants: Development, assessment, and intervention*. Englewood Cliffs, NJ: Prentice Hall.

Zero to Three. (1995). *Diagnostic classification: 0–3*. Arlington, VA: National Center for Clinical Infant Programs.

Zero to Three Work Group. (1994). Toward a new vision for the developmental assessment of infants and young children. *Zero to Three, 14*, 1–8.

CHAPTER 10

Issues in Preschool Assessment

Terms to Know	▌ transdisciplinary play-based assessment	▌ portfolios
	▌ developmentally appropriate practice	

CHAPTER OVERVIEW   This chapter traces the use of assessment systems in preschool settings. Links are made to selection of children for participation in limited and competitive enrollment situations. The limitations of screening instruments for enrollment decisions are discussed. Next, issues surrounding the connection from assessment to curriculum, instruction, and the return are made. A section is included regarding referral to special services. Included in the discussion are links to appropriate teacher roles in the process and transdisciplinary play-based assessment. Transition to first grade issues are discussed.

Topics Discussed

▌ Preschool assessment system issues

▌ Selection for the preschool program

▌ Selection of children in competitive situations

▌ Planning for instruction

▌ Transition to kindergarten or first grade

Preschool assessment system issues

At the preschool level, young children may attend a child-care center, a family child-care, a half-day nursery school, a part-time play group, all day care, or a regular or special education program. Teachers in each of these settings have similar demands for assessment measures. They plan instruction and keep track of child progress. Sometimes teachers participate in decisions that require consultation and professional assistance. The most common preschool assessment decisions include selection for the preschool program, planning for instruction, referral for special services, and transition to kindergarten/first grade. In each of these situations, preschool teachers are problem solvers who use assessment to teach.

Selection for the preschool program

Parent convenience

Parents often choose a program close to their home and enroll their children there. Children are accepted on a first-come, first-served basis. These community-based programs generally select children because of age, religious affiliation, ability to pay, or other demographic characteristics. Child ability is not usually the basis for selection decisions.

Limited enrollment decisions

Choosing children deemed "academically at risk" currently happens due to restricted public funds. Selection criteria may apply to family and child characteristics. Family demographics included are poverty, limited English fluency, or teen mothers. After agencies and school districts collect a pool of demographically eligible children, they employ an efficient method to choose those most in need of the special program. School districts frequently choose screening instruments for this purpose. These measures give a general overview of a child's ability and achievement in self-help skills, cognition, language, fine and gross motor, and social/emotional development. The opportunity for participation in screening should be open to all children to secure this developmental review.

Screening programs survey many children in a short period. Thus, most children pass through the screen and are not identified as in need of an at-risk program. The screening procedure acts as a selection device. Because screening procedures typically survey developmental milestones, the results have a short time of usability. The younger the child, the more limited is the time line. This is due to the rapid nature of developmental change in young children. When there is a long time delay between screening and program delivery, re-screening is necessary.

Choosing a screening instrument

Many factors must be considered in choosing a screening instrument or procedure. First, a developmental screening review should be comprehensive, reviewing all aspects of development: cognitive, physical and social/emotional. Activities conducted with the children should be seen as play; concrete materials should form the basis of the activity. The procedure should reflect the cultural diversity of a particular community. Parents should be involved in providing primary information about a child's history and perceptions of current functioning. Of course, technical qualities of reliability, validity, and over-referral/under-referral should be considered in choosing a screening system. The procedure or plan should be quick to administer to individual children. Young children can give limited attention to formal screening tasks. Quickly administered measures function efficiently for the screening agency.

Limitations of screening instruments

Screening procedures and instruments have limitations. These tools cannot diagnose children. They are appropriately used to select children who may be at risk of academic failure. However, they cannot be used to definitively decide individual developmental profiles. Further assessment is necessary to decide eligibility for special education placement or to plan for educational intervention. (Goldenberg & Mindes, 1989; Mindes, 1993).

"Screening programs identify those children who may need special kinds of help to function well in school. They should not exclude them from a program for which they are legally eligible. Sound, ethical practice is to accept children in all their variety, identify any special needs they have, and offer them the best possible opportunity to grow and learn" (Hills, 1987, p. 2).

⊞ Selection of children in competitive situations

Highly touted programs may find parents camping in the parking lot overnight to secure applications for the few available places in the program. If child assessment measures decide eligibility for these programs, the criteria should be published for parents to review. Sometimes, these settings use individualized intelligence tests to select children (Robinson, 1988). A qualified psychologist should administer intelligence tests. Utilizing intelligence tests professionally with parent permission may be a better practice than using *homemade* tests that may have limited validity or reliability. Sometimes these homemade tests are criterion-referenced measures that are inappropriate as selection measures.

The pinch of salt to keep in mind: Whenever children are screened for eligibility to participate in a program, all of the limitations and cautions for these instruments apply. The primary tenet of appropriate assessment is to match the method to the purpose.

Planning for instruction

Once children enter a program, the program philosophy guides the curriculum and instruction. Assessment links the instructional strategies to individual children. *Observation* of children forms the backbone of the preschool assessment program. This assessment method is an integral part of the play-based curriculum found in preschool settings. Play-based curricula incorporate concrete experiential activities. Planned projects are grounded on the interests and needs of the children. Commonly, curricula are divided into knowledge, skills, and attitudes. Knowledge is the content or subject matter for the program. Typically, curricular themes for preschool include those rooted in the immediate social world of the children—my family, my community, my friends, our garbage, etc. The skills of the instructional process include problem solving; communicating in words, pictures and writing; cooperating with friends; and following schedules and routines, etc. Attitudes include curiosity, risk taking, self-confidence; respect for others, etc. Learning of knowledge, skills, and attitudes occurs in activities that tap the intellectual, creative, social/emotional, and physical domains.

Themes and projects organized around a topic provide children opportunities to develop in holistic fashion in each of the domains. Opportunities for children to experience the topics occur in small groups, at interest centers, individually, and with the whole class. The teacher provides the environment and activities for children to explore in their relationships with children, materials, and the teacher.

Teachers plan activities around themes that offer multiple outcomes, so that a wide range of child ability and interests can be served. These complicated activities accommodate the typical range of development as well as mixed age groups and children with special needs. Choosing activities that accommodate the diverse social experiences of children permits the enrichment of their basic understanding of their broadening social world.

By starting with their interests, knowledge, and skills, teachers create an excitement for learning. Children learn by experimenting with materials, observing their environment, conversing with others and sharing their insights. The teacher sets the stage for the integration of learning by starting with complex topics that lead in many directions.

This child initiated theme is an example of a complex topic that is developed with multilevel experiences to meet the needs of the diverse group of four year olds in Ms. Berg's class as discussed in Box 10.1. Parents are

---

BOX 10.1

Garbage in Our World

Ms. Berg's four year olds attend a school that recycles papers, magazines, glass, and cans. The children see recycling efforts made by the whole school in the cafeteria that uses donated silverware and dishes to avoid paper plates. The dishes don't match. One day at lunch, Kimberly asks Ms. Berg why the dishes don't match. From this discussion, the children decide that they want to explore other ways to help the school and their families conserve and recycle. Ms. Berg prepares a number of interest centers for the children that will elaborate the theme. The children develop a compost heap, interview their families about garbage awareness and recycling habits, read books about ecology, draw pictures representing a world full of garbage, etc. The children begin a school-wide drive to collect cloth napkins as a further recycling effort.

---

drawn into the process as the experience evolves. The theme offers opportunities to develop knowledge, skills, and attitudes in the intellectual, social/emotional, physical, and creative domains. Experiences in this theme are concrete and active. (cf Berry & Mindes, 1993; Seefeldt & Barbour, 1994).

This approach is explicitly outlined and explained in *Developmentally Appropriate Practice from Birth to 8 Years* (Bredekamp, 1987). One important principle of this approach is that process and presentation—the how—is as important as the specific content. Complex activities that have multiple outcomes form the content. The presentation of the activity and the teacher's interaction helps and stimulates the acquisition of content and/or skills. In this curricular approach, the teacher plays a critical role as "decision maker," motivator, model, innovator, environmental planner, and evaluator (Berry & Mindes, 1993). The teacher shifts role, based on observation of the children in action.

Teacher instructional role

As they observe, teachers change their roles in instruction from observer to validator, participant/converser, extender, problem initiator, model, instructor, and manager/organizer/provider (Lee-Katz, Ellis, & Jewett, 1993). Role shifting by teachers is based not only on inference through observation. Teachers also ask children to describe and interpret their work. In this way, the teacher can explicitly understand the child's thinking and goals. Teachers design games, interviews, contracts for specific work, and directed assignments to further understand children's development and to plan instruction (Hills, 1992).

Teachers establish the baseline for the program: routines, room arrangement, rules and expectations, schedule, and interpersonal relationships (Berry & Mindes, 1993). Once the stage is set and the theme chosen, teachers assess the curriculum effectiveness for individual children and for the group by watching the children. Teachers then adjust the baseline to meet the needs of children. For example, if an objective of the program is to increase knowledge of the functional uses of print, then how does a teacher know whether Maria understands? In a dramatic play setting, she observes Maria grabbing a message pad and scribbling as she listens to the phone call. Maria shows that writing is a substitute for oral messages (Vukelich, 1992). Teachers instruct and assess simultaneously. Seefeldt & Barbour (1994) offer the following focus questions for this kind of integrated teaching.

- Are children showing progress in relationships?
- Are they expressing joy, anger, jealousy, or fear in ways that facilitate coping?
- Do they run, skip, climb, and move with greater ability?
- Can they handle scissors, pencils, and tools more efficiently?
- Do they show increased knowledge about their world?
- Are they using language effectively?
- How do they solve problems?
- Does the play seem rich in ideas, flexible, and fluid?
- Do shy children find ways of entering into play?
- Do aggressive children share ideas and cooperate?
- Can children sustain play episodes for longer periods?
- Do the play themes become more varied and complex?
  (Seefeldt & Barbour, 1994, pp. 325–326)

Teachers should adjust their interactions with children, create an environment that promotes self-discipline, and assist children in mediating their own interactions. Sensitive response and adjustment to observed problems help children grow and succeed. Teachers can decide what to teach by watching the children. Who is interested in leaves? What do the children know about squirrels? Can they identify red, blue, or green? Checklists and discussions of materials, room arrangement, and activities are available in the child guidance and curriculum literature (cf Kostelnik, M. J., Stein, L. C., Whiren, A. P., & Soderman, A. K., 1993; Dodge, D. T. & Colker L. J., 1992; Ashton-Lilo, L. J., 1981).

Link to philosophy

Teachers should carefully select recording methods and the particular goal for observation based on the philosophy and goals of instruction for the program. Examples of different traditions in action are described by Genishi (1992). In this book, teachers talk about how they have incorporated assessment in the teaching-learning process. Teachers discuss how philosophy, planning, and assessment go together. Assessment is not an extra, it's part of what a teacher does.

Assessment is developmentally appropriate to the extent that the processes are

- continuous,
- directed to all developmental areas,
- sensitive to individual and cultural diversity,
- completely integrated with curriculum and instruction,
- based on a defensible theory of child development and learning,
- collaborative between teachers and parents,
- helpful to teachers in their planning to meet the needs of children and the goals of the program, and
- unequivocally in the best interests of the children.
  (Hills, 1992, p. 61)

Thus, the preschool way of teaching is active, and involves problem solving and decision making. Teachers show children how to learn by observing, questioning, and developing interesting projects for children. Teachers establish what children can do through their interactions with them. Using their knowledge, teachers individualize instruction. This is possible in the optimum preschool setting because the activities and procedures are broad. Multiple outcomes and levels of success are possible. For example, a teacher plans a theme on Where Do We Live? Houses and Shelter. "This theme allows children the opportunity to develop a knowledge of the physical properties of their immediate family and the home environment. In addition, the theme fosters scientific inquiry about building materials." (Berry & Mindes, 1993, p. 87). One of the activities for the theme is "4.3.6 Make House Structures/Use paste, liquid cornstarch, sticks, etc., to make buildings with paper and wallpaper samples. Glue on vinyl tiles for roofs. Discuss what makes these structures work or fall apart." (Berry & Mindes, 1993, p. 94)

Every child who attempts this activity can be successful. There is no right answer to the "house" or the "apartment." Not all children are required to make a shelter. Some may choose to read about houses, some may choose to draw, or some may choose to build houses with blocks. Because children are not forced into a "one size fits all" activity, all can be successful. Children build confidence in themselves as learners and dare to try new things. Teachers inventory knowledge, skills, and attitudes of children in the intellectual, social/emotional, and physical domains. They search for ways to stretch and encourage children as learners and achievers. Successful preschool teachers braid assessment and teaching into a smooth coil.

Collecting assessment information in portfolios

As discussed in earlier chapters, **portfolios** serve as documentation for assessment information. Teacher observation, informal assessments, and student work products are collected, reviewed, and shared with parents and students. The portfolios are a more dynamic record of child practice than records of formal screening tests and other measures.

One promising use of portfolio is a parent-education piece. That is, you review the portfolio with parents. Besides seeing child progress, parents learn about **developmentally appropriate practice** in a practical, specific way. Examples of organizational categories for portfolios include products from a theme on personal growth, favorite stories, special science projects, or other materials chosen by child and teacher to show to parent (Gelfer & Perkins, 1992).

Referral for special services

After adjusting the baseline and the activities, teachers will find some children who need special services. These include speech and language therapy, occupational therapy, physical therapy, play therapy, and other special services to the family. In these situations, teachers need to document their observations in a child study. The child study serves as a basis for communicating with parents and other professionals. Increasingly, special services for children are delivered in the regular preschool setting. The preschool teacher is an integral member of the team serving the child and the family. Therefore, teacher observations serve as a source of information for choosing appropriate referral starting points and for ongoing assessment of the effectiveness of the interventions planned and carried out.

Standard ingredients in a child study and questions to ask include birth history, motor development, language history, family composition and history, interpersonal relationships, and medical history. This information may be obtained by teacher interview of the parent. In Chapters Seven and Eight these questions are discussed in more detail. A social worker, psychologist, or counselor may conduct more in-depth interviews as the diagnostic process proceeds.

Teacher contribution to the process

The teacher offers observations, strategies used to modify the curriculum, and the instructional process. Strategies employed may address variations in classroom organization and instructional techniques. Instructional activity individualization considers the child's particular social responsiveness, cognitive style, interactive competencies, and developmental progress (Raab, Whale, & Cisar, 1993). Depending on the complaint presented or set of symptoms of concern, the child should then be evaluated by a qualified professional. These include speech and language clinicians, occupational therapists, physical therapists, psychologists, and social workers. Sometimes only one specialist will be necessary. For example, if a teacher observes difficulty with the form of language that a three year old uses, an on-site evaluation by a speech and language therapist may be necessary. The teacher's role in this situation is to help the therapist pick a good time to visit the class to assess the target child's use of language in the play setting and to help the therapist in establishing rapport for an interview. Sometimes, the teacher may interview the child to obtain information for the therapist.

A child with behavioral problems usually is interviewed by a social worker, psychologist, child psychiatrist, or counselor. The nature of the problem and the kind of services most conveniently available to the community and family will influence the choice of the mental health professional. For a child presenting severe symptoms such as hitting, kicking, screaming, or biting, a comprehensive look by the team of professionals may be required.

Of course, for any evaluation, parents must give written permission. This is in keeping with good practice and federal law (P.L. 99–457; P.L. 94–142). Appropriate and best practice in preschool settings involves teachers in creating a regular dialogue with parents about child progress and adjustment. Thus, parents and teachers form an ongoing partnership in the best interests of the child.

Transdisciplinary play-based assessment

In some settings, agencies use **transdisciplinary play-based assessment** (Linder, 1990). Observation categories include cognitive development, social/emotional development, communication and language development, and sensorimotor development. The team of professionals, including the preschool teacher, observe and record information according to a protocol. This method of assessment is regarded as best practice in infant/toddler programs. Parents are an integral part of the process (McGonigel, Woodruff, & Rosmann-Millican, 1994). Preschool teachers must be familiar with this approach to assessment as a possibility for their programs, but also as part of their responsibility for articulation with infant/toddler programs. The approach is discussed more fully in Chapter Nine.

The continuum of referral

Referral of young children for special services operates on a continuum. At the beginning, teachers observe and interact with the children, adjusting various aspects of the program—routines, relationships, room arrangement, and activities. In these situations the teacher seeks to individualize the preschool setting so the child can be successful.

Next in the continuum, teachers may contact parents to obtain suggestions and insights for helping a child participate successfully. Sometimes teachers will discover a family event or crisis that requires special support for the child and his family. Stressors for children include a new baby, the loss of a pet, a move, a change of child-care arrangements, an illness, a death, or a divorce. Whatever the situation, teachers and parents need to work together to support the child in adjusting.

At the next step of the continuum, teachers and parents exhaust their ideas and resources for solutions to the child's symptoms. Then a specialist evaluates and makes suggestions for modification to the preschool program or special services. Speech therapy is a commonly required special service. It is critical that teachers and parents prepare young children for the experience of a formal assessment (diagnostic test). Children will have many questions such as "What will the examiner do?" "Can mom or my teacher stay with me?" "Do I have to? Why me?"

Agencies and schools need to be sure that examiners are experienced with young children. To assist the examiner, teachers and schools must

- give a clear and specific referral question,
- supply information and materials that will help the examiner understand the history of the problem,
- identify all the relevant people to be included in the assessment,
- assist in identifying all areas that need to be emphasized, and
- assist the examiner in developing an overall testing strategy (Romero, 1992, pp. 57–58).

On rare occasions, teachers, parents, and specialists will decide to remove a child from the typical preschool program. In these situations, a specialized setting may be necessary to help a child. Children with profound hearing loss, for example, may profit from a class where sign language is taught.

At each point of the continuum, assessment results will suggest intervention modifications. Intervention modifications succeed or other strategies are tried. The process of intervention modification continues until something works.

Mrs. Martin cannot say, for example: "I tried seating Jerard next to me at large group time and it doesn't work. He continues to get up and leave the group." Another modification must be tried. Maybe offering Jerard the opportunity to listen to the large group from the block corner, house corner, water table, or other favorite area would be more effective.

At the same time, communicate to the rest of the children that modifications are being made for Jerard as an individual in the group, just as modifications are made for them as individuals. Mary Lou doesn't drink milk because she is allergic to milk. Muhammad doesn't eat pork because it is against his religion. Alice doesn't eat birthday cake because it is against her religion. Arnold doesn't run since he is recovering from heart surgery. Marta stays away from chalk since she is allergic to chalk dust. James doesn't have to count to 20 because he is still learning to talk.

The team of parent, teacher, and specialists strives to strengthen child successes in the preschool setting so that the child becomes a confident learner.

Formal identification for special education

For any child identified and classified as a child with a disability, the provisions of P.L. 94–142 and P.L. 99–457 apply. Assessment must

- be given in the child's native language.
- be given by personnel having the requisite training and licensure.
- be tests that are valid for the purpose used.
- be comprehensive, multifactored, and conducted by a multidisciplinary team.
- be equitable to children with specific sensory or communication disorders and thus assess their genuine abilities separate from their disabilities (Nuttall, Romero, & Kalesnik, 1992).

Formal planning and documentation

Federal law requires an Individualized Family Service Plan (IFSP). This document serves as a record of goals, interventions, and results. The child manager or teacher convenes regular meetings with the family to review and change this planning document. All records of assessment and intervention are confidential. The Family Educational Rights and Privacy Act governs access and confidentiality specifications (FERPA, 1974).

Transition to kindergarten or first grade

Leaving a comfortable early childhood setting to go to the *big school* is a major adjustment for young children. While they may look forward to the idea of being *grown up* enough for this next step, the unknown is scary. Preschool teachers can make the process less scary. The best way to help children and their families is to be familiar with the diverse settings where

the children will be transferring. This happens through regularly scheduled meetings with kindergarten and primary teachers. Discussions can
focus on curricula and transition plans.

Articulation of preschool/kindergarten goals

Preschool programs need not change philosophy and goals in response
to pressure from primary teachers, if such practices seem developmentally inappropriate. Teachers should articulate child progress and the
preschool program philosophy in developmentally appropriate language
and function.

For example, instead of responding to the demand from school districts to interpret reading readiness as letter recognition, letter writing, and
other specific skills, describe readiness to learn in broader terms with illustrations of child performance to support this broader response to Goal
One—by the year 2000 all children in America shall come to school ready
to learn. As developed by legislators this goal may have meant that all children should come to school and sit in their seats and read. As interpreted
by early-childhood advocates, Goal One is reinterpreted to include activities that will support the development of children, including physical well-
being, emotional maturity, social confidence, language richness, and
general knowledge (cf Jensen & Goffin, 1993).

Appropriately planned preschool settings can describe child progress
in terms of these broad categories. Summative or final/cumulative reports should describe children in terms that highlight their knowledge,
skills, and attitudes as problem solvers, self-confident and independent
learners, cooperative group workers, etc. This gives schools or parents the
big picture about individual children. Descriptions of children as curious
learners or effective group participants are the global behaviors that will
serve children well in tackling learning to read, compute, and write.
Preschool programs form the foundation of exploration and socialization
for children to begin the discovery of the primary school educational
agenda. By describing children in this way, you have redefined *readiness*
in service to individual children. The list of narrowly defined concepts
such as knowledge of colors and numbers, ability to write name and alphabet, ability to count, etc., may cast some children in a *bad* light if they
are missing some of these concepts or skills. To the receiving teacher, it
may sound as if the absence of these items is yielding a class of *slow learners* when quite the contrary is true. The children in your program have
learned to investigate the answers to questions of concern to them, and
they are expressing their thinking in words, pictures, and invented
spelling. They have learned to work together, to respect diversity, to appreciate stories, to memorize favorite songs, etc. Rich preschool reports

describing learning style and accomplishments can go a long way to bridging the transition to primary school.

Teachers should arm parents with information about the appropriate use and misuse of tests. In settings where school districts have adopted screening tests as placement tests, teachers can help parents lobby for a differentiated diagnosis, if necessary. This avoids the heartache experienced by Sue Long of Denver City, TX, (Atkins, 1990) who discovered that one of her twin daughters was scheduled for the developmental kindergarten and the other for the regular kindergarten, based on the results of a screening test. Screening tests are inappropriately used for this purpose.

Preschool teachers who assist parents in understanding and anticipating kindergarten issues such as screening, entrance age, extra-year kindergarten programs, and readiness as a child characteristic (Graue, 1993) make the process of going to school a smooth one for children and families. Preschool teachers pave the way for continuity in education. They articulate the *real* characteristics of successful students—motivated, curious partners with teachers and parents, proud of accomplishments, appreciative for the process of inquiry, and communicative (Chapel Hill Training-Outreach Project, 1986).

Preschool teachers can advocate that the only true criterion for admission to kindergarten is chronological age. It is not *child readiness* that should concern teachers, schools, and parents, but broad curricula that allow the acceptance of all children. (NAEYC, 1990; Kagan, 1990). Broadly focused teacher descriptions of children address the attention to this approach. "Early childhood education research provides for preschool teachers a clear notion of child development, an awareness of the role of play in the young child's life, and an understanding of the collaborative role of parents. Early childhood educators, as the experts, must present facts, illustrations, and a firm commitment to best practices in kindergarten" (Mindes, 1990). In this way preschool teachers serve children and families for the foundation of a rewarding trip through the educational system.

⊞ Summary

The preschool teacher is a busy professional. Child assessment is a vital part of the job. Teachers share the responsibility for choosing wisely when informal and formal instruments are selected. They must serve as reflective, conscientious teachers of young children. This involves knowing the children, planning, and making changes based on children's work. Responsible and responsive teaching of children involves sensitivity. Sensitive teachers report their knowledge to parents and others, based on their observations and routinely collected, fair assessments.

ACTIVITIES

1. If possible, observe a screening session at a local child-care or school setting. Are appropriate safeguards for privacy and confidentiality in place?
2. Interview a teacher about her experiences with screening procedures. Focus some of the discussion on the way she uses screening results in planning instruction.
3. With permission, observe a multidisciplinary staffing. Note the diverse ways that assessment data are included. After the meeting, plan how you would instruct the children in your class.
4. Visit the first grades in your community. Outline an articulation procedure for a preschool of your choice.

CHAPTER 10 Suggested further readings

McAffee, O., & Leong, D. (1994). *Assessing and guiding young children's development and learning*. Needham, MA: Allyn & Bacon.

Puckett, M. B., & Black, J. (1994). *Authentic assessment of the young child*. Columbus, OH: Merrill.

Spodek, B., & Saracho, O. N. (1994). *Dealing with individual differences in the early childhood classroom*. New York: Longman.

CHAPTER 10 Study questions

1. How is assessment appropriately used in enrollment decisions? What are some practices that are unnecessary or unfair to children and families?
2. What is transdisciplinary play-based assessment and how is it used in preschool programs?
3. Describe the process for making formal assessment decisions in the lives of preschool children. What is the appropriate role for the early childhood teacher in these situations?
4. How does the planned articulation between programs assist in smooth transition for children? What part does assessment play in this process? Who are the players?
5. Describe appropriate screening processes. What are the benefits and limitations of developmental screening?
6. Identify the components of developmentally appropriate preschool assessment practices. What errors in practice are frequently made?

7. Under which circumstances should portfolios be included in the preschool program? What ingredients contribute to successful routines in gathering and processing the material for preschool portfolio assessment?

8. What are developmental milestones? What role do these play in program planning and evaluation of children?

9. How does an early-childhood teacher use informal assessment? What are the strengths and limitations of this approach in an assessment system?

⁘ References

Ashton-Lilo, L. J. (1981). Pinpointing teacher goals to assist in a successful preschool classroom. *Topics in Early Childhood Special Education, 1,* 37–44.

Atkins, A. (1990). Do kindergarten tests fail our kids? Don't let a misused test direct your child to the wrong classroom. *Better Homes and Gardens, 68,* 22–24.

Berry, C. F., & Mindes, G. (1993). *Planning a theme-based curriculum: Goals, themes, and planning guides for 4s and 5s.* Chicago: Good Year.

Bredekamp, S. (Ed.). (1987). *Developmentally appropriate practices in early childhood programs serving children from birth to age 8.* Washington, DC: National Association for the Education of Young Children.

Bredekamp, S., & Rosegrant, T. (Eds.). (1992). *Reaching potentials: Appropriate curriculum and assessment for young children.* Washington, DC: National Association for the Education of Young Children.

Chapel Hill Training-Outreach Project. (1986). Transition from preschool to public school, a slide/tape presentation. Chapel Hill, NC: Chapel Hill Training-Outreach Project and the National Interagency Committee on Transition.

Dodge, D. T., & Colker, L. J. (1992). *The creative curriculum for early childhood* (3rd ed.). Washington, DC: Teaching Strategies.

Family Education Rights and Privacy Act of 1974. 20U.S.C.A. Section 123g with accompanying regulations set down in 45 C.F.R. part 99.

Gelfer, J. I., & Perkins, P. G. (1992). Constructing student portfolios: A process and product that fosters communication with families. *Day Care and Early Education, 20,* 9–13.

Genishi, C. (Ed.). (1992). *Ways of assessing children and curriculum: Stories of early childhood practice.* New York: Teachers College.

Goldenberg, D., & Mindes, G. (1989). *Early childhood screening: A position statement by the IASCD Early Childhood Committee.* Normal, IL: Illinois Association for Supervision and Curriculum Development.

Graue, M. A. (1993). *Ready for what? Constructing meanings of readiness for kindergarten.* Albany: SUNY.

Hills, T. W. (1987). *Screening for school entry, ERIC Digest.* Champaign, IL: ERIC Clearinghouse on Elementary and Early Childhood Education.

Hill, T. W. (1992). In S. Bredekamp, & T. Rosegrant (Eds.), *Reaching potentials: Appropriate curriculum and assessment for young children.* Washington, DC: National Association for the Education of Young Children.

Jensen, M. A., & Goffin, S. G. (Eds.). (1993). *Visions of entitlement: The care and education of young children.* Albany, NY: SUNY

Kagan, S. L. (1990). Readiness 2000: Rethinking rhetoric and responsibility. *Phi Delta Kappan, 272–279.*

Kostelnik, M. J., Stein, L. C., Whiren, A. P., & Soderman, A. K. (1993). *Guiding children's social development* (2nd ed.). Albany: Delmar.

Lee Katz, L., Ellis, M., & Jewett, J. (1993). *There's math in deviled eggs: Strategies for teaching young children.* Bloomington, IN: Agency for Instructional Technology.

Linder, T. (1990). *Transdisciplinary play-based assessment.* Baltimore: Brookes.

McGonigel, Woodruff, & Rosmann-Millican. (1994). Parents in the infant-toddler assessment process. *Zero to Three, 14,* 59–65.

Mindes, G. (1993). Assessing young children in the at-risk program. In *Early childhood handbook.* Springfield, IL: Illinois State Board of Education.

Mindes, G. (1990). Kindergarten in our nation. In C. Seefeldt, *Continuing issues in early childhood education.* Columbus, OH: Merrill.

National Association for the Education of Young Children. (1990). Position statement on school readiness. *Young Children, 46,* 21–23.

Nuttall, E. V., Romero, I., & Kalesnik, J. (1992). *Assessing and screening preschoolers: Psychological and educational dimensions.* Needham Heights, MA: Allyn & Bacon.

Raab, M. M., Whaley, K. T., & Cisar, C. L. (1993). Looking beyond instructional interactions: An ecological perspective of classroom programming. Presentation made at the 20th International Early Childhood Conference on Children with Special Needs, San Diego, CA, December.

Robinson, J. (1988). *The baby boards: A Parents' guide to preschool & primary school entrance tests.* New York: Arco.

Romero, I. (1992). Individual assessment procedures with preschool children. In E. V. Nuttall, I. Romero, & J. Kalesnik, *Assessing and screening preschoolers: Psychological and education dimensions.* Needham Heights, MA: Allyn & Bacon.

Seefeldt, C., & Barbour, N. (1994). Play: The integrator of the Curriculum. In *Early childhood education: An Introduction* (3rd ed., pp. 296–330). Columbus, OH: Merrill.

Vukelich, C. (1992). Play and assessment: Young children's knowledge of the functions of Writing. *Childhood Education, 68,* 202–207.

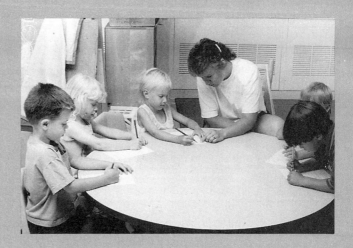

CHAPTER 11

Special Issues in Primary Grades

Terms to Know

- accountability
- learner outcomes
- informal evaluation
- portfolios
- individualized academic tests
- textbook tests

CHAPTER OVERVIEW   This chapter presents the special assessment issues in the primary grades. Teachers must assess the diverse population of children in the programs. Children in the primary grades have different learning styles and developmental and educational strengths. Teachers can use many informal methods to determine the learning needs of these children. Learner outcomes and accountability are discussed. Special issues of urban and nontraditional learners are incorporated in the discussion. Portfolios in the assessment system are presented. Achievement tests in the primary grades are discussed, as well as potential alternatives to the use of these measures. Finally, textbook and individual academic tests are described.

Topics Discussed

- Primary assessment systems issues
- Transition from preschool
- Assessing teaching level
- Learner outcomes

■ Urban and nontraditional learner issues

■ Portfolios

■ Achievement testing

Primary assessment systems issues

Primary teachers are responsible for formal assessment decisions for all the children they serve. In addition, teachers must prepare report cards, keep cumulative records, and use assessment to plan. Primary teachers must give standardized tests. They are accountable for meeting learner goals or outcomes. **Learner outcomes** are expectations for children's performances as defined by professional associations, the federal government, state legislatures, and school districts. In most cases, these various government bodies are not concerned with the learner outcomes for preschool children. The notable exception is Goal One of Goals 2000—All children shall come to school ready to learn. Nevertheless, preschool children are busy learning and have already entered the assessment system.

Transition from preschool

Today, 4.2 million young children attend some preschool program. According to a report on the state of America's children by the Children's Defense Fund (1994), more than 6.5 million children younger than five whose mothers were employed were cared for by someone other than their parents in 1990. Family child-care homes (26.6%) and child-care centers (37.9%) accounted for 64.5% of the 4.2 million children in care. In the best situations, children have discovered how to learn, feel confident about themselves, possess basic self-help skills, and know some basic concepts—colors, numbers, shapes, etc. They are curious and ready to hit the big school running. Unfortunately, not all children have optimum preschool experiences. Some children are coping with risk factors in their lives. Not everyone is on the same developmental step. Even under the best family and social conditions, development occurs in an uneven fashion. So, a big part of a teacher's job is assessment of developmental and educational progress.

Assessing teaching level

In September, when children transfer schools, and throughout the year, teachers must quickly find out the instructional needs and levels of their children. Besides observation, the primary mode of assessment for young children, teachers review records of children. When records are not available, not complete, or not definitive, teachers must quickly assess children as they teach.

Informal evaluation

Informal evaluation is comprised of techniques to be used in these circumstances. These techniques are task activities for the learner to solve. The activities fit into the routine of the day. They are similar to the tasks or activities that engage children in learning centers and in didactic experiences with the teacher, both solely and in small groups. The tasks specify scoring criteria or rubrics. In the boxes that follow, examples of these techniques are shown.

⊞ Learner outcomes

From the perspective of educators, learner outcomes are a discrete expression of a philosophy of education. That is, what do we want children to know and be able to do or how do we want them to behave? Once we have decided the goals—learner outcomes, we can match the teaching method with the assessment method.

Specification of learner outcomes is usually by subject area. For example, a math curriculum for kindergarten (Addison School District 4, 1993) may have the following categories:

- shapes
- classification
- spatial relationships
- comparisons
- patterns
- counting
- numbers and numerals
- addition and subtraction operations
- calendar
- measurement
- estimating
- graphing

One way to teach this curriculum is to select workbooks that contain all or most of these activities. The teacher then divides the children into groups by ability or by convenience. On day one, children count from one to ten, discuss counting, and then go to their seats and practice writing numbers and counting objects in pictures in their workbooks. Everyone marches through the same pages of the workbook. The teacher plans extra sheets for those who don't grasp the particular concept being taught.

BOX 11.1

Math Assessment

As children take part in classroom activities, the role of the teacher is to observe how they participate in

- group games involving logico-mathematical thinking (Kamii, 1985, 1989b, 1994). An example is the game "Always 12" consisting of seventy-two round cards bearing the numbers 0 through 6. The object of play is to make a total of 12 with four cards. Two to four children can play. The winner is the child with the most cards (Kamii, 1989b).

- using calculators and computers.

- counting and using numbers as names.

- activities involving demonstration of number facts, properties, procedures, algorithms, skills (Schultz, Colarusso, Strawderman, 1989).

- geometry, including activities that require children to "describe, model, draw, and classify shapes; investigate and predict the results of combining, subdividing, and changing shapes; develop spatial sense; relate geometric ideas to number and measurement ideas; recognize and appreciate geometry in their world." (National Council of Teachers of Mathematics, 1989, p. 48).

- measurement, including activities that involve the development of "the attributes of length, weight, area, volume, time, temperature, and angle; the process of measuring and concepts related to units of measurement; making and using estimates of measurement; making and using measurements in problem and everyday situations." (National Council of Teachers of Mathematics, 1989, p. 51).

Examples of specific informal tasks that can be used are the following.

M & M® Task for Pre-K to 2nd Grade

Materials

small bags of M & M's®, napkins, paper, crayons, markers, or other recording materials

The Task

Conduct this task in small groups or with individual children. Give each child a bag of M & M's®. Ask each child to show the color distribution in the bag. Explain that each bag will have a different amount of candy of each color, so that there is not one right answer, but multiple answers to this problem.

BOX 11.1 (continued)

Allow children to express their answers in diverse ways. Children may draw circles to represent the numbers of red, green, yellow, etc. They may summarize their count—2 green, 3 red, etc. They may prepare a graph.

The teacher's role in this task is to observe. Ask the children to give a product showing their work. When finished, children may eat the M & M's®.

Scoring the Task

0 = unable

1 = can sort by color, but cannot illustrate the solution

2 = can identify same, more, less

3 = illustrates task

4 = makes a pictorial graph

5 = makes a numerical or tabular graph

Pizza Party for Second Grade

Materials

a large cardboard circle, resembling a pizza.

The Task

Conduct this task in small groups or with individual children. Show the cardboard pizza form to the children. Tell the children to pretend that they have two pizzas that size. The two pizzas are for a party. Seven boys and five girls will attend the party. Then say, "We want to give everyone a piece the same size. How can we do that?" Ask children to illustrate the answer to this question. Explain that each child may answer this question in different ways.

Supply paper, crayons, markers, pencils, or other recording materials and scissors for children to show their work. Allow children to express their answers in diverse ways. Children may draw circles and divide the pizza; they may cut out paper to represent pieces and children; they may illustrate the answer with fractions, etc.

The teacher's role in this task is to observe, and ask the children to give a product showing their work.

Scoring of the Task

0 = no idea

1 = drawing stick children (or hatch marks) to decide the number of pieces needed

2 = cutting up paper to show the answer

3 = drawing fractional representations of circles

4 = showing the answer arithmetically with numbers

BOX 11.2

Informal Language Arts Assessment

As the children move in the room around the interest centers, observe literacy development. Categories of observation and informal assessment include the following:

- Interest in books: Teachers can see which children are interested in books. Children and teachers can record lists of favorite books. Parents can be involved in this recording of favorites.

- Concept of print: Teachers can evaluate students' ability to read environmental print, own words as sight vocabulary, attempts to read predictable book, identification of letters of the alphabet, association of letters and sounds, use of story books (Morrow, 1989).

- Story concept awareness: Teachers observe how students attend to pictures, but not stories; attend to pictures and form oral stories; attend to a mix of pictures, reading and storytelling; attend to pictures but form written stories, attend to print (Sulzby, 1985). This can be evaluated by observing story retelling, attempted reading of favorite storybooks, role playing, picture sequencing, use of puppet or felt board and questions and comments during story reading (Morrow, 1989).

- Reading strategies: This includes evidence of how the children approach reading. Where does each child fall in the continuum toward conventional reading?

- Using reading: In which ways do children use reading: for pleasure, to discover information, etc.?

- Writing strategies: Developmentally, writing begins with scribbling and proceeds through a number of stages to conventional spelling and grammar (cf Teale & Sulzby, 1986).

- Handwriting mechanics: This task includes use of pencils and markers, and ability to form letters, stay on line, etc.

- Listening strategies: This task includes child's ability to grasp information in one-to-one situations, small groups, large group, note taking, etc.

- Speaking strategies as evidence of language development: This task includes phonology, syntax, and semantics (cf Morrow, 1989).

Examples of informal performance tasks include the following.

Morris Ten Words (Morris & Perney, 1984)

This is a means to assess invented spelling (child's creation of a word, based on his understanding of the sounds involved) and potential readiness for formal reading instruction. Model phonetic spelling for children by showing them how to sound out the word: mat. Write it on the chalkboard or on chart paper as you sound out the word. Continue this process with the words: let and stop. Use these words in sentences, so the children have a context.

BOX 11.2 (continued)

Give the children paper and pencils. Then dictate the following ten words and sentences.

1. fit: These shoes do not fit correctly.
2. side: I have one hand on each side of my body.
3. dress: Latoya's new dress is pretty.
4. stick: Juan found a stick under the tree.
5. rice: I like to have rice with dinner.
6. beg: The dog likes to beg at the table.
7. seed: The flower grew from a tiny seed.
8. gate: The gate on the fence was open.
9. drop: If you drop the plate, it will break.
10. lake: Jennifer is swimming in the lake.

Scoring

0 = only unrelated letters are used

1 = first or last letter of word

2 = part of the sounds represented

3 = initial consonant, vowel, and final consonant

4 = conventional English spelling

Composition Assessment

Assign a topic. For example, "One day, I found a magic hat . . . " Then ask the child to dictate, write and/or illustrate the story, as age appropriate.

Scoring

0 = undecipherable or blank composition

1 = random words or child repeats prompts

2 = ideas have little or no relationship to the magic hat or simply repeats ideas from the story

3 = at least one new idea present, ideas lack development or are contradictory, writing may simply list ideas or wishes

4 = several new ideas present; ideas are not fully developed; sentence structure is repetitions; lacks structure

5 = ideas are fairly well developed and expressed; writing has some structure (beginning, middle, end); development and organization could be improved

BOX 11.2 (continued)

6 = ideas are very well-developed and expressed; fully developed structure with beginning, middle, and end; logical and well organized; good sentences, variety, and expression

Each of these informal assessment procedures can be incorporated into the day-to-day activity of the classroom. These activities are performance-based assessments. The examples are drawn from teachers in the field. In implementing these procedures, teachers think about what they need to know about the children so they can provide the activities that lead the children to academic success. Starting from learner outcomes, specified by school districts and state legislatures, teachers plan what to teach. Using the tools of books and other materials in their classroom, they carry out the required curriculum. Knowing where the children are, developmentally speaking, is the key to creating meaningful activities and successful experiences.

She judges success by right answers on the workbook pages and the answers in small group discussion.

In this scene, children are discussing the calendar every day. Today is Tuesday, October 15. It is sunny and bright. We go to gym today. It is Audrey's birthday and she is five years old. In some classes, children would then copy this story from the chalkboard. This example shows inappropriate practice (Bredekamp, 1987).

In an appropriate classroom, teachers will look at the goals for math, science, social studies, and language arts. Using the predetermined goals, the teacher will build an integrated curriculum. The curriculum should be based on a significant theme in the lives of young children. A common theme at the beginning of the year in kindergarten is "My Self." Possible learning activities that relate to the goals or learner outcomes for this theme are the following:

- How Tall Am I?
  Attach a long piece of construction paper to the wall. Use the children's foot and hand tapes to measure their heights. Later use a standard inch/foot measure and compare.

- Height Guesstimate
  Have children choose partners. Then ask one partner of each pair to guess how many feet long the other child is. Have the children verify their guesses by measuring each other (Berry and Mindes, 1993, p. 39).

Another more comprehensive way to organize math outcomes is according to the following categories:

BOX 11.3

Social/Emotional Assessment

Teachers need to plan assessment to measure social/emotional adjustment to school. Zvetina and Guiterrez (1994) have described this adjustment as "the school self." It is the child's sense of oneself as a learner and as a member of the community of learners that influences behavioral adjustment to academic demands of the environment. The school self can be seen in children who participate and invest in the community of learners. Zvetina and Guiterrez suggest that such students will

- show a sense of themselves as competent learners.
- display increasing motivation manifested by their own curiosity, interest, and persistence toward school-related tasks and experiences.
- initiate, participate, and connect in relationships with their peers and teachers.
- use problem-solving skills to work through and resolve problems related to tasks and interpersonal conflicts.
- draw upon a repertoire of internal and external coping strategies for controlling their impulses, modulating these affects, and effectively using time and space.

Through their work with teachers in urban classrooms, Zvetina and Guitterez (1994) have developed this concept of the child role in behavioral adjustment. They are developing observational criteria for assessing this adjustment.

Traditionally, teachers have used categories such as self-esteem, achievement motivation, peer relationships, relationships with teachers, persistence, and attention to describe social/emotional adjustment. Today's teachers must be aware of contextual and cultural factors relating to adjustment as they develop distinct specific criteria for describing the *successful* learner. Henning-Stout (1994) reminds us that learning is a personal process mediated by the culture of a given community, as well as the community of the school. In schools where cooperative learning and child-initiated activity are valued, social emotional assessment must include opportunities for students and teachers toward the assessment of these valued practices.

- attitudes
- concepts and processes:
    - problem solving
    - communication
    - reasoning
    - connections
    - patterns and relationships
    - estimation
    - number sense and numeration

- concepts of whole number operations and computation
- geometry and spatial sense
- measurement
- data analysis
- common fractions (Nebraska Department of Education, 1993).

Math objectives carried out in a theme on "Trees and Growing Things" could include:

- counting rings
- marking shadows of the tree
- comparing the sizes of trees
- observing the geometric shapes
  (Nebraska Department of Education, 1993, p. 4).

The topic includes science, music, social studies, arts, health, safety, physical education, cooking, language arts, and reading activities. Assessment follows the theme through several activities.

- Group evaluation of the topic
    Children discuss what they know, what they want to know about the topic, collect information, then decide whether they learned what was necessary. Of course, as the project evolves, they learn more and become curious about additional phenomena. Thus, they practice formative and summative evaluation as well as problem solving. How shall we gather this information and establish whether we have learned it?

- Student evaluation of self-progress
    Children keep logs, notes, and experimental records. They decide and discuss with the teacher whether they have added to their store of knowledge.

- Teacher evaluation of student products
    Teachers review graphs, notebooks, drawings, stories, models, videos, plays, and all products produced by children.

- Journal writing, stories written
    Notes and stories can be reviewed not only for content obtained, but also for writing conventions followed. (Nebraska Department of Education, 1993, p. 8).

Another thematic example is a six-week theme for third graders on ecology from the perspective of the Native American philosophy with nature (Zielinsky, 1994). The plan is to begin the theme by an introduction to the sustained yield practices of the Menominee Tribal Enterprises, a lumber and wood producer. The sustained yield practices philosophy includes

- waste not, want not
- life giving water
- creatures of the world
- the plants do fine without us
- it's in your hands

Objectives for the sixth week include:

- *math:* greater than and less than, using a balance to show the benefits of more people joining the environmental movement
- *science:* examination of recycling and pollution controls from the view of third graders
- *social studies:* acquaintance with the worldwide environmental effort
- *reading: Simple Things Kids Can Do to Save the Earth*
- *writing:* newsletter for the school to share learning and to gain whole-school cooperation in the environmental movement
- *spelling:* related new words

Assessment and evaluation will mainly be addressed through two means. One of these is detailed observation of students during class time. Participation will be an important factor, but so will an ability to concentrate and work alone. As responsibility is emphasized, children will be expected to complete their work and this material will also be used in evaluation. The main emphasis of evaluation, however, will be through examination of the child's Specialized Activity Center work as collected in a portfolio and through student-teacher conferences.

Class time holds the important responsibility of socialization and active thinking rather than performance at a task. The purpose of the Activity Centers and the assignments that correspond is to provide an outlet for children to express what it is that they know and learn through actively engaging with subject matter. The main thrust of this classroom method is complete learning and comprehension. Therefore much class time will be spent in discussion and discovery rather than production of graded materials.

As this third-grade classroom is expected to meet the requirement of testing and assessment, of course children will take the standardized tests as required, and the material which children need to learn at the specified grade levels and times during the year will be integrated in their entireness. Children will be at a disadvantage when compared to other third graders and what is being learned. These children will be at an advantage because they are learning how subject matter crosses boundaries and that what is learned in one area can be related to the next. Interdisciplinary themes are important for total comprehension and for making knowledge usable. When children realize that their schoolwork is more than just *schoolwork,* they become eager learners.

There is little question that there will continue to be children who do not want to be in school who are not inclined to learn in such a setting. These are the times when individualization and parent-teacher communication are essential. It may be that the student requires more structure and so might receive specially designed assignments to complete while other children are involved with the activity centers. Additional guidelines may be provided during class activities as long as other children are not limited by them. Creative thinking is essential for lifelong learning and for development of independence. Those who can think for themselves will be more successful in life than those who are limited to following others' directions. Children should be given as much freedom of expression as possible, particularly because we know that children enter school with different talents and aptitudes and also a variety of home and early education experience. Children should be given every opportunity to use and integrate their knowledge and to gain confidence in themselves as problem solvers themselves and in terms of community and society (Zielinsky, 1994).

An example of a state plan for coordination of a plan to coordinate assessment and learning goals is the Model Learner Outcomes in Early Childhood Education (Minnesota Department of Education, 1990). An observation instrument suggests the following categories:

- Personal
  - emotional development
  - independence
  - self-concept
  - health and safety
  - moral development
- Social outcome
  - sense of self as a social being
  - social relations
  - social skills
- Physical outcome
  - gross motor
  - fine motor
- Cognitive outcome
  - attention
  - curiosity

- perception
- memory
- problem solving
- logical thinking
- Aesthetic/creative outcome
  - creates
  - responds
  - evaluates
- Communication outcome
  - receptive communication-nonverbal
  - receptive communication-listening
  - receptive communication-reading
  - expressive communication-nonverbal
  - expressive communication-speaking
  - expressive communication-writing

Minnesota specifies observation at the chronological age points of 2.5, 4.5, 6.5, and 9.0. Target sub-skills focus observer attention at each point.

Kentucky (Guskey, 1994) has also developed a comprehensive system that encompasses learning goals comprised of basic skills and the core concepts of self-sufficiency, group membership, problem solving, and integration of knowledge. These are specified in 75 learner outcomes. Assessment is divided into an accountability strand and a continuous strand. Included in the accountability strand are

- scheduled performance events
  On demand, children are asked to complete performance tasks, including observation of experiments and recording and reporting results.
- portfolio performance tasks
  Initially, only a writing portfolio was required. The goal now includes paper products, video, and computer products.
- scheduled transitional times/tasks
  At specified intervals, students complete both multiple choice and open-ended standardized tasks.

These are mandatory and include statewide assessment at grades 4, 8, and 12; an annual assessment, and accountability every two years.

Within the continuous assessment strands there are formal procedures that include performance assessments and portfolio tasks and informal instructional-embedded assessments. Kentucky's system is complex but it is a good example of a comprehensive high-stakes approach to school reform.

Outcomes and accountability

Other state legislatures are concerned more with **accountability** when outcomes are specified. Legislators are influenced by the input/output philosophy of business. The debate then becomes: "What is worthwhile to know?" If definitions for academic success change toward more holistic definitions, then assessment must change as well. Performance on the outcomes shows success. The risks, of course, are the re-creation of another set of *high stakes* test hurdles for children. Performance tests that are not sensitive to the curriculum available and to the social context of learning may serve children in the same way that IQ tests and poorly chosen achievement tests have served children in the past.

From an educational policy perspective, learner outcomes and performance assessment should be used to improve programs for all children. The weight of the assessment should not fall on the back of an individual child and thus deny access in an unfair way. That is, a child who is judged on the basis of performance tasks must be assured that prior educational experience has included tasks similar to those requiring proficiency at specified age or grade levels. It is easy to see that a standardized achievement test requiring an in-depth knowledge of static electricity is not *fair* for children who have not studied electricity. Teachers must also keep well in mind that performance tasks have the capacity to be biased, as well. If children have not participated in *hands on* science, for example, they may not be able to handle problems that are presented by asking, "How many ways can you use a widget?" Many states have defined outcomes for the purpose of accountability (O'Neil, 1994).

The Georgia Kindergarten Assessment Program (Stanley, 1991) is designed by educators to meet the demands of accountability and to be useful for teachers. Both observation and performance assessment tasks are included. Categories include communicative capability, logical-mathematical capability, physical capability, personal capability, and social capability.

The State of Illinois (Illinois State Board of Education, 1985) developed a system of standards for reading, mathematics, writing, science, social science, fine arts, and physical development and health. These standards, as designed, are performance definitions and levels. School effectiveness is reported annually in the newspapers around the state. The scores are used to recognize effective schools, rather than for grading, promotion, retention, or graduation. Although these performance standards apply to school recognition, they reflect on individual children by default. A child is a member of a school community. If a whole school is a Level One school, where students are not meeting performance standards as established by the state, a child or children may feel that they have failed or are in some other way unworthy. A Level One school in reading is one where students "may not read material that is appropriate to their grade. Particularly at the upper grades, such students do not think of themselves as readers and often fail to value reading for personal purposes. As a result, they may exhibit aberrant response patterns on tests or give up. (Illinois State Board of Education, 1993, 7–8). The blame for nonachievement is usually laid at the door of the children, rather than at the door of the teachers and principal. Most often schools that do not meet state goals are beset with at-risk children—children who are poor, who may be malnourished, or who may live in violent situations.

Urban and nontraditional learner issues

The task for the teacher in urban and nontraditional settings is to look beyond the traditional academic readiness rubric: assess the child's conformity to traditional learning settings. What bridges must be provided? Does Erica need a bit of phonics instruction because she has not been exposed to standard English? Should the seven year old who has not been to school before be shown how to use lockers? To what extent have teachers incorporated an understanding of cultural groups in their approach to education in these urban schools?

Independence and interdependent functioning are not universally accepted values by all cultures in our society. For example, doing your own work is a traditional American value—part of the self-actualization ethic of America. Some cultures value teamwork more than independence. Not putting yourself forward is yet another value held by many cultures (Greenfield & Cocking, 1994). Thus, if a teacher is measuring initiative as maturity, without consideration for the traditional values of the children she teaches, she may misjudge the child and decide that he is lazy or dumb or mentally assign another negative characteristic.

The Boston College Center for the Study of Testing, Evaluation and Educational Policy, Urban District Assessment Consortium, made up of Boston schools and other urban settings, puts performance assessment in action with guidelines for practice. In collaboration with teachers, the Center developed assessment for reading, writing, math, and science. The components were drawn from the National Assessment of Education Progress, open-ended questions derived from subjects and performance tasks. Writing performance is assessed by presenting a culturally rich urban mural picture as the stimulus. Students brainstorm for 8–10 minutes, then write for 35 minutes (Urban District Assessment Consortium, 1994, p. 34). Children read a story called "A Bicycle for Rosaura." They record on tape a retelling of the story (Urban District Assessment Consortium, 1994, p. 36).

In many state plans, "student assessment is increasingly used to leverage systematic reform. The goal of education reform is to provide students with a better balance between the old core of memorizing and repeating and the new core of inquiry, thinking, communicating, and problem solving. Seventeen states report using performance assessment and six states report using portfolios" (Bond, 1992).

Collecting evidence on learner outcomes with performance tasks requires a new format for record keeping. The most common method is evidence collection in a portfolio. Portfolios are regarded as dynamic and inclusive—involving the child, teacher, and parent.

⊞ Portfolios

The collection and development of **portfolios** is the most current way to link teaching and assessment. Most approaches to the collection of portfolios suggest that the process be as important as the products stored. Teachers and students must think critically about what to include in these folders/boxes/baskets. Parents are sometimes involved in helping teachers and children.

"Portfolios serve several important purposes:

- integration of instruction and assessment,
- provide students, teachers, parents, administrators, and other decision makers with essential information about child progress and overall classroom activities,
- make it possible for children to participate in assessing their own work,
- keep track of individual child progress,
- form the basis for evaluating the quality of a child's total performance" (Meisels & Steele, 1991).

In an ideal way, portfolios are used according to an established purpose. Goals are defined. Activities are designed to carry out the goals. Students and teachers determine the criteria for success. Students choose, under teacher guidance, examples of their work for their efforts for the year.

Examples of categories for math portfolios (Stenmark, 1991) include:

- problem comprehension
- approaches and strategies
- relationships
- flexibility
- communication
- curiosity and hypotheses
- equality and equity
- solutions
- examining results
- mathematical learning
- self assessment

In portfolio development, students help teachers generate criteria for effective work (Loughlin, 1992). Children form criteria for good and great work. They evolve clear models for the required assignments. Children refer to the criteria for success as they work. The teacher's job is to provide resources for quality work.

Donovan (1994b) developed procedures for teachers to use to tie teaching, assessment, and the Illinois Goals Assessment Program (IGAP) together. She makes teachers conscious of the connection of the processes. She breaks the strands of the reading assessment portion of the IGAP into teaching activities. For example: "The first evaluation strand of the IGAP measures the student's ability to make predictions about the general content of a selection about to be read and the second background knowledge of a topic before reading about it. Reading process components assessed word identification and recognition and comprehension."

Donovan continues the delineation of the tasks on the IGAP as they relate to reading: constructing meaning, vocabulary items, characterization items, reading process components, and author's craft/purpose/bias. She then suggests that teachers routinely include each item that will be assessed in the activities planned for lessons.

Similarly, Donovan (1994a) has broken down the IGAP writing objectives:

- integration
- focus
- support and elaboration
- organization
- conventions

She has done this grouping for kindergarten, and first, second, and third grades.

Meisels, Jablon, Marsden, Dichtelmiller, and Dorfman (1994) have been working with school districts to develop a comprehensive approach to assessment. The Work Sampling System™ yields developmental guidelines and checklists as well as portfolios that include core items to show growth over time and individualized items that reflect original characteristics of learners. Summary reports are produced three times per year by teachers to guide planning and to summarize growth. The system is designed to separate developmental readiness and progress from academic knowledge and skills. Parents, students, and teachers are involved in creating the system. The system attempts to model a comprehensive approach for the assessment of young children.

In all of these examples of portfolio assessment, hopefully, the reader gains an appreciation for the similarity of day-to-day curriculum with the periodic assessment tasks. The assessment procedure is not designed as a *get the learner* activity, but as part of the check on learning progress. Where is the learner in relation to goals? Teachers, parents, and children collaborate to address these issues. Many examples of performance tasks and portfolio examples are available in published form today. (cf Darling-Hammond, Einbender, Frelow, & Ley-King, 1993). Teachers must use good judgment in choosing published tasks or portfolios. The crucial factors are the relationships of philosophy, goals, activities, and assessment strategy. There must be a crossmatch.

Achievement testing

Many schools across the country continue to use achievement testing as part of the early-childhood program. Tests are used to assess readiness for reading at kindergarten level. In schools that receive Chapter 1 funds, pre- and post-achievement test assessment is required. Proposed changes in Chapter 1 Regulations (Olson, 1994) will end heavy reliance on multiple choice tests for Chapter 1 programs. The same procedures as used for the whole school district will apply for these special programs. Legislation is pending. States and school districts may require regular achievement testing. Frequently this is done as a way to check the curriculum and instruction process. Often, the results are used as documentation for referral of children for retention or special education. These applications of tests are developmentally inappropriate for young children. Speaking for the National Association for the Education of Young Children, Kamii (1989) has edited a publication called *Achievement Testing in the Early Grades*. All of the reasons for not using achievement tests with young children are outlined and explained. Inappropriate uses that are discussed include:

▮ Using tests to decide which children should fail kindergarten and other grades.

▮ Ignoring the limitations and technical aspects of tests, i.e. using instruments that are not matched to the curriculum.

▮ Placing inappropriate weight on the statistics of tests, e.g., ignoring stanines and percentiles, but placing great faith in grade-level equivalents.

▮ Using closed-answer instruments to judge effectiveness of constructionist curriculum.

▮ Relying on test scores to evaluate success of students, schools, and teachers.

▮ Accepting without question "the science" of tests.

One of the potentially most devastating ways that schools misuse tests with young children is in readiness testing. These tests are administered at the beginning of a child's career in school. Children are treated to failure experiences that shape their entire lives. Relying on a readiness test to determine placement in grades is inappropriate. Such measures neglect the social/cultural context and typical individual developmental deviation found in all groups of children. *Reading readiness* can be more appropriately assessed by redesigning the concept of reading to include the topics thought of as emergent writing and reading (Sulzby, 1990). "Children appear to add new understandings about writing, somewhat as a repertoire of understandings in the sociolinguistic sense. . . . Their development does not follow one invariant, hierarchical order. We see several patterns of development, with a general progressive track" . . . to conventional writing (p. 85). Sulzby defines conventional writing as "the child's production of text that another conventionally literate person can read and that the child himself or herself reads conventionally" (Sulzby, 1990, p. 88).

Children learn to read contextually and specifically, simultaneously. That is, young children can read the word "Stop" when it appears on a sign, but not in a book or on a chalkboard (Teale, 1990, p. 49). They have read the word in context. Through exposure to familiar words—dog, pat, dinosaur, Barney—in favorite stories, they learn the specifics. Gradually, they can form greater understandings from contextual situations.

Replacing mandated tests

Pre- and post-achievement can be assessed by reexamining learner outcomes and tracking accomplishments according to the goals. For example, by third grade, children should know how to "Describe how scientists could conclude cause and effect relationships between different factors and the weather" (Illinois State Board of Education, 1992). How can this knowledge be documented? What experiences will show that children know this?

There are many other ways to identify children in need of special services besides standardized achievement testing. Observation, trial teaching, task analysis, and all of the other special methods available are more appropriate. If special services are needed, then a child study is developed. That is soon enough to use an individualized standardized test done by a trained clinician. The test is part of the clinical material that the professional uses in considering the recommendation for special intervention strategies.

When teachers do use achievement tests

Teachers should involve the decision makers in carrying out the testing practice in the classroom. A kindergarten teacher in a suburban school district, Ms. Green, was told that she must administer a reading readiness test to her group in November. The teacher, an experienced early-childhood teacher of three to five year olds, had been hired late in August. Her assignment was to teach a group of 25 children whose parents had just registered them for school. The parents had not registered the children in the spring round up, as many families had done. The group of children had limited experience in a formal learning situation—many were learning English. She was given a classroom with workbooks, dittos, crayons, and a limited number of table games. She immediately went to garage sales to find housekeeping center materials, borrowed big books from the library, and reorganized the room into interest centers. Ms. Green created a developmentally appropriate environment. She developed an assessment system based on district goals as stated on the kindergarten report card. She organized folders for each child, kept work samples, and made anecdotal notes. Ms. Green created partnerships with parents and children. They (teacher, children, and parents) all knew what they were doing:

- learning how to be students,
- satisfying their curiosity,
- enjoying the group experience,
- discovering new information,
- learning English,
- writing and reading at the pre-literacy level,
- solving problems,
- using numbers and equations.

All of this information about achievement was available by teacher report. What would a reading readiness test add?

Ms. Green protested to the district test coordinator. She gave all the reasons about why not to test. She even pulled out the National Association for the Education of Young Children Position Statement on Assessment of Young Children (1989). The test coordinator remained firm. All kindergarten children would be tested.

The teacher asked for help to administer the test. She was working alone in the room with 25 children, except an occasional parent volunteer. Test day arrived. The children were prepared. The test director could not get the children to cooperate! Testing was abandoned. Ms. Green served as an advocate for the young children in her program. She did so at personal risk to her career in that district. When teachers choose to resist tests, they must be prepared to show why the tests are inappropriate and how the necessary progress and accountability information can be obtained in a different way.

On a case-by-case basis, school districts have received permission to drop achievement testing for Chapter 1 students because they could show how learner outcomes were matched to student performance. The performance measures documented progress toward achievement goals. This trend has expanded as protests against premature testing of young children have gained momentum.

When you plan to use an achievement test, keep the following in mind:

- Help the district be aware of the limitations of testing for young children.

- Point them in the direction of some newer standardized tests that attempt to include problem solving and multiple correct answers.

- Lobby to have testing begin at the earliest at third grade. Then at least, children have some capacity for sustained attention to detail and writing and reading skills.

- Prepare the children in advance for the experience.

There are two distinct aspects of preparation—preparation for the actual administration of the test and cluing the children into the activity. Teachers must review the test and available samples so that they know what tasks children will be required to complete. Teachers must also be thoroughly familiar with the required testing conditions. This familiarity is not *teaching to the test*, but providing appropriate experience so that children can be successful. Once teachers have completed their homework, then they may help the children in the following ways:

- provide opportunities to mark papers in the same way required by the test,

- provide directions as limited by the test,

- include opportunities to work under time pressure,
- use separate answer sheets for assignments if children will be required to juggle these,
- use the real machine scorable sheets,
- describe and practice appropriate test behavior: do one's own work, be quiet,
- talk about guessing,
- identify strategies for managing the number of items, i.e., which ones to do first,
- help children cope with the anxiety of the task through story reading,
- incorporate test materials in the literacy or other interest center so children can cope through play.

To be fair to children, teachers must be thoroughly familiar with the test, its components, and procedures; follow the directions explicitly; adhere strictly to the time components; note any deviations made inadvertently; record notes about any unusual circumstances that occur with individual children; and be prepared to help children live with the stress that they feel during the test administration.

Once the test is over, skillful teachers go back to business-as-usual in the classroom. However, starting where children are comfortable or with favorite activities is a good way to recapture the momentum of life in the classroom. The test is just one of the cycles of student life.

Using achievement test results

The tests are given—now what? Look at the results for individual children. Put the scores into the context of what a teacher knows about the child. Do the scores make sense? Often the answer will be "yes." For those cases where the answer is "no"—the child's performance is higher, lower, or different—gather support for the position through observation, task analysis, or individualized academic assessment. Then document the results. When it will be in the best interest of a particular child, ask that the results be set aside, considered as a minimal estimate of performance, and supply corroborating evidence.

The next major task is to interpret the test results to parents. To do this most effectively, be thoroughly familiar with the technical terms of the test, know what the scores mean, and be able to explain the results to parents in comparison to classroom functioning.

Parents will want to understand what the test means about their child. Is it a fair assessment? Does the test measure the curriculum? Can the parents help their child to improve? Will the score influence school practices? That is, will it entitle their child to special services?

Explain the terms of percentile, stanine, standard scores, mean, median, and variance to parents. The best preparation is a thorough understanding of the terms and the limitations of testing in the early years.

Textbook tests

Publishers of textbooks publish **textbook tests.** These include sample test items, chapter reviews, and other assessment materials to go with instructional materials. Examine these materials with the same intensity that you apply to the texts. Are the materials harmonious with the philosophy of education? If teaching from a process approach, use the suggested performance tasks that can be set up for children to solve. Use the record keeping forms that are compatible with your learner outcome requirements.

Because these items say "test," do not assume that they are necessarily appropriate to use. Examine the materials as if they were tests. Are the materials valid? Do they match what is taught? Is there another way to gather the information that will be more efficient? Do the materials fit into the portfolio plan?

Individualized academic tests

Sometimes it may be convenient to use an individualized academic test for determining reading or math instructional level. These instruments may be particularly helpful when children move to the classroom without records or when you are puzzled about how a child is learning. **Individualized academic tests** are formal interviews of children on a topic such as reading or mathematics. Through the standardized interview process, the teacher learns not only first hand what the second or third grader knows, but also how she approached the task. For example, if assessing knowledge of double digit addition, watch Marcey at work. Give her some double digit addition problems. You can readily assess Marcey's ability with this problem, $22 + 49 = 611$.

Such information can be gathered through informal means if that is the only question. But if more information is needed about math facts, math concepts, or math vocabulary—spend 30 minutes in a structured interview with an individualized math test and Marcey and gather this information. It may take several days of observation to gather as much information. Used selectively, tests can be helpful efficiency tools.

⊞ Summary

At the primary level, tests and testing frequently become a formal part of student life. While best early-childhood practice eschews the use of tests for the most part, assessment in the service of instruction is required. Sometimes tests are the most efficient way to quickly gather information. Sometimes tests are required as part of the accountability mechanism. Teachers must pick the procedure to match the philosophy of their school's program and be prepared to answer responsibly when asked to describe child progress.

⊞ CHAPTER 11 Suggested further readings

Armstrong, T. (1994). *Multiple intelligences in the classroom.* Alexandria, VA: Association for Supervision and Curriculum Development.

Hart, D. (1994). *Authentic assessment: A handbook for educators.* Menlo Park, CA: Addison-Wesley.

McAffee, O., & Leong, D. (1994). *Assessing and guiding young children's development and learning.* Needham, MA: Allyn & Bacon.

Puckett, M. B., & Black, J. K. (1994). *Authentic assessment of the young child.* Columbus, OH: Merrill.

⊞ CHAPTER 11 Study questions

1. Describe the appropriate early childhood teacher role in assessing progress toward learner outcomes. Where does this material fit in the accountability portion of an assessment system?

2. What is an achievement test? How are these appropriately used with young children? What are the limitations of such measures?

3. How does learning style influence the collection of assessment information on individual children? How does an early childhood teacher plan for the diverse needs of her class so that learning style variables are appropriately addressed?

4. When should early childhood teachers appropriately use informal evaluation methods? How do these measures contribute to the comprehensive assessment system?

5. What are the issues in portfolio development and its use in the primary classroom? How do these issues compare to those in preschool classrooms?

ACTIVITIES

1. With a small group of children, try one or more of the informal assessment measures described. Report the results—respecting confidentiality—to your class.
2. For your state, find out about the required learning goals or learning outcomes. Make a plan for assessing children for the acquisition of these for a grade level of your choice.
3. Examine portfolios in a local school. Discuss with your classmates the similarities or differences across grades and schools.
4. Review the test manual for a standardized achievement test. Try giving the test to a classmate. Critique your efforts. Discuss ways to improve performance on subsequent administrations.
5. Look at textbook tests and compare them to the curricular goals for a theme of your choice. How would these measures assist your efforts in assessment? What limitations did you find?
6. Review an individualized academic test. Try administering part or all of it to a volunteer child. How will you use these measures in your program of the future?

6. Individualized achievement tests and textbook tests serve what functions in a primary classroom assessment program? What must early childhood teachers consider in the balance?

7. When are readiness tests commonly used? What are the liabilities in the practice?

8. Why do schools and states mandate tests? How can teachers serve as child advocates in changing to developmentally appropriate practice? What are the limits of the teacher role?

References

Addison School District 4. (1993). *Kindergarten guide to curriculum and instruction.* Addison, IL.: School District 4.

Berry, C., & Mindes, G. (1993). *Planning a theme based curriculum: Goals, themes, activities, and planning guides for 4's and 5's.* Chicago: Good Year.

Bond, L. (1992). *Surveying the landscape of state educational assessment programs.* Washington, DC: Council for Educational Development and Research, Boston College.

Bredekamp, S. (1987). *Developmentally appropriate practice.* Washington, DC: National Association for the Education of Young Children.

Children's Defense Fund. (1994). *The State of America's Children.* Washington, DC: Author.

Darling-Hammond, L., Einbender, L., Frelow, F., & Ley-King, J. (1993). *Authentic assessment in practice: A collection of portfolios, performance tasks, exhibitions, and documentation.* New York: Teachers College, National Center for Restructuring Education, Schools, and Teaching.

Donovan, M. (1994a). *Illinois Goals Assessment Program (IGAP) Writing Definitions.* Chicago: Erikson Institute for Early Education.

Donovan, M. (1994b). *Reading assessment inventory.* Chicago: Erikson Institute for Early Education.

Greenfield, P. M., & Cocking, R. R. (1994). *Cross-cultural roots of minority child development.* Hillsdale, NJ: Laurence Erlbaum.

Guskey, T. R. (Ed.). (1994). *High-stakes performance assessment: Perspectives on Kentucky's educational reform.* Thousand Oaks, CA: Corwin.

Henning-Stout, M. (1994). *Responsive assessment: A new way of thinking about learning.* San Francisco: Jossey-Bass.

Illinois State Board of Education. (1985). *The Illinois goals assessment program.* Springfield, IL: Illinois State Board of Education.

Illinois State Board of Education. (1993). *An overview of IGAP performance standards for reading, mathematics, writing, science, social sciences* (2nd Ed.). Springfield, IL: Illinois State Board of Education.

Illinois State Board of Education. (1992). *Illinois goal assessment program: science sample items.* Springfield, IL: Illinois State Board of Education.

Kamii, C. (1985). *Young children reinvent arithmetic: Implications of Piaget's theory.* New York: Teachers College.

Kamii, C. (1989a). *Achievement testing in early childhood: Games grown-ups play.* Washington, DC: National Association for the Education of Young Children.

Kamii, C., (with Joseph, L.). (1989b). *Young children continue to reinvent arithmetic, 2nd grade: Implications of Piaget's theory.* New York: Teachers College.

Kamii, C., (with Sally Jones Livingston). (1994). *Young children continue to reinvent arithmetic: Implications of Piaget's theory.* New York: Teachers College.

Loughlin, S. (1992). Quality by design through portfolios. *ASCD Update, 34.* 5, 2.

Meisels, S. J., Jablon, J. R., Marsden, D. B., Dichtelmiller, M. L., & Dorfman, A. B. (1994). *The Work Sample Method:™ An overview* (3rd ed.). Ann Arbor: Rebus Planning Associates, Inc.

Meisels, S. J., & Steele, D. M. (1991). *The early childhood portfolio collection process.* Ann Arbor: Center for Human Growth and Development, The University of Michigan.

Minnesota Department of Education. (1990). *Model learner outcomes in early childhood education.* St. Paul: Minnesota Department of Education.

Morris, D., & Perney. (1984). Developmental spelling as a predictor of first grade reading achievement. *Elementary School Journal, 84,* 441–457.

Morrow, L. M. (1989). *Literacy development in the early years.* Columbus, OH: Merrill.

National Association for the Education of Young Children. (1989). NAEYC position statement on standardized testing of young children 3 through 8 years of age. *Young Children, 43,* 42–47.

National Council for Teachers of Mathematics. (1989). *Curriculum and evaluation standards for school mathematics.* Reston, VA: National Council for Teachers of Mathematics.

Nebraska Department of Education. (1993). *Primary programs: Growing and learning in the heartland.* Lincoln, NE: Nebraska Department of Education.

Olson, L. (1994, August 3). Major changes in Chapter 1 testing are in the offing. *Education Week,* p. 26+.

O'Neil, J. (1994). Aiming for new outcomes: The promise and the reality. *Educational Leadership, 51.6,* 6–10.

Schultz, K. A., Colarusso, R. P., & Strawderman, V. W. (1989). *Mathematics for every young child.* Columbus, OH: Merrill.

Stanley, S. J. (1991, April). *The Georgia kindergarten assessment program: Distinctive features.* Paper presented at the meeting of the National School Board Association, San Francisco.

Stenmark, J. K. (1991). Math portfolios: A new form of assessment. *Teaching K–8, 21,* 62–68.

Sulzby, E. (1985). Children's emergent reading of favorite storybooks. *Reading Research Quarterly, 20,* 458–481.

Teale, W. H. (1990). Promise and challenge of informal assessment. In L. M. Morrow & J. K. Smith (Eds.), *Assessment for instruction in early literacy.* Englewood Cliffs, NJ: Prentice Hall.

Teale, W. H., & Sulzby, E. (Eds.). (1986). *Emergent literacy: Writing and reading.* Norwood Park, NJ: Ablex.

Urban District Assessment Consortium. (1994). *Implementation manual: A guide to administering, rating, and reporting the results of UDAC's alternative accountability assessments.* Chestnut Hill, MA: Center for the Study of Testing, Evaluation, and Educational Policy, Boston College.

Zeilinsky, S. (1994). *A Portfolio for ecology from the perspective of the Native American philosophy of harmony with nature.* Chicago: DePaul University, unpublished paper.

Zevtina, D., & Guitterez, J. (1994). *Social emotional observation criteria.* Chicago: Erikson Institute.

Early Childhood Tests

Brief descriptive information useful for teachers on a variety of tests designed for young children is listed below. All tests are individually administered except for those followed by an asterisk (*), which indicates that group administration is possible. The tests are grouped in ten categories:

1. School Readiness and Screening Tests
2. Diagnostic Tests of Development, Ability, and Aptitude
3. Tests of Academic Achievement
4. Tests of Achievement in Language
5. Tests of Achievement in Reading
6. Tests of Achievement in Spelling
7. Tests of Achievement in Mathematics
8. Tests to Identify Giftedness
9. Tests of Perceptual and/or Motor Skills
10. Tests of Behavior and Conduct

1. School Readiness and Screening Tests

Name: Ages and Stages Questionnaires (ASQ)
Author(s): Bricker, D., et al.
Publisher: Paul H. Brookes
Copyright Date: 1995
Age Range: 4 months to 4 years
Purpose: A parent-completed questionnaire used to identify children at risk for developmental delays and to monitor the child's progress at four- to six-month intervals. Records child's abilities in five areas: gross motor, fine motor, communication, personal-social, and problem solving. Also available in Spanish.
Approximate Testing Time: 10 Minutes
Type(s) of Response: Rater

Name: Basic School Skills Inventory–Screen (BSSI–S)
Author(s): Hammill, D., & Leigh, J.
Publisher: Pro-Ed
Copyright Date: 1983
Age Range: 4-0 to 6-11

Appendix A compiled by Lynn Van Stee, School of Education, Loyola University.

Purpose: Designed to predict school readiness and identify those at risk for school failure or in need of more in-depth assessment. A more in-depth diagnostic version is also available (BSSI–D).
Approximate Testing Time: 5–10 minutes
Type(s) of Response: Verbal, nonverbal, rater

Name: **Boehm Test of Basic Concepts–Revised (BTBC–R)***
Author(s):   Boehm, A.
Publisher: Psychological Corporation
Copyright Date: 1986
Age Range: 3 to 5 and kindergarten to second grade
Purpose: Measures children's mastery of the concepts considered necessary for achievement in the first years of school. Concepts tested include those of space (location, direction, orientation, and dimension), time, and quantity (number).
Approximate Testing Time: 15–30 minutes
Type(s) of Response: Nonverbal (pencil and booklet)

Name: **Brigance Early Preschool Screen***
Author(s):   Brigance, A.
Publisher: Curriculum Associates
Copyright Date: 1990
Age Range: 2 to 2 1/2
Purpose: A test of age-appropriate skills in general knowledge, language development, gross- and fine-motor skills, and body awareness. Also includes supplemental advanced assessments. A Spanish direction booklet is available.
Approximate Testing Time: 12–15 minutes
Type(s) of Response: Verbal and nonverbal

Name: **Brigance K&1 Screen–Revised***
Author(s):   Brigance, A.
Publisher: Curriculum Associates
Copyright Date: 1992
Age Range: 5 to 6
Purpose: A criterion- and curriculum-referenced test of developmental readiness and early academic skills. Samples language, motor ability, number skills, body awareness, auditory and visual discrimination, and early reading and math skills. Supplemental advanced assessments are also included. A Spanish direction booklet is available.
Approximate Testing Time: 12–15 minutes
Type(s) of Response: Verbal and nonverbal

Name: **Brigance Preschool Screen***
Author(s):   Brigance, A.
Publisher: Curriculum Associates
Copyright Date: 1985
Age Range: 3 to 4
Purpose: Assesses a sampling of developmental skills in the domains of general knowledge and comprehension, speech and language, gross- and fine-motor

skills, and math. Supplemental advanced assessments are also included. A Spanish direction booklet is available.

Approximate Testing Time: 12–15 minutes

Type(s) of Response: Verbal and nonverbal

Name: Children-At-Risk Screener: Kindergarten & Preschool (CARS)

Author(s):   Aaronson, M., & Aaronson, D.

Publisher: CTB/McGraw-Hill

Copyright Date: 1991

Age Range: 2 to 6

Purpose: Designed to identify children at risk for educational failure and in need of more in-depth assessment. CARS tests a variety of skills including following directions, abstract reasoning, spatial relationships, receptive language, and cognitive concepts. Includes a magnetic board and figures as testing tools.

Approximate Testing Time: 8–15 minutes.

Type(s) of Response: Expressive language not necessary.

Name: Comprehensive Identification Process (CIP)

Author(s):   Zehrbach, R.

Publisher: Scholastic Testing Service

Copyright Date: 1976

Age Range: 2-5 to 5-5

Purpose: Identifies children who may need special medical, psychological, or educational assistance before they enter school. Assesses various areas of development: fine motor, gross motor, cognitive-verbal, speech-expressive, language, hearing, vision, social-affective, and medical.

Approximate Testing Time: 30 minutes

Type(s) of Response: verbal and nonverbal

Name:

Author(s):   Fewell, R., & Langley, M.

Publisher: Pro-Ed

Copyright Date: 1977, 1984

Age Range: Birth to 60 months

Purpose: An informal test for early diagnosis of developmental disabilities. Covers fifteen skill categories such as sensory intactness, reasoning, and means-end relationships. This test can be adapted for children with visual impairment.

Approximate Testing Time: 25–30 minutes

Type(s) of Response: Nonverbal

Name: Developmental Indicators for the Assessment of Learning–Revised (DIAL–R)

Author(s):   Mardell-Czudnowski, C., & Goldenberg, D.

Publisher: American Guidance Service

Copyright Date: 1990

Age Range: 2-0 to 5-11

Purpose: Designed to identify children with potential learning problems or potential giftedness. Areas measured include motor, concepts, and language.

Although this test is administered individually, it is designed to handle screening of large numbers of children with different examiners administering each of the three areas.

Approximate Testing Time: 20–30 minutes

Type(s) of Response: Verbal, nonverbal

Name: **Early Screening Inventory–2nd Edition (ESI)**

Author(s): Meisels, S., & Wiske, M.

Publisher: Teacher's College Press

Copyright Date: 1987

Purpose: Identifies children who are at-risk in the areas defined by IDEA (Individuals with Disabilities Education Act). Domains include cognition, communication, and motor. An optional social-emotional scale and adaptive behavior checklist are also available.

Approximate Testing Time: 15 minutes

Type(s) of Response: Verbal, nonverbal, rater

Name: **LAP Kindergarten Screen**

Author(s): Chapel Hill Training Outreach Project

Publisher: Kaplan School Supply

Copyright Date: 1980

Age Range: 5

Purpose: Provides a measure of skills in the areas of fine motor-writing and manipulation, language comprehension and naming, gross motor, and cognitive.

Approximate Testing Time: 15 minutes

Type(s) of Response: Verbal and nonverbal

Name: **McCarthy Screening Test (MST)**

Author(s): McCarthy, D.

Publisher: Psychological Corporation

Copyright Date: 1978

Age Range: 4-0 to 6-6

Purpose: Measures a variety of abilities that are important in achieving success in school. Some of the six subtests are reported as predictive in identifying children with learning disabilities or perceptual difficulties.

Approximate Testing Time: 20 minutes

Type(s) of Response: Verbal and nonverbal

Name: **Miller Assessment for Preschoolers (MAP)**

Author(s): Miller, L.

Publisher: Psychological Corporation

Copyright Date: 1982

Age Range: 2-9 to 5-8

Purpose: The MAP is a screening tool used to identify children who exhibit moderate "pre-academic problems," which may affect one or more areas of development, but who do not have obvious or serious problems. Domains tested include foundations (basic motor and sensory tasks), coordination, verbal, nonverbal, and complex (sensorimotor abilities in conjunction with cognitive and visual-spatial abilities).

Approximate Testing Time: 20–30 minutes
Type(s) of Response: Verbal and nonverbal

Name: Minneapolis Preschool Screening Instrument (MPSI)
Author(s): Lichtenstein, R.
Publisher: Minneapolis Public Schools
Copyright Date: 1980
Age Range: 3-7 to 5-4
Purpose: Measures skills in various areas which are combined into a single score to determine referrals for further assessment. Domains include building, copying shapes, information, matching, sentence completion, hopping and balancing, naming colors, prepositions, identifying body parts, and repeating sentences.
Approximate Testing Time: 12–15 minutes
Type(s) of Response: Verbal, nonverbal, rater

Name: Preschool Behavior Rating Scale
Author(s): Barker, W., & Doeff, A.
Publisher: Child Welfare League of America
Copyright Date: 1980
Age Range: 3-0 to 5-11
Purpose: Rates coordination, receptive and expressive language, environmental adaptation, and social relations to indicate typical and atypical preschool behavior.
Approximate Testing Time: 5–10 minutes
Type(s) of Response: Rater

Name: Preschool Inventory–Revised Edition
Author(s): Caldwell, B.
Publisher: Educational Testing Service
Copyright Date: 1970
Age Range: 3 to 6
Purpose: Assesses the child's knowledge and skills in areas necessary for school achievement: personal facts, social roles, number concepts, colors, and geometric designs.
Approximate Testing Time: 15 minutes
Type(s) of Response: Verbal and nonverbal

Name: School Readiness Test (SRT)*
Author(s): Anderhalter, O., & Perney, J.
Publisher: Scholastic Testing Service
Copyright Date: 1977
Age Range: End of kindergarten to first three weeks of first grade
Purpose: A tool for evaluating a child's readiness for first grade. The eight subtests are administered over several sessions and include vocabulary, identifying letters, visual discrimination, auditory discrimination, comprehension and interpretation, number knowledge, handwriting ability, and developmental spelling ability.
Approximate Testing Time: 90 minutes
Type(s) of Response: Nonverbal (pencil and booklet)

Name: **Screening Children for Related Early Educational Needs (SCREEN)**
Author(s): Hresko, W., et al.
Publisher: Pro-Ed
Copyright Date: 1988
Age Range: 3 to 7
Purpose: This test of educationally relevant abilities provides a measure of both global and specific abilities. Useful for identifying mildly handicapped students and monitoring progress.
Approximate Testing Time: 25–50 minutes
Type(s) of Response: Verbal and nonverbal

Name: **Test of Basic Experiences 2 (TOBE 2)***
Author(s): Moss, M.
Publisher: CTB/McGraw-Hill
Copyright Date: 1979
Age Range: Preschool to first grade
Purpose: Assesses important concepts which contribute to readiness for school. Contains one level for preschool and kindergarten and another for kindergarten and first grade, neither of which requires reading. Areas addressed are mathematics, language, science, and social studies. A practice test is included, and a Spanish edition is available.
Approximate Testing Time: Practice test, 20 minutes; Battery, 45 minutes
Type(s) of Response: Nonverbal (pencil and booklet)

2. Diagnostic Tests of Development, Ability, and Aptitude

Name: **Batelle Developmental Inventory (BDI)**
Author(s): Batelle Memorial Institute
Publisher: DLM Teaching Resources
Copyright Date: 1978, 1984 (norms recalibrated in 1988)
Age Range: Birth to 8-0
Purpose: A measure of basic developmental skills in five domains: personal-social, adaptive, motor, communication, and cognitive. Information is gained by means of observations of the child in a natural setting, parent interview, and a structured test format. Developed for planning and designing educational programs and for program evaluation. A 10–30 minute screening component is also available.
Approximate Testing Time: Varies
Type(s) of Response: Verbal, nonverbal, rater

Name: **Bracken Basic Concept Scale (BBCS)**
Author(s): Bracken, B.
Publisher: Psychological Corporation
Copyright Date: 1984
Age Range: 2-6 to 8-0
Purpose: Measures knowledge of general concepts usually acquired during preschool and early school years. Subtests include colors, letter identification,

numbers and counting, comparisons, shapes, direction/position, social/
emotional, size, texture/material, quantity, and time/sequence.
Approximate Testing Time: 20–30 minutes
Type(s) of Response: Nonverbal

Name: Brigance Diagnostic Inventories—Early Development & Basic Skills
Author(s):   Brigance, A.
Publisher: Curriculum Associates
Copyright Date: 1978
Age Range: Early Development, birth to 7; Basic Skills, kindergarten to 6th grade
Purpose: These easel format, criterion-referenced inventories are part of a three-
part series which provides information on mastered and unmastered skills, con-
cepts, and behavior. This information can be used to determine strengths and
weaknesses and to plan instruction.
Approximate Testing Time: Not reported (test is untimed)
Type(s) of Response: Verbal and nonverbal

Name: Carolina Developmental Profile–Revised (CDP)
Author(s):   Harbin, G., & Lillie, D.
Publisher: Kaplan School Supply
Copyright Date: 1980
Age Range: 2 to 5
Purpose: An observation tool for monitoring progress of individual students so
that goals and instruction can be personalized for each child. The skills are di-
vided into major developmental categories: gross motor, fine motor, reasoning,
receptive and expressive language, and social-emotional. A Spanish edition is
available.
Approximate Testing Time: Varies
Type(s) of Response: Verbal and nonverbal

Name: Child Observation Record (COR)
Author(s):   Publisher
Publisher: High/Scope Educational Research Foundation
Copyright Date: 1992
Age Range: 2 1/2 to 6
Purpose: Measures a young child's developmental status using teacher observa-
tions throughout the year. The teacher makes note of child behavior in six do-
mains: initiative, social relations, creative representation, music and movement,
language and literacy, and logic and mathematics. The information gained from
on-going administration of the COR is useful for evaluating programs, monitoring progress, and planning developmentally appropriate experiences for
each child. Initial training is recommended.
Approximate Testing Time: Varies (on-going process)
Type(s) of Response: Rater

Name: Child Development Inventory (CDI)
Author(s):   Ireton, H.
Publisher: Behavior Science Systems

Copyright Date: 1992

Age Range: 15 months to 6 years

Purpose: Measures a young child's present development according to the parent's report. Includes eight scales: Social Development, Self Help, Gross Motor, Fine Motor, Expressive Language, Language Comprehension, Letters, and Numbers. Also a 30-item problems checklist. Profiles child's development, strengths, and problems.

Approximate Testing Time: 45 minutes

Type(s) of Response: Verbal, nonverbal, rater

Name: **Comprehensive Scale of Student Abilities (CSSA)**

Author(s): Hammill, D., & Hresko, W.

Publisher: Pro-Ed

Copyright Date: 1994

Age Range: 6 to 16

Purpose: A rating scale to quantify students' school-related developmental abilities. For use in referral for special education services.

Approximate Testing Time: Varies

Type(s) of Response: Rater

Name: **Developing Skills Checklist (DSC)**

Author(s): Publisher

Publisher: CTB/McGraw-Hill

Copyright Date: 1990

Age Range: 4 to 6-2

Purpose: A comprehensive assessment package that measures a full range of skills and behavior that children typically develop between pre-kindergarten and the end of kindergarten. Test domains include mathematical concepts and operations, language, memory, visual, auditory, print concepts, writing and drawing concepts, plus a social-emotional observational record. A Spanish edition is available.

Approximate Testing Time: 30–45 minutes total administered over 3 sessions

Type(s) of Response: Verbal, nonverbal, rater

Name: **Developmental Observation Checklist System (DOCS)**

Author(s): Hresko, W., et al.

Publisher: Pro-Ed

Copyright Date: 1994

Age Range: Birth to 6

Purpose: A checklist completed by parents or caregivers. DOCS uses a systems approach, assessing three areas: general development, adjustment behavior, and parent stress and support.

Approximate Testing Time: Varies

Type(s) of Response: Rater

Name: **Developmental Profile II (DP–II)**

Author(s): Alpern, G., et al.

Publisher: Western Psychological Services

Copyright Date: 1986

Age Range: Birth to 9-6
Purpose: A parent- or teacher-interview technique designed to screen large populations and to clinically assess individual children's developmental competencies in the areas of physical, self-help, social, academic, and communication development. The DP–II contains enough information to construct individual programs and to provide pre- and post-evaluative information.
Approximate Testing Time: 20–40 minutes
Type(s) of Response: Rater

Name: Early Learning Accomplishment Profile (E-LAP)
Author(s): Glover, M., et al.
Publisher: Kaplan School Supply
Copyright Date: 1980
Age Range: Birth to 36 months
Purpose: A criterion-referenced measure of gross- and fine-motor, cognitive, language, self-help, and social/emotional development.
Approximate Testing Time: Varies
Type(s) of Response: Verbal, nonverbal, rater

Name: Early School Assessment (ESA)*
Author(s): Publisher
Publisher: CTB/McGraw-Hill
Copyright Date: 1990
Age Range: Pre-kindergarten to beginning first grade
Purpose: Assesses pre-math and pre-reading skills to guide the teacher in developing appropriate instruction and identifying children who qualify for Chapter 1 programs. The ESA probes language, visual, auditory, number concepts, logical operations and memory.
Approximate Testing Time: 15–30 minutes for each of 6 sessions
Type(s) of Response: Nonverbal (pencil and booklet)

Name: Gesell Developmental Schedules–Revised
Author(s): Knobloch, H., et al.
Publisher: Developmental Evaluation Materials
Copyright Date: 1987
Age Range: 4 weeks to 36 months
Purpose: Designed to assist in the early identification of developmental problems in infants and young children. The schedules sample a variety of behaviors: adaptive, gross motor, fine motor, language, and personal-social. Test data is gathered through both observation and direct testing. A parent questionnaire can also be administered.
Approximate Testing Time: 45 minutes
Type(s) of Response: Verbal, nonverbal, rater

Name: Hiskey-Nebraska Test of Learning Aptitude (NTLA)
Author(s): Hiskey, M.
Publisher: Author
Copyright Date: 1966
Age Range: 3 to 16

Purpose: An assessment of learning aptitude for deaf and hearing children with separate norms for each. Instructions for the deaf are pantomimed.
Approximate Testing Time: 50 minutes
Type(s) of Response: Nonverbal

Name: **Inventory of Early Development–Revised (IED)**
Author(s): Brigance, A.
Publisher: Curriculum Associates
Copyright Date: 1991
Age Range: Birth to 7
Purpose: In addition to helping identify at-risk infants and preschoolers, the IED tracks development, assists with instructional planning, and assists in communicating with parents. It includes 11 major skill areas: pre-ambulatory motor, gross motor, fine motor, self-help, speech and language, general knowledge and comprehension, social and emotional development, readiness, basic reading, manuscript writing, and basic math.
Approximate Testing Time: Varies
Type(s) of Response: Verbal, nonverbal, and rater

Name: **Learning Accomplishment Profile Diagnostic Assessment Kit (LAP–D)**
Author(s): Sanford, A., et al.
Publisher: Kaplan School Supply
Copyright Date: 1975
Age Range: 2-6 to 6-0
Purpose: Originally a criterion-referenced test, the LAP–D is now norm-referenced. It provides assessment in five areas of development: motor, social, self-help, language, and cognition.
Approximate Testing Time: 45 minutes
Type(s) of Response: Verbal, nonverbal, and rater (parent)

Name: **Metropolitan Readiness Tests–5th Edition (MRT)***
Author(s): Nurss, J., & McGauvran, M.
Publisher: Psychological Corporation
Copyright Date: 1986
Age Range: Preschool to fall of first grade
Purpose: The MRT consists of two levels. Level 1, for preschool through fall of kindergarten, measures a wide range of pre-reading skills. Level 2, for spring of kindergarten through fall of first grade, measures more advanced beginning reading and math skills. The 6th edition, a component of a new program called M-KIDS which will be available sometime in 1995, will be designed for optional one-on-one administration in order to aid teachers in assessing emergent literacy strategies and processes in their students.
Approximate Testing Time: 80–100 minutes total administered over five to seven sittings
Type(s) of Response: Nonverbal (booklet and pencil)

Name: **Mullen Scales of Early Learning**
Author(s): Mullen, E.
Publisher: American Guidance Service

Copyright Date: 1989
Age Range: Birth to 36 months and 36 to 69 months
Purpose: These scales provide an assessment of the child's learning style, strengths, and needs, focusing on five areas: visual receptive organization, visual expressive organization, language receptive organization, language expressive organization, and gross motor base. These scales are available in two levels: infant and preschool. Administration of this test requires training in clinical infant assessment.
Approximate Testing Time: 10–45 minutes
Type(s) of Response: Verbal and nonverbal

Name: System to Plan Early Childhood Services (SPECS)
Author(s):   Bagnato, S., et al.
Publisher: American Guidance Service
Copyright Date: 1990
Age Range: 2 to 6
Purpose: SPECS is a three-part system: first, "Developmental Specs" is a rating scale for the child's developmental and behavioral status and is to be completed by all members of the child's team; next, "Team Specs" provides a summary of the individual ratings of the team members; and finally, "Program Specs" helps the team design an individualized plan and evaluate progress.
Approximate Testing Time: Not reported
Type(s) of Response: Rater

3.   Tests of Academic Achievement

Name: Aprenda: La prueba de logros en espanol*
Author(s):   Publisher
Publisher: Psychological Corporation
Copyright Date: 1990
Age Range: Kindergarten to eighth grade
Purpose: A norm-referenced test of achievement for Spanish-speaking students. This is not a translation of an English language test, rather it was specifically developed for the Spanish-speaking population. Subtests include sounds and letters, word reading, sentence reading, listening to words and stories, and mathematics.
Approximate Testing Time: 2 hours 25 minutes for kindergarten, ranging to 4 hours 45 minutes at higher levels
Type(s) of Response: Nonverbal (pencil and booklet)

Name: Basic Achievement Skills Individual Screener (BASIS)
Author(s):   Sonnenschein, J.
Publisher: Psychological Corporation
Copyright Date: 1983
Age Range: First to twelfth grade
Purpose: A norm- and criterion-referenced test to assess the basic skill areas of reading, mathematics, spelling, and writing.
Approximate Testing Time: Less than one hour
Type(s) of Response: Verbal and nonverbal

Name: California Achievement Tests–5th Edition (CAT–5)*
Author(s): Publisher
Publisher: CTB/McGraw-Hill
Copyright Date: 1992
Age Range: Kindergarten to 12th grade
Purpose: A set of norm-referenced tests that assess mastery of instructional objectives. Content areas include reading, spelling, language, mathematics, study skills, science and social studies. Braille and large print editions are available.
Approximate Testing Time: 1 hour 30 minutes for kindergarten, ranging to 5 hours 30 minutes at higher levels
Type(s) of Response: Nonverbal (pencil and booklet)

Name: Comprehensive Tests of Basic Skills–4th Edition (CTBS/4)*
Author(s): Publisher
Publisher: CTB/McGraw-Hill
Copyright Date: 1990
Age Range: Kindergarten to 12th grade
Purpose: Used to assess academic achievement progress in basic skills areas: reading, language, spelling, mathematics, study skills, science, and social studies. Braille and large print editions are available.
Approximate Testing Time: 1 hour 30 minutes for kindergarten, ranging to 5 hours 15 minutes at higher levels
Type(s) of Response: Nonverbal (pencil and booklet)

Name: CTB Portfolio Assessment
Author(s): Publisher
Publisher: CTB/McGraw-Hill
Copyright Date: 1992
Age Range: 1st to 8th grade
Purpose: A method of assessment that is incorporated into regular classroom activities. Through 8–20 real-life experiences, students create original responses to be included in their portfolios. Emphasis is on development, improvement, and teacher/student co-monitoring progress. May be used alone or to complement more traditional assessment methods.
Approximate Testing Time: Varies (on-going process)
Type(s) of Response: Verbal and nonverbal

Name: Diagnostic Achievement Battery–2nd Edition (DAB–2)*
Author(s): Newcomer, P.
Publisher: Pro-Ed
Copyright Date: 1990
Age Range: 6 to 14
Purpose: Assesses performance in listening, speaking, reading, writing, and mathematics.
Approximate Testing Time: 40–50 minutes
Type(s) of Response: Verbal and nonverbal

Name: Diagnostic Screening Test: Achievement (DSTA)*
Author(s): Gnagey, T., & Gnagey, P.

Publisher: Slosson Educational Publications
Copyright Date: 1977
Age Range: Kindergarten to 12th grade
Purpose: Provides a measure of achievement in science, social studies, literature, and the arts, plus a total achievement score and an estimated mental age.
Approximate Testing Time: 5–10 minutes
Type(s) of Response: Nonverbal (pencil & booklet)

Name: GOALS: A Performance-Based Measure of Achievement*
Author(s):   Publisher
Publisher: Psychological Corporation
Copyright Date: 1992
Age Range: 1st to 12th grade
Purpose: An assessment of academic achievement that uses open-ended questions and requires students to use reasoning skills while writing, drawing diagrams, completing charts and pictures, and editing. The test items are designed to resemble classroom activities. Can be used alone or in combination with more traditional achievement tests.
Approximate Testing Time: One class period
Type(s) of Response: Nonverbal (pencil & booklet)

Name: Hudson Educational Skills Inventory (HESI)
Author(s):   Hudson, F., et al.
Publisher: Pro-Ed
Copyright Date: 1989
Age Range: Kindergarten to 12th
Purpose: A criterion-referenced, "curriculum-based" assessment series to aid teachers in planning appropriate instruction in math, reading, and writing.
Approximate Testing Time: Not reported
Type(s) of Response: Verbal and nonverbal

Name: Iowa Tests of Basic Skills (ITBS)*
Author(s):   Hieronymus, A., et al.
Publisher: Riverside
Copyright Date: 1990
Age Range: Kindergarten to 9th
Purpose: A criterion-and norm-referenced set of tests which measure overall functioning rather than specific content. The tests can provide a continuous measure of the development of fundamental skills necessary for school and life success.
Approximate Testing Time: 125–150 minutes
Type(s) of Response: Nonverbal (pencil and booklet)

Name: Kaufman Test of Educational Achievement (KTEA)
Author(s):   Kaufman, A., & Kaufman, N.
Publisher: American Guidance Service
Copyright Date: 1985
Age Range: 1st to 12th grade
Purpose: A norm-referenced, easel format test of multiple skills. The KTEA contains both a Brief and Comprehensive Form. Either can be used for pro-

gram planning and placement decisions. Additionally, the Brief Form is useful for screening, and the Comprehensive Form for identifying strengths and weaknesses.

Approximate Testing Time: Brief Form, 10–35 minutes; Comprehensive, 20–75 minutes

Type(s) of Response: Verbal and nonverbal

Name: Metropolitan Achievement Tests–7th Edition (MAT–7)*
Author(s):   Prescott, G., et al.
Publisher: Psychological Corporation
Copyright Date: 1992
Age Range: Kindergarten to grade 12-9
Purpose: The MAT-7 provides a global assessment of the student's skill development in reading, mathematics, language, social studies, and science. The battery is useful for screening, monitoring group performance, and evaluating programs. A Short Form is also available.
Approximate Testing Time: 1 hour 35 minutes for kindergarten, ranging to 4 hours 10 minutes at higher levels
Type(s) of Response: Nonverbal (pencil and booklet)

Name: Monitoring Basic Skills Progress (MBSP)
Author(s):   Fuchs, L., et al.
Publisher: Pro-Ed
Copyright Date: 1990
Age Range: 1st to 6th grade
Purpose: A computer-assisted measurement program that both tests and monitors progress in reading, math, and spelling. Students are tested at the computer, each time with a different test form. Results are computer-plotted graphically over time so that teachers can easily monitor progress. The program also reports a performance analysis and remedial program recommendations.
Approximate Testing Time: Varies
Type(s) of Response: Nonverbal (keyboard)

Name: Peabody Individual Achievement Test–Revised
Author(s):   Markwardt, F.
Publisher: American Guidance Service
Copyright Date: 1989
Age Range: Kindergarten to 12th grade
Purpose: Provides a wide-range screening of basic curriculum areas: mathematics, reading recognition, reading comprehension, spelling, general information, and written expression. This test is useful for individual evaluation, guidance and counseling, admissions and transfers, grouping students, and progress evaluation.
Approximate Testing Time: 30–40 minutes
Type(s) of Response: Verbal and nonverbal

Name: Riverside Performance Assessment Series (R–PAS)*
Author(s):   Publisher

Publisher: Riverside
Copyright Date: 1993
Age Range: 1st to 12th grade
Purpose: A set of free-response assessments for reading, mathematics, and writing. For each activity, students are presented with a scenario in which they must take an active part, using strategic thinking and problem-solving skills while writing and completing charts and diagrams. A Spanish edition is available.
Approximate Testing Time: Varies
Type(s) of Response: Nonverbal

Name: SRA Achievement Series*
Author(s): Naslund, R., et al.
Publisher: Science Research Associates
Copyright Date: 1978
Age Range: Kindergarten to 12th grade
Purpose: A norm- and criterion-referenced test battery which assesses skill development in reading, mathematics, language arts, social studies, sciences, and use of reference materials.
Approximate Testing Time: 2 hours to 2 hours 47 minutes for grades K–3
Type(s) of Response: Nonverbal (pencil and booklet)

Name: The Stanford Early School Achievement Test–3rd Edition (SESAT)*
Author(s): Madden, R., et al.
Publisher: Psychological Corporation
Copyright Date: 1989
Age Range: Kindergarten to 1st grade
Purpose: The first of a series of three tests (SESAT, SAT, TASK) which provide comprehensive, continuous assessment of skill development in key content areas: sounds and letters, word reading, sentence reading, mathematics, environment, and listening to words and stories.
Approximate Testing Time: Level 1 (K-0 to K-5), 3 hours 10 minutes; Level 2 (K-5 to 1-5), 3 hours 45 minutes
Type(s) of Response: Nonverbal (pencil and booklet)

Name: Wechsler Individual Achievement Test (WIAT)
Author(s): Publisher
Publisher: Psychological Corporation
Copyright Date: 1992
Age Range: 5 to 19
Purpose: A comprehensive battery for measuring academic difficulties. Measures eight areas: basic reading, mathematics reasoning, spelling, reading comprehension, numerical operations, listening comprehension, oral expression, and written expression. A shorter screening battery can also be given.
Approximate Testing Time: Comprehensive Battery, 30–50 minutes for young children; Screener, 10–18 minutes
Type(s) of Response: Verbal and nonverbal

Name: Wide Range Achievement Test–3 (WRAT–3)* (Group administration for spelling and arithmetic sections only)

Author(s):   Wilkinson, G.
Publisher: Jastak Associates
Copyright Date: 1940, 1984, 1993
Age Range: 5 to 75
Purpose: Measures achievement with a focus on the coding skills of reading, spelling, and arithmetic.
Approximate Testing Time: 15–30 minutes
Type(s) of Response: Verbal and nonverbal

Name: **Woodcock-Johnson Psycho-Educational Battery–Revised (WJ–R): Tests of Achievement**
Author(s):   Woodcock, R., & Johnson, M.
Publisher: DLM Teaching Resources
Copyright Date: 1990
Age Range: 2 to 90
Purpose: An easel-format set of tests for assessing achievement level in reading, mathematics, written language and knowledge. The standard battery yields five cluster scores and includes nine tests. A supplemental battery of five additional tests can also be administered if additional diagnostic information is needed. Computer scoring and books on test interpretation are available.
Approximate Testing Time: (*Information not found*)
Type(s) of Response: Verbal and nonverbal

Name: **Work Sampling System**
Author(s):   Meisels, S.
Publisher: Author
Copyright Date: 1992
Age Range: 3 to 9
Purpose: An on-going evaluation process designed as an alternative to standardized achievement tests. The System is composed of three elements: developmental checklists, portfolios, and summary reports, which are all intended to be classroom-focused and relevant to instruction.
Approximate Testing Time: Varies (on-going process)
Type(s) of Response: Verbal, nonverbal, rater

4.   Tests of Achievement in Language

Name: **Bankson Language Test–2nd Edition (BLT–2)**
Author(s):   Bankson, N.
Publisher: Pro-Ed
Copyright Date: 1977, 1990
Age Range: 3-0 to 6-11
Purpose: Useful for establishing the presence of a language disorder or need for further testing. The BLT–2 provides a measure of a child's linguistic skills in terms of semantic knowledge, morphological/syntactical rules, and pragmatics. A short form is also available for screening purposes.
Approximate Testing Time: 30 minutes
Type(s) of Response: Verbal and nonverbal

Name: Clark-Madison Test of Oral Language
Author(s):   Clark, J., & Madison, C.
Publisher: Pro-Ed
Copyright Date: 1981, 1984
Age Range: 4 to 8-11
Purpose: Provides a measure of expressive language capacity as evaluated through a spoken exchange. Categories evaluated are syntax, modifiers, determiners and prepositions, verbs, pronouns, and inflections.
Approximate Testing Time: 10–20 minutes
Type(s) of Response: Verbal

Name: Clinical Evaluation of Language Fundamentals–Preschool (CELF–Preschool)
Author(s):   Wiig, E., et al.
Publisher: Psychological Corporation
Copyright Date: 1992
Age Range: 3 to 6
Purpose: Assesses a wide range of expressive and receptive language skills: basic concepts, sentence structure, word structure, formulating labels, recalling sentences in context, and linguistic concepts.
Approximate Testing Time: 30–45 minutes
Type(s) of Response: Verbal and nonverbal

Name: Comprehensive Receptive and Expressive Vocabulary Test (CREVT)
Author(s):   Wallace, G., & Hammill, D.
Publisher: Pro-Ed
Copyright Date: 1993
Age Range: 4 to 17
Purpose: Used to identify students with difficulties, define strengths and weaknesses, and measure progress. The CREVT measures two skills: receptive language, for which the student points to the correct picture for the word spoken by the examiner, and expressive language, for which the student defines the word spoken.
Approximate Testing Time: 20–30 minutes
Type(s) of Response: Verbal and nonverbal

Name: Diagnostic Screening Test: Language–2nd Edition (DSTL)*
Author(s):   Gnagey, T., & Gnagey, P.
Publisher: Slosson Educational Publications
Copyright Date: 1977, 1980
Age Range: 1st to 12th grade
Purpose: Provides a measure of language achievement in terms of sentence structure, grammar, punctuation, capitalization, and formal spelling rules.
Approximate Testing Time: 10–20 minutes
Type(s) of Response: Nonverbal (pencil and booklet)

Name: Expressive One-Word Picture Vocabulary Test–Revised (EOWPVT–R)
Author(s):   Gardner, M.

Publisher: Academic Therapy Publications
Copyright Date: 1979, 1990
Age Range: 2-0 to 11-11
Purpose: Provides a measure of a child's expressive vocabulary through the presentation of picture cards. The test can be used to appraise definitional and interpretational skills, estimate fluency in English, and indicate possible speech or language difficulties.
Approximate Testing Time: 5–10 minutes
Type(s) of Response: Verbal

Name: **Illinois Test of Psycholinguistic Abilities (ITPA)**
Author(s): Kirk, S., et al.
Publisher: University of Illinois Press
Copyright Date: 1968
Age Range: 2-4 to 10-3
Purpose: Assesses both verbal and nonverbal psycholinguistic ability. The "representation level" tests skills with language symbols, and the "automatic level" assesses skills in retention and retrieval of language.
Approximate Testing Time: 1 hour
Type(s) of Response: Verbal and nonverbal

Name: **Kaufman Survey of Early Academic and Language Skills (K-SEALS)**
Author(s): Kaufman, A., & Kaufman, N.
Publisher: American Guidance Service
Copyright Date: 1993
Age Range: 3 to 6
Purpose: A norm-reference measure of children's language (expressive and receptive), articulation, and pre-academic skills with numbers, letters, and words.
Approximate Testing Time: 15–25 minutes
Type(s) of Response: Verbal and nonverbal

Name: **Kindergarten Language Screening Test (KLST)**
Author(s): Gauthier, S., & Madison, C.
Publisher: Pro-Ed
Copyright Date: 1983
Age Range: Kindergarten
Purpose: A screener to identify children with language problems either in reception or expression.
Approximate Testing Time: Less than five minutes
Type(s) of Response: Verbal and nonverbal

Name: Language Arts Assessment Portfolio
Author(s): Karlsen, B.
Publisher: American Guidance Service
Copyright Date: 1992
Age Range: 1st to 6th grade
Purpose: A classroom assessment system of student progress in four areas of language arts: reading, writing, listening, and speaking. It provides a means for in-

dividualizing both assessment and instruction, using teacher evaluation and a portfolio of student work documenting student growth.

Approximate Testing Time: Varies (on-going process)

Type(s) of Response: Verbal, nonverbal, rater

Name: **Oral and Written Language Scales (OWLS)**

Author(s):   Carrow-Woolfolk, E.

Publisher: American Guidance Service

Copyright Date: 1994

Age Range: 3 to 21

Purpose: OWLS samples a wide range of language tasks: listening comprehension, oral expression, and written expression. The scales assess semantic, syntactic, pragmatic, and supralinguistic (higher-order thinking) aspects of language.

Approximate Testing Time: Listening Comprehension, 5–15 minutes; Oral Expression, 10–25 minutes. (Written Expression time not reported.)

Type(s) of Response: Verbal and nonverbal

Name: **Peabody Picture Vocabulary Test–Revised (PPVT–R)**

Author(s):   Dunn, L., & Dunn, L.

Publisher: American Guidance Service

Copyright Date: 1981

Age Range: 2-6 to 40

Purpose: An easel format, receptive vocabulary test intended to measure verbal ability and scholastic aptitude. A suitable test for students with reading or writing difficulties or those who are severely physically impaired since any method of indicating "yes" or "no" is an acceptable response.

Approximate Testing Time: 10–15 minutes

Type(s) of Response: Verbal and nonverbal

Name: **Picture Articulation and Language Screening Test (PALST)**

Author(s):   Rodgers, W.

Publisher: Pro-Ed

Copyright Date: 1976

Age Range: 1st grade

Purpose: A test of articulation of sounds and formation of language which presents the child with pictures in order to elicit sounds spontaneously. Tests 27 different phonemes.

Approximate Testing Time: Less than two minutes

Type(s) of Response: Verbal

Name: **Pre-LAS (Language Assessment Scales)**

Author(s):   Duncan, S., & DeAvila, F.

Publisher: CTB/McGraw-Hill

Copyright Date: 1987

Age Range: Preschool to 1st grade

Purpose: Assesses the oral language proficiency of children in three areas: morphology, syntax, and semantics. There are two separate tests, English and Spanish. Useful for identifying limited or non-English speaking students.

Approximate Testing Time: 10 minutes
Type(s) of Response: Verbal and nonverbal

Name: **Preschool Language Scale–3 (PLS–3)**
Author(s): Zimmerman, I., et al.
Publisher: Psychological Corporation
Copyright Date: 1992
Age Range: Birth to 6
Purpose: A norm-referenced test of pre-language skills (attention, vocal development, social communication), and receptive and expressive skills (semantics, structure, and integrative thinking skills). Uses play-like test activities. Spanish edition available.
Approximate Testing Time: 20–30 minutes
Type(s) of Response: Verbal and nonverbal

Name: **Prueba del Desarrollo Inicial del Lenguaje**
Author(s): Hresko, W., et al.
Publisher: Pro-Ed
Copyright Date: 1982
Age Range: 3 to 7
Purpose: A measure of both receptive and expressive spoken Spanish.
Approximate Testing Time: 15 minutes
Type(s) of Response: Verbal and nonverbal

Name: **Receptive-Expressive Emergent Language Test (REEL–2)**
Author(s): Bzoch, K., & League, R.
Publisher: Pro-Ed
Copyright Date: 1972, 1991
Age Range: Birth to 3
Purpose: Measures children's language development in the first three years of life. The test covers areas of receptive, expressive, and inner language through an interview with a parent or other caregiver. The REEL–2 is useful for developing interventions for at-risk infants and toddlers.
Approximate Testing Time: 30–40 minutes
Type(s) of Response: Rater

Name: **Receptive One-Word Picture Vocabulary Test (ROWPVT)**
Author(s): Gardner, M.
Publisher: Academic Therapy Publications
Copyright Date: 1985
Age Range: 2-0 to 11-11
Purpose: Designed as a companion test to the EOWPVT, this test assesses receptive language skills and is especially useful for bilingual, speech-impaired, immature and withdrawn, and emotionally or physically impaired children.
Approximate Testing Time: 20 minutes
Type(s) of Response: Nonverbal

Name: **Screening Kit of Language Development (SKOLD)**
Author(s): Bliss, L., & Allen, D.

Publisher: University Park Press
Copyright Date: 1983
Age Range: 2 to 5
Purpose: Designed to identify language disorders and delays. Includes norms for speakers of both Standard and Black English.
Approximate Testing Time: 15 minutes
Type(s) of Response: Verbal

Name: Speech-Ease Screening Inventory
Author(s):   Speech-Ease
Publisher: Pro-Ed
Copyright Date: 1985
Age Range: Kindergarten to 1st grade
Purpose: A quick assessment of articulation, expressive and receptive vocabulary, and auditory comprehension abilities for identifying children in need of further diagnostic evaluation.
Approximate Testing Time: 7 to 10 minutes
Type(s) of Response: Verbal and nonverbal

Name: Test de Vocabulario en Imagenes Peabody (TVIP)
Author(s):   Dunn, L., et al.
Publisher: American Guidance Service
Copyright Date: 1986
Age Range: 2-5 to 18
Purpose: For use with Spanish-speaking or bilingual students. The TVIP is based on the PPVT–R; however, each test item has been appropriately selected for Spanish-speaking communities.
Approximate Testing Time: 10–15 minutes
Type(s) of Response: Nonverbal

Name: Test of Auditory Comprehension of Language-Revised (TACL-R)
Author(s):   Carrow-Woolfolk, E.
Publisher: DLM Teaching Resources
Copyright Date: 1985
Age Range: 3-0 to 9-11
Purpose: Provides a measure of receptive language functioning in a number of areas including command of vocabulary, concepts, prepositions, agreement, active and passive voice, interrogatives, and coordination.
Approximate Testing Time: 25 minutes
Type(s) of Response: Nonverbal

Name: Test of Early Language Development–2nd Edition (TELD–2)
Author(s):   Hresko, W., et al.
Publisher: Pro-ed
Copyright Date: 1981, 1991
Age Range: 2-0 to 7-11
Purpose: Provides an overall score of language proficiency as well as a diagnostic profile of a child's language skills in both reception and expression.

Approximate Testing Time: 20 minutes
Type(s) of Response: Verbal and nonverbal

Name: Test of Early Written Language (TEWL)
Author(s):   Hresko, W.
Publisher: Pro-Ed
Copyright Date: 1988
Age Range: 3 to 7
Purpose: An assessment of emergent written language skills. Useful for measuring progress and evaluating programs and appropriate for identifying mildly handicapped students.
Approximate Testing Time: 10–30 minutes
Type(s) of Response: Verbal and nonverbal

Name: Test of Language Development–Primary, 2nd Edition (TOLD–P:2)
Author(s):   Newcomer, P., & Hammill, D.
Publisher: Pro-Ed
Copyright Date: 1977, 1988
Age Range: 4-0 to 8-11
Purpose: Designed to identify and isolate disorders through testing the basic linguistic skills of listening, speaking, semantics, syntax, and phonology
Approximate Testing Time: 30–60 minutes
Type(s) of Response: Verbal and nonverbal

Name: Test of Phonological Awareness (TOPA)*
Author(s):   Torgesen, J., & Bryant, B.
Publisher: Pro-Ed
Copyright Date: 1994
Age Range: Kindergarten to 2nd grade
Purpose: Provides a measure of a child's ability to hear individual sounds in words. Since this ability is related to ease in learning to read, this test can be used to identify children in kindergarten who may benefit from specialized instruction to prepare them for reading. One test is available for kindergarten and another for 1st and 2nd grade.
Approximate Testing Time: 20 minutes
Type(s) of Response: Nonverbal

Name: Test of Pragmatic Language (TOPL)
Author(s):   Phelps-Terasaki, D., & Phelps-Gunn, T.
Publisher: Pro-Ed
Copyright Date: 1992
Age Range: 5-0 to 13-11
Purpose: A comprehensive test of the student's pragmatic language, meaning language used socially and for a purpose. It is a measure of not just what is said, but why.
Approximate Testing Time: 45 minutes
Type(s) of Response: Verbal

5. Tests of Achievement in Reading

Name: **The Classroom Reading Inventory–5th Edition**
Author(s): Silvaroli, N.
Publisher: Wm. C. Brown

Name: **Gilmore Oral Reading Test**
Author(s): Gilmore, J., & Gilmore, E.
Publisher: Psychological Corporation
Copyright Date: 1968
Age Range: 1st to 8th grade
Purpose: Assess a student's accuracy, comprehension, and rate of reading. Types of errors are analyzed and categorized as substitutions, mispronunciations, words aided by the examiner, omissions, repetitions, hesitations, insertions, and disregard of punctuation.
Approximate Testing Time: 15–20 minutes
Type(s) of Response: Verbal

Name: **Gray Oral Reading Test–Revised (GORT–R)**
Author(s): Wiederholt, L., & Bryant, B.
Publisher: Pro-Ed
Copyright Date: 1967, 1986
Age Range: 7-0 to 7-11
Purpose: This test requires students to read passages aloud and answer literal, inferential, critical, and affective comprehension questions. The GORT–R identifies students who may benefit from additional help, indicates strengths and weaknesses, and monitors progress.
Approximate Testing Time: 15–30 minutes
Type(s) of Response: Verbal

Name: **New Sucher-Allred Reading Placement Inventory**
Author(s): Sucher, F., & Allred, R.
Publisher: The Economy Company
Copyright Date: 1968, 1973, 1981
Age Range: Primer to 9th grade
Purpose: This test of reading ability has two forms and includes word recognition and oral reading sections. The student's independent, instructional, and frustration levels of reading are assessed.
Approximate Testing Time: 20 minutes
Type(s) of Response: Verbal

Name: **Slosson Oral Reading Test–Revised (SORT–R)**
Author(s): Slosson, R.
Publisher: Slosson Educational Publications
Copyright Date: 1994
Age Range: Preschool to adult
Purpose: A quick estimate of target-word recognition useful for identifying individuals with reading difficulties.

Approximate Testing Time: 3–5 minutes
Type(s) of Response: Verbal

Name: Stanford Diagnostic Reading Test–3rd Edition (SDRT)*
Author(s):   Karlsen, B., & Gardner, E.
Publisher: Psychological Corporation
Copyright Date: 1985
Age Range: Late 1st grade to post high-school
Purpose: A norm- and criterion-referenced test designed to indicate areas of strength and weakness in reading decoding, vocabulary, comprehension, and rate of reading. The SDRT is primarily for use with low achievers and thus contains a greater number of easy items than some other achievement tests.
Approximate Testing Time: 105 minutes for grades K-3
Type(s) of Response: Nonverbal (pencil and booklet)

Name: Test of Early Reading Ability–2nd Edition (TERA–2)
Author(s):   Reid, D., et al.
Publisher: Pro-Ed
Copyright Date: 1981, 1989
Age Range: 3 to 9-11
Purpose: Provides a measure of the student's reading ability in terms of contextual meaning, alphabet, and the conventions of print.
Approximate Testing Time: 15–30 minutes
Type(s) of Response: Verbal

Name: Test of Early Reading Ability–Deaf or Hard of Hearing (TERA–D)
Author(s):   Reid, D., et al.
Publisher: Pro-Ed
Copyright Date: 1991
Age Range: 3-0 to 13-11.
Purpose: An adaptation of the TERA–2 designed for simultaneous communication or American Sign Language.
Approximate Testing Time: 20–30 minutes
Type(s) of Response: Verbal or sign language

Name: Woodcock Reading Mastery Tests–Revised (WRMT–R)
Author(s):   Woodcock, R.
Publisher: American Guidance Service
Copyright Date: 1987
Age Range: 5 to 75+
Purpose: Provides an assessment of reading skills in six areas: visual-auditory learning, letter identification, word identification, word attack, word comprehension, and passage comprehension. Computer scoring is available.
Approximate Testing Time: 10–30 minutes
Type(s) of Response: Verbal

6.   Tests of Achievement in Spelling

Name: Diagnostic Screening Test: Spelling–3rd Edition (DSTS)*
Author(s):   Gnagey, T.

Publisher: Slosson Educational Publications
Copyright Date: 1979
Age Range: 1st to 12th grade
Purpose: A quick measure of spelling ability that assesses phonetic and sight spelling. Additional verbal and written spelling scores can be obtained when the test is administered individually.
Approximate Testing Time: 5–10 minutes
Type(s) of Response: Nonverbal (and verbal when administered individually)

Name: **Test of Written Spelling–3rd Edition (TWS–3)***
Author(s):   Larsen, S., & Hammill, D.
Publisher: Pro-Ed
Copyright Date: 1994
Age Range: 1st to 12th grade
Purpose: An assessment of spelling ability which includes a comparison between ability with predictable sound-letter patterns and with less predictable patterns.
Approximate Testing Time: 20 minutes
Type(s) of Response: Nonverbal

7.   Tests of Achievement in Mathematics

Name: **Diagnostic Test of Arithmetic Strategies (DTAS)**
Author(s):   Ginsburg, H., & Mathews, S.
Publisher: Pro-Ed
Copyright Date: 1984
Age Range: 1st to 6th grade
Purpose: Provides a measure of the student's procedural ability in addition, subtraction, multiplication, and division. Identifies faulty strategies as well as potential strengths. Information on remedial instruction is included in the manual.
Approximate Testing Time: 79–90 minutes
Type(s) of Response: Verbal and nonverbal

Name: **Diagnostic Screening Test: Math–3rd Edition (DSTM)***
Author(s):   Gnagey, T.
Publisher: Slosson Educational Publications
Copyright Date: 1980
Age Range: 1st to 10th grade
Purpose: Assesses students' conceptual and computational skills in basic math processes and special areas such as time and money.
Approximate Testing Time: 5–20 minutes
Type(s) of Response: Nonverbal (pencil and booklet)

Name: **Keymath–Revised**
Author(s):   Conolly, A.
Publisher: American Guidance Service
Copyright Date: 1988
Age Range: Kindergarten to 9th grade

Purpose: A norm- and criterion-referenced, easel-format test of math skills in three areas: basic concepts, operations, and applications. Two forms and computer scoring are available.
Approximate Testing Time: 35–50 minutes
Type(s) of Response: Verbal and nonverbal

Name: Sequential Assessment of Mathematics Inventory (SAMI)
Author(s): Reisman, F.
Publisher: Psychological Corporation
Copyright Date: 1985
Age Range: Kindergarten to 8th grade
Purpose: A measure of mathematical ability in eight areas: mathematical language, ordinality, number and notation, computation, measurement, geometric concepts, mathematical applications, and word problems.
Approximate Testing Time: 20 to 60 minutes
Type(s) of Response: Verbal and nonverbal

Name: Test of Early Mathematics Ability–2nd Edition (TEMA–2)
Author(s): Ginsburg, H., & Baroody, A.
Publisher: Pro-Ed
Copyright Date: 1983, 1990
Age Range: 3-0 to 8-11
Purpose: Measures both formal and informal math skills and identifies specific strengths and weaknesses. Useful for assessing specific difficulties, measuring progress, designing instruction and remediation, and identifying gifted students. A book of remedial techniques and instructional activities for each area tested is also available.
Approximate Testing Time: 20–30 minutes
Type(s) of Response: Verbal and nonverbal

8. Tests for Identifying Giftedness

Name: Creativity Assessment Packet (CAP)*
Author(s): Williams, F.
Publisher: Pro-Ed
Copyright Date: 1980
Age Range: 6 to 18
Purpose: The CAP is a set of three instruments for identifying creativity. Two are completed by the student: the Test of Divergent Thinking and the Test of Divergent Feeling. The third instrument, the Williams Scale, is a rating scale completed by teachers or parents. Factors measured include fluency, flexibility, elaboration, originality, vocabulary, and comprehension.
Approximate Testing Time: Divergent Thinking, 25 minutes for younger students; Divergent Feeling, 20–30 minutes; Williams Scale, 30 minutes
Type(s) of Response: Nonverbal (pencil and booklet), rater

Name: Screening Assessment for Gifted Elementary Students–Primary (SAGES–P)*
Author(s): Johnson, S., & Corn, A.

Publisher: Pro-Ed
Copyright Date: 1992
Age Range: 5-0 to 8-11
Purpose: Useful for helping to identify gifted children in grades K to 3. SAGES–P contains two sections: a reasoning subtest which serves as a measure of aptitude, and a general information subset which serves as a measure of achievement.
Approximate Testing Time: 30 minutes
Type(s) of Response: Nonverbal (pencil and booklet)

Name: **Torrance Tests of Creative Thinking***
Author(s):   Torrance, E.
Publisher: Scholastic Testing Service
Copyright Date: 1974, 1990, 1992
Age Range: Kindergarten to adult
Purpose: Evaluates creative potential in a wide variety of areas. The test has 2 sections: Figural (involves thinking creatively with pictures) and Verbal (involves thinking creatively with words). Tests of thinking creatively with actions and movement are also available for ages three to kindergarten.
Approximate Testing Time: Figural, 30 minutes; Verbal, 45 minutes
Type(s) of Response: Nonverbal

9.   Tests of Perceptual and/or Motor Skills

Name: Bruininks-Oseretsky Test of Motor Proficiency
Author(s):   Bruininks, R.
Publisher: American Guidance Service
Copyright Date: 1978
Age Range: 4 1/2 to 14 1/2
Purpose: A measure of both gross- and fine-motor functioning. Skills sampled include running, speed and agility, balance, bilateral coordination, strength, upper limb coordination, response speed, visual-motor control, and upper limb speed and dexterity.
Approximate Testing Time: 45–60 minutes
Type(s) of Response: Nonverbal

Name: **Developmental Test of Visual Perception–2nd Edition (DTVP–2)**
Author(s):   Hammill, D., et al.
Publisher: Pro-Ed
Copyright Date: 1993
Age Range: 4 to 10
Purpose: An eight-subtest measure of visual-perception and visual-motor integration skills. Useful for identifying children with difficulties in these areas, determining eligibility for special programs, and monitoring intervention progress.
Approximate Testing Time: 35 minutes
Type(s) of Response: Nonverbal

Name: **Developmental Test of Visual-Motor Integration (VMI)***
Author(s):   Beery, K., & Buktenica, N.

Publisher: Modern Curriculum Press
Copyright Date: 1967, 1982
Age Range: 2 to 15
Purpose: Designed to determine the level at which visual-motor perception and motor performance are integrated. The VMI consists of geometric figures that are copied by the student as accurately as possible.
Approximate Testing Time: 15–20 minutes
Type(s) of Response: Nonverbal

Name: Goldman-Fristoe-Woodcock Test of Auditory Discrimination (G-F-WTAD)
Author(s): Goldman, R., Fristoe, M., & Woodcock, R.
Publisher: American Guidance Service
Copyright Date: 1990
Age Range: 3-8 to adult
Purpose: Evaluates an individual's ability to discriminate among speech sounds in both quiet and noisy backgrounds. Words are presented on cassette.
Approximate Testing Time: 15 minutes
Type(s) of Response: Nonverbal

Name: Motor-Free Visual Perception Test (MVPT)
Author(s): Colarusso, R., & Hammill, D.
Publisher: Academic Therapy Publications
Copyright Date: 1972
Age Range: 4-0 to 8-0
Purpose: Useful for screening or diagnosis with learning disabled, mentally challenged, or physically challenged children. The MVPT measures visual perception by presenting a student with a line drawing which he or she must match with an identical drawing presented in a multiple choice format.
Approximate Testing Time: 10 minutes
Type(s) of Response: Nonverbal

Name: Peabody Developmental Motor Scales (PDMS)
Author(s): Folio, M., & Fewell, R.
Publisher: DLM Teaching Resources
Copyright Date: 1983
Age Range: Birth to 83 months
Purpose: Assesses both gross- and fine-motor skills in children. The PDMS was developed to meet the programming needs of handicapped children in physical education. Gross-motor items are classified into five skill categories: reflexes, balance, nonlocomotor, locomotor, and receipt and propulsion of objects. Fine-motor items are classified into four skill categories: grasping, hand use, eye-hand coordination, and manual dexterity.
Approximate Testing Time: 45–60 minutes
Type(s) of Response: Nonverbal

Name: Test of Auditory-Perceptual Skills (TAPS)
Author(s): Gardner, M.
Publisher: Pro-Ed

Copyright Date: 1985
Age Range: 4 to 12
Purpose: Useful for identifying auditory-perceptual difficulties, imperceptions of auditory modality, and language and learning problems.
Approximate Testing Time: 10–15 minutes
Type(s) of Response: Verbal

Name: Test of Gross Motor Development (TGMD)
Author(s):   Ulrich, D.
Publisher: Pro-Ed
Copyright Date: 1985
Age Range: 3 to 10
Purpose: Assesses appropriate motor skills in the areas of locomotion and object control. The TGMD is useful for identifying children who are significantly behind their peers and may be eligible for special physical education services.
Approximate Testing Time: 15 minutes
Type(s) of Response: Nonverbal

10.   Tests of Behavior and Conduct

Name: AAMR Adaptive Behavior Scale–School Edition (ABS–S:2)
Author(s):   Nihira, K., & Lambert, N.
Publisher: American Association on Mental Retardation
Copyright Date: 1993
Age Range: 3 to 16
Purpose: A 16-domain measure of social competence and independence for use with mentally retarded, emotionally maladjusted, and developmentally disabled individuals.
Approximate Testing Time: 60–90 minutes
Type(s) of Response: Rater (teacher or other school personnel)

Name: Adaptive Behavior Inventory for Children (ABIC)
Author(s):   Mercer, J., and Lewis, J.
Publisher: Psychological Corporation
Copyright Date: 1978
Age Range: 5 to 11
Purpose: A rating scale covering six areas: family, peers, community, school, earner-consumer, and self-maintenance. A Spanish edition is available.
Approximate Testing Time: Varies
Type(s) of Response: Rater

Name: Anxiety Scales for Children and Adults (ASCA)*
Author(s)   Battle, J.
Publisher: Pro-Ed
Copyright Date: 1993
Age Range: School age to adult
Purpose: A series of self-report scales to identify individuals experiencing intense anxiety.

Approximate Testing Time: 15 minutes
Type(s) of Response: Nonverbal (pencil and booklet)

Name: Behavior Assessment System for Children (BASC)
Author(s):   Reynolds, C., & Kamphaus, R.
Publisher: American Guidance Service
Copyright Date: 1992
Age Range: 4 to 18
Purpose: A set of rating scales for describing an individual's behavior and emotions. Contains teacher, parent, and self-reports plus directly observed classroom behavior and a structured developmental history. Computer scoring is available.
Approximate Testing Time: Varies
Type(s) of Response: Nonverbal (pencil and booklet), rater

Name: Comprehensive Test of Adaptive Behavior (CTAB)
Author(s):   Adams, G.
Publisher: Psychological Corporation
Copyright Date: 1984
Age Range: Birth to 60
Purpose: Assesses level of independent behavior in individuals with mental and/or physical disabilities. Includes both a student test and a parent/guardian survey.
Approximate Testing Time: Varies
Type(s) of Response: Rater

Name: Conners' Rating Scales
Author(s):   Conners, C.
Publisher: Multi-Health Systems
Copyright Date: 1989
Age Range: 3 to 17
Purpose: A standard scale for identifying attention deficit disorder and other problem behaviors. The test can also be used for charting progress and evaluating intervention programs. A "Hyperactivity Index" is included or can be administered separately as "Conners' Abbreviated Symptom Questionnaire" (CASQ). Long and short forms of the CRS are available for both teachers and parents.
Approximate Testing Time: Varies
Type(s) of Response: Rater

Name: Coping Inventory
Author(s):   Zeitlin, S.
Publisher: Scholastic Testing Service
Copyright Date: 1985
Age Range: 3 to 16
Purpose: An observation form for assessing behavior patterns used by children to deal with personal and environmental needs. Coping style is described on three scales: productive-nonproductive, active-passive, and flexible-rigid.

Approximate Testing Time: Varies
Type(s) of Response: Rater

Name: **Culture-Free Self-Esteem Inventories–2nd Edition (CFSEI–2)**
Author(s):   Battle, J.
Publisher: Pro-Ed
Copyright Date: 1992
Age Range: 5-0 to adult
Purpose: A series of self-report scales which measure an individual's self-esteem in a variety of contexts: general, peers, school, and parents. A "lie" (defensiveness) scale is also included.
Approximate Testing Time: 15–20 minutes
Type(s) of Response: Verbal and nonverbal

Name: **Depression and Anxiety in Youth Scale (DAYS)**
Author(s):   Newcomer, P., et al.
Publisher: Pro-Ed
Copyright Date: 1994
Age Range: 6-0 to 19-0
Purpose: Used to identify major depressive disorder and overanxious disorders in children. The teacher and parent scales have a true/false format regarding the presence or absence of a symptom. Students also report the degree to which they experience certain feelings.
Approximate Testing Time: Student scale, 15–20 minutes for readers and 30 minutes when items must be read to the student; teacher and parent scales, 5–10 minutes
Type(s) of Response: Nonverbal or verbal, rater

Name: **Early Coping Inventory**
Author(s):   Zeitlin, S., et al.
Publisher: Scholastic Testing Service
Copyright Date: 1988
Age Range: 4 months to 36 months
Purpose: An observation form for assessing young children's coping (adaptive) behaviors in common situations. Three areas are assessed: sensorimotor organization, reactive behaviors, and self-initiated behaviors.
Approximate Testing Time: Varies
Type(s) of Response: Rater

Name: **Normative Adaptive Behavior Checklist (NABC)**
Author(s):   Adams, G.
Publisher: Psychological Corporation
Copyright Date: 1984
Age Range: Birth to 21
Purpose: A brief descriptive scale which identifies individuals with deficiencies in adaptive behavior and independent living skills through a questionnaire format.
Approximate Testing Time: 20 minutes
Type(s) of Response: Rater

Name: Scales of Independent Behavior (SIB)
Author(s): Bruininks, R., et al.
Publisher: DLM Teaching Resources
Copyright Date: 1984
Age Range: Infant to adult
Purpose: Assesses functional independence and adaptive behavior in motor, so-
cial, and communication, personal-living and community-living skills. A Span-
ish edition is available.
Approximate Testing Time: 45–50 minutes
Type(s) of Response: Rater

Name: Social-Emotional Dimension Scale (SEDS)
Author(s): Hudson, J., & Roberts, T.
Publisher: Pro-Ed
Copyright Date: 1986
Age Range: 5 1/2 to 18 1/2
Purpose: A rating scale to screen for students at risk for conduct disorders, be-
havior problems, or emotional disturbance.
Approximate Testing Time: Not reported
Type(s) of Response: Rater

Name: Teacher's Report Form
Author(s): Achenbach, T., & Edelbrock, C.
Publisher: Author
Copyright Date: 1986
Age Range: 6 to 11 and 12 to 16
Purpose: Provides a profile of problem-behavior syndromes, adaptive behavior,
and school performance. Eight scales are included: anxious, social withdrawal,
unpopular, self-destructive, obsessive-compulsive, inattentive, nervous-over-
active, and aggressive.
Approximate Testing Time: Varies
Type(s) of Response: Rater

Name: Test of Early Socioemotional Development (TOESD)
Author(s): Hresko, W., & Brown, L.
Publisher: Pro-Ed
Copyright Date: 1984
Age Range: 3-0 to 7-11
Purpose: Identifies young children with behavior problems, documents the de-
gree of behavioral difficulty, identifies specific settings in which problem be-
haviors most often occur, and evaluates the impressions a child makes on
different observers.
Approximate Testing Time: Varies
Type(s) of Response: Rater

Name: T.M.R. School Competency Scales
Author(s): Levine, S., et al.
Publisher: Consulting Psychologists Press

Copyright Date: 1976
Age Range: 5 to 10 and 11+
Purpose: A measure of the personal and social skills of trainable mentally retarded children. Five scales are included: perceptual motor, initiative-responsibility, cognition, personal-social, and language.
Approximate Testing Time: Varies
Type(s) of Response: Rater

Name: Vineland Adaptive Behavior Scales
Author(s):   Sparrow, S., et al.
Publisher: American Guidance Service
Copyright Date: 1984
Age Range: 1 month to adult
Purpose: Provides a measure of social maturity, competence, and independence for both handicapped and nonhandicapped individuals. Items are designed to elicit factual descriptions of the examinee's behavior from parents, teachers, or other caregivers. Areas probed include daily living skills, communication, motor skills, and socialization. There are three versions: survey, expanded, and classroom.
Approximate Testing Time: 20–90 minutes
Type(s) of Response: Rater

Test Publishers

Achenbach, Thomas
Department of Psychiatry
University of Vermont
1 South Prospect Street
Burlington, VT 05405

Academic Therapy Publications
20 Commercial Blvd.
Novato, CA 94947

American Association on Mental
    Retardation
5101 Wisconsin Avenue, NW
Washington, DC 20007

American Guidance Service
Publishers Building
Circle Pines, MN 55014–1796

Behavior Science Systems
Box 580274
Minneapolis, MN 55458

Child Welfare League of America
67 Irving Plaza
New York, NY 10003

Consulting Psychologists Press
577 College Avenue
Palo Alto, CA 94306

CTB/McGraw-Hill
Del Monte Research Park
2500 Garden Road
Monterey, CA 93940-5380

Curriculum Associates
5 Esquire Road
North Billerica, MA 01862–2589

Developmental Evaluation Materials
Houston, TX 77277

DLM Teaching Resources
One DLM Park
Allen, TX 75002

Economy Publishing Company
E. 7915 Elk Chattaroy Rd.
Chattaroy, WA 99003

Educational Testing Service
P.O. Box 995
Princeton, NJ 08540

High/Scope Educational Research Foundation
600 N. River St.
Ypsilanti, MI 48198–2898

Hiskey, Marshall
5640 Baldwin
Lincoln, NE 68507

Jastak Associates
P.O. Box 4460
Wilmington, DE 19807

Kaplan Supply Company
600 Jonestown Road
Winston-Salem, NC 27103

Ladoca Publishing Foundation
5100 Lincoln Street
Denver, CO 80216

Meisels, Samuel
Center for Human Growth and Development
University of Michigan
Ann Arbor, MI 48103

Minneapolis Public Schools
Prescriptive Instruction Center
Special Education Division
254 Upton Avenue South
Minneapolis, MN 55405

Modern Curriculum Press
13900 Prospect Road
Cleveland, OH 44136

Multi-Health Systems
908 Niagara Falls Blvd.
North Tonawanda, NY 14120–2060

Paul H. Brookes
P.O. Box 10624
Baltimore, MD 21285–0624

Pro-Ed
5341 Industrial Oaks Blvd.
Austin, TX 78735

Psychological Corporation
7500 Old Oak Blvd.
Cleveland, OH 44130

Riverside Publishing Company
8420 Bryn Mawr Avenue
Chicago, IL 60631

Scholastic Testing Service
480 Meyer Road
Bensenville, IL 60106

Science Research Associates
259 East Erie Street
Chicago, IL 60611

Slosson Educational Publications
P.O. Box 280
East Aurora, NY 14052

Teachers's College Press
Columbia University
New York, NY 10010

University of Illinois Press
Urbana, IL 61801

University Park Press
300 North Charles Street
Baltimore, MD 21201

Western Psychological Services
12031 Wilshire Blvd.
Los Angeles, CA 90025

William C. Brown
2460 Kerper Blvd.
Dubuque, IA 52001

Test Evaluation Form

When reviewing tests, consult the catalog, the test manual, reviews of the test, and Chapter Four to answer the following questions.

Descriptive Information

Title _____

Author _____ Copyright date _____

Publisher _____

Cost _____ Qualifications for Administrator _____

Time required to administer _____ Individual _____ Group _____

What is the purpose of the test? _____

Is this a standardized test? _____

Who is it designed to assess? _____

Is the test available in another language? _____

How clear are the directions? _____

Is extra equipment required? _____

How easy is it to administer? _____

What kind of scores does the test yield? _____

What information is given about the technical qualities? _____

- norms _____
- reliability _____
- validity _____

Summary of strengths _____

- technical adequacy _____
- efficiency _____
- matches purpose planned _____

Do the claims made match the evidence you have available? _____

Does it match your purpose? _____

CEDSIT II

CHICAGO EARLY DEVELOPMENT
SCREENING INVENTORY
FOR TEACHERS II

By: Evelyn Baumann, Jack Kavanagh, and Gayle Mindes

CEDSIT II: Field Test Version of Screening Inventory for Teachers of 3 and 4 Year Olds

IDENTIFYING INFORMATION   Date: _____

Child's Name:_____ **Sex:** _____
first   middle   last

Parent or Guardian: _____

Date of Birth:_____ **Age:** _____
year   month   day

Preschool Center:_____ **Teacher:** _____

BACKGROUND INFORMATION

- This checklist has been designed as a screening instrument to identify those children who are "at high risk". It is developed to quickly find those children who may require referral and special services. It has been standardized on Head Start children and is designed to reflect each child's strengths and special needs.

- For greater accuracy in using this checklist, it is recommended that it be completed after the child has been in the program for a period of four weeks. Also, it is recommended that teachers or other program staff complete a parent interview, as the child enters the program. The **CEDSI II,** the parent interview instrument has been specifically designed for this purpose and has been standardized on Head Start children.

- Following the scoring of the **CEDSIT II**, if the child is found to be at risk for special needs, an appropriate referral for professional diagnosis should be made. The **CEDSI II** Interview Form and the **CEDSIT II** Form can be of help to the diagnostians and should be utilized for periodic review.

DIRECTIONS

- Please read over the entire checklist before planning to complete the **CEDSIT II**. You will then be familiar with the kinds of skills that you must plan to observe.

- Plan to complete the **CEDSIT II** on individual children when you can observe the child. Answer each item carefully with a firm decision that the child does or does not possess the particular skill on the checklist.

- It will ordinarily take 30 to 40 minutes to complete this observation on each child.

DEVELOPMENTAL ASSESSMENT, INC. ■ P.O. Box 148186 ■ Chicago Heights, Illinois 60614

CHICAGO EARLY DEVELOPMENT SCREENING INVENTORY FOR TEACHERS II (CEDSIT II)

Motor / Communication / Cognitive Skills

This child:

	YES	NO
1. Cannot catch a large ball	___	___
2. Cannot throw a ball or bean bag	___	___
3. Often bumps into things	___	___
4. Cannot walk on tiptoes when asked to	___	___
5. Seems unusually clumsy	___	___
6. Cannot pull pants down	___	___
7. Cannot pull pants up	___	___
8. Cannot undress completely	___	___
9. Cannot unbutton front buttons	___	___
10. Cannot pull on shoes	___	___
11. Cannot eat with a spoon without spilling	___	___
12. Cannot wash hands when asked to do so	___	___
13. Very seldom copies actions he/she has seen others perform	___	___
14. Cannot match three primary colors (red, blue, yellow)	___	___
15. Cannot group balls into groups of large and small	___	___
16. Has trouble telling how old he/she is (or showing the correct number of fingers)	___	___
17. Cannot run forward	___	___
18. Cannot run backward	___	___
19. Cannot grasp a small cube	___	___
20. Cannot stack blocks when shown how	___	___
21. Has trouble stating correctly whether he/she is a boy or a girl	___	___
22. Cannot name more than one or two parts of his/her face	___	___
23. Cannot state his/her first name	___	___
24. Cannot state his/her whole name	___	___
25. Has trouble naming items in a picture	___	___
26. Cannot repeat five word sentence spoken to him/her	___	___
27. Cannot make a two word sentence	___	___

Social / Emotional Skills

This child:

	YES	NO
1. Is unable to join in play with other children for brief periods	___	___
2. Is unable to enjoy toys or equipment with child next to him	___	___
3. Does not seem to enjoy pretending (driving, putting dolls to sleep)	___	___
4. Flits from activity to activity	___	___
5. Clings to favorite toy (blanket, truck, doll)	___	___
6. Has to be asked two or three times to do something	___	___
7. Will do what is asked, but dawdles and needs to be reminded	___	___
8. Seems more restless and fidgety than other children	___	___
9. Is easily distracted from his on-going activities	___	___
10. Will not put toys away unless helped by an adult	___	___
11. Always wants what other children have	___	___
12. Often asks for food other than at snack or mealtimes	___	___
13. Tends to cry easily	___	___
14. Mostly whines and complains when asked to wait for something he/she wants	___	___
15. Tends to react to strange adults by clinging to that person	___	___
16. Seems mostly shy and withdrawn	___	___
17. Does not seem to be liked by the other children	___	___
18. Seems, in general, to not find eating pleasurable	___	___

19. Tends to wet his/her pants more than most children _____
20. Often provokes other children (starts fights, hits, throws things) _____
21. Always demands certain classroom toys (truck, doll, tricycle) _____
22. Clings to the teacher _____
23. Appears to be sad _____
24. Often pouts or is sullen when he/she does not get what he/she wants _____
25. Tends to give up easily when things are not going his/her way _____
26. When not given his/her way, tends to withdraw or retreat into isolation (in a cubby, under a table) _____
27. Seems to suck thumb excessively _____
28. Tends to let other children take his/her toys away _____
29. Has trouble accepting the teacher's limits _____
30. Is excessively demanding of the teacher _____
31. Seems to often indulge in body play (rocking, finger twiddling, masturbation) _____
32. Cannot ask for toys, foods, activities without crying, whining _____

Teacher Notes: _____

_____

_____

_____

_____

_____

_____

28. **Has trouble singing songs** _____
29. Has trouble telling a story about a picture shown him/her _____
30. Has trouble repeating (in his/her own words) a simple story _____
31. Very seldom uses two or more sentences to tell something _____
32. Has not begun to ask questions (what and where) _____
33. Has trouble when required to do two things, one right after the other ("Put the book on the table and then close the door.") _____
34. Does not seem to like to look at books _____
35. Cannot follow a simple direction (Come here) _____
36. Seems to hear directions, but seems to have trouble understanding what is expected of him/her _____
37. Cannot put together puzzle with single shape pieces _____
38. Cannot string large beads _____
39. Cannot roll, pound, or pull clay _____
40. Cannot match geometric shapes (circle, square) _____
41. Cannot name two body parts (arms, legs, head) _____
42. Cannot point to pictures of familiar objects, when named (fork, spoon, ball) _____
43. Cannot point to pictures of animals (dog, cat, horse) _____
44. Cannot match pictures of letters or numbers _____
45. Cannot match lotto pictures _____
46. Cannot point to on, under the table _____
47. Often says "huh" or "what" when I talk to him/her _____
48. Seems to have trouble hearing from across the room _____
49. Seems to have trouble hearing when spoken to in a whisper _____
50. May have a speech problem _____
51. Seems afraid to talk _____

CEDSIT II SCORING (Field Test Version)

DIRECTIONS

1. Give one point for each **YES** answer on the **Motor / Communication / Cognitive Skills Scale**. Add the points together to make a total.

2. Give one point for each **YES** answer on the **Social / Emotional Skills Scale**. Add the points together to make a total.

3. Record the scores in the space provided below and interpret the scales according to the directions.

INTERPRETATION

TOTALS: _____ Motor / Communication / Cognitive

_____ Social / Emotional

Refer for evaluation:

$12 - 20^{*}$ on **Motor / Communication / Cognitive Scale**

$7 - 11^{*}$ on **Social / Emotional Scale**

Observe further:

$4 - 11$ on **Motor / Communication / Cognitive Scale**

$2 - 6$ on **Social / Emotional Scale**

Not likely to require referral:

$0 - 3$ on **Motor / Communication / Cognitive Scale**

$0 - 1$ on **Social / Emotional Scale**

*or scores above

PLEASE NOTE A high score on either scale indicates a need to refer the child for an in-depth diagnostic assessment.

Teacher's Comments _____

_____

_____

_____

_____ Teacher's Signature

CHICAGO EARLY DEVELOPMENT SCREENING INVENTORY FOR TEACHERS II

By: Evelyn Baumann, Jack Kavanagh, and Gayle Mindes

CEDSIT II: Version of Screening Inventory for Teachers of 4 and 5 Year Olds

IDENTIFYING INFORMATION

Date: _____

Child's Name: _____ Sex: _____
       first   middle   last

Parent or Guardian: _____

Date of Birth: _____ Age: _____
      year   month   day

Preschool Center: _____ Teacher: _____

BACKGROUND INFORMATION

- This checklist has been designed as a screening instrument to identify those children who are "at high risk". It is developed to quickly find those children who may require referral and special services. It has been standardized on Head Start children and is designed to reflect each child's strengths and special needs.

- For greater accuracy in using this checklist, it is recommended that it be completed after the child has been in the program for a period of four weeks. Also, it is recommended that teachers or other program staff complete a parent interview, as the child enters the program. The **CEDSI II**, the parent interview instrument has been specifically designed for this purpose and has been standardized on Head Start children.

- Following the scoring of the **CEDSIT II**, if the child is found to be at risk for special needs, an appropriate referral for professional diagnosis should be made. The **CEDSI II** Interview Form and the **CEDSIT II** Form can be of help to the diagnostians and should be utilized for periodic review.

DIRECTIONS

- Please read over the entire checklist before planning to complete the **CEDSIT II**. You will then be familiar with the kinds of skills that you must plan to observe.

- Plan to complete the **CEDSIT II** on individual children when you can observe the child. Answer each item carefully with a firm decision that the child does or does not possess the particular skill on the checklist.

- It will ordinarily take 30 to 40 minutes to complete this observation on each child.

KBM DEVELOPMENTAL ASSESSMENT, INC. • 507 N. Elmhurst Road • Prospect Heights, Illinois 60070

Chicago Early Development Screening Inventory for Teachers II (CEDSIT II)

Motor / Communication / Cognitive Skills

This child: YES   NO

1. Often bumps into things
2. Seems unusually clumsy
3. Has trouble using buttons
4. Has trouble using zippers
5. Has trouble putting on coat
6. Has trouble tying shoes
7. Has trouble washing self when told to do so
8. Has trouble hopping on one foot
9. Has trouble catching a ball
10. Has trouble copying a square
11. Has trouble copying a circle
12. Tends to scribble rather than draw shapes or pictures of things
13. Has trouble using scissors
14. Has trouble assembling puzzles
15. Has trouble naming the primary colors (red, blue, yellow)
16. Has trouble counting beyond three
17. Has trouble naming the letters of the alphabet
18. Has trouble telling how old he/she is (or showing the correct number of fingers)
19. Has trouble stating correctly whether he/she is a boy or girl
20. Has trouble naming more than one or two body parts of his/her body
21. Has trouble stating his/her full name

Social / Emotional Skills

This child: YES   NO

1. Has difficulty sitting still seems to be in continual motion
2. Frequently has temper tantrums
3. Often provokes other children (starts fights, hits, and throws things)
4. Has trouble accepting limits
5. Shows considerable frustration when his/her activities are interfered with
6. Is excessively demanding of the teacher
7. Very seldom shares with others
8. Seems more restless and fidgety than other children
9. Is easily distracted from his activities
10. Often asks for food other than at snack or mealtimes
11. Tends to cry easily or frequently
12. Mostly whines and complains when asked to do or get something
13. Often pouts and is sullen when he/she doesn't get what he/she wants
14. Tends to react to strange adults by clinging to that person
15. Tends to react to strange adults by showing fear and withdrawal
16. Tends to give up easily when things are not going his/her way
17. Seems mostly shy and withdrawn
18. Tends to interact more with adults than with other children
19. Seems to prefer toys or activities more appropriate for younger children (pull toys, stack blocks or rings)

20. Seems to prefer repetitious involvement with records, puzzles or other toys _____

21. In general does not seem to be liked by other children _____

22. In general does not find eating pleasurable _____

23. Tends to wet his/her pants more than other children _____

24. Seems to often indulge in body-play (rocking, finger-twiddling, or masturbation) _____

Teacher notes: _____

_____

_____

_____

_____

_____

_____

_____

_____

_____

_____

_____

_____

22. Has trouble describing items in a picture _____

23. Has trouble repeating a sentence spoken to him/her _____

24. Has trouble singing songs or nursery rhymes _____

25. Has trouble telling a story about a picture shown to him/her _____

26. Has trouble repeating (in his/her own words) a simple story _____

27. Has trouble when required to do two things, one right after the other ("Put the book on the table and close the door.") _____

28. Has trouble following directions _____

29. Does not seem to like to look at books _____

30. Often says "huh?" or "what?" or asks for repetition of what is said _____

31. Very seldom copies actions he/ she has seen others perform _____

32. Very seldom uses two or more sentences to tell me something _____

33. Very seldom asks questions _____

34. Very seldom asks questions about how things work _____

35. Very seldom asks questions about why _____

36. Has trouble understanding and responding when I talk to him/ her _____

37. Seems to have trouble hearing from across the room _____

38. Seems to have trouble hearing when spoken to in a whisper _____

39. May have a speech problem _____

40. Tends to stutter _____

41. Speech seems unclear and hard to understand _____

42. Seems afraid to talk _____

43. Tends to use "me" rather than "I" when speaking _____

CEDSIT II SCORING

DIRECTIONS

1. Give one point for each **YES** answer on the **Motor / Communication / Cognitive Skills Scale**. Add the points together to make a total.

2. Give one point for each **YES** answer on the **Social / Emotional Skills Scale**. Add the points together to make a total.

3. Record the scores in the space provided below and interpret the scales according to the directions.

INTERPRETATION

TOTALS: _____ **Motor / Communication / Cognitive**

_____ **Social / Emotional**

Refer for evaluation:

$12-20^*$ on **Motor / Communication / Cognitive Scale**

$7-11^*$ on **Social / Emotional Scale**

Observe further:

$4-11$ on **Motor / Communication / Cognitive Scale**

$2-6$ on **Social / Emotional Scale**

Not likely to require referral:

$0-3$ on **Motor / Comminication / Cognitive Scale**

$0-1$ on **Social / Emotional Scale**

***or scores above**

PLEASE NOTE A high score on either scale indicates a need to refer the child for an in-depth diagnostic assessment.

Teacher's Comments _____

_____

_____

_____

_____Teacher's Signature

Glossary

accountability   being responsible for the proper education of all children.

age-equivalent score   derived score giving a child's performance as that which is normal for a certain age.

amniocentesis   a prenatal test in which amniotic fluid is withdrawn from the embryonic sac of a fetus.

anecdotal notes   brief notes of significant events or critical incidents in a particular child's day.

Apgar Rating Scale   screening test given to newborn infants one minute and five minutes after birth.

arena approach to assessment   *see* transdisciplinary team.

assessment   process for gathering information to make decisions.

atypical development   unusual developmental pattern of children.

authentic assessment   *see* performance assessment.

behavioral questionnaires   questionnaires designed to give parents an opportunity to report any behavior problems of their children.

biological risk   risk to infant because of prenatal, perinatal, or neonatal difficulty.

checklists   forms for recording the skills or attributes of the children in a class.

child find team   group of professionals whose responsibility it is to determine children with special needs.

child study   in-depth look at a particular child at a specific point in time.

chorionic villus biopsy   a prenatal test in which chorionic tissue is removed from the developing placenta.

concurrent validity   relationship between a test and another criterion when both are obtained at about the same time.

confidentiality   allowing a child's assessment and other records to be available only to school personnel, agency officials, and parents.

content validity   extent of how well a test tests the subject matter it is supposed to test.

construct validity   the extent to which a test measures a theoretical characteristic or trait.

correlation coefficient   degree of relationship between two variables.

criterion-referenced measures   tests that compare performance in certain skills to accepted levels.

criterion-referenced test   a standardized test that compares a child's performance to his or her own progress in a certain skill or behavior.

criterion-related validity   relationship between the scores on a test and another criterion.

curriculum-based measures   diagnostic tests for specific subjects.

derived scores   score obtained by comparing the raw score with the performance of children of known characteristics on a standardized test.

developmentally appropriate practice   planning instruction for preschool children around topics rooted in the children's social world.

developmental questionnaires   questionnaires that focus on a child's present development.

deviation quotients   standard scores with a mean of 100 and a standard deviation of usually 15.

diagnostic evaluation   *see* diagnostic tests.

diagnostic tests   tests used to identify a child's specific areas of strength and weakness, determine the nature of the problems, and suggest the cause of the problems and possible remediation strategies.

drug-exposed babies   babies born to mothers who used drugs during pregnancy.

dynamic assessment   one-to-one interview approach between teacher and student using available assessment information for teaching a specific skill.

environmental risk   risk to infants because of family or social stress.

established risk   risk to infants because of gene abnormality, malformation or structural problems, or in utero drug exposure.

event sampling   record of skills or behaviors a teacher wants the children to know or to do.

extrapolated score   derived score estimated from norm scores because the raw score is either less than or greater than anyone in the normative sample.

face validity   whether a test looks as if it is testing what it is supposed to be testing.

family involvement   including the parents in all phases of the assessment of a child with a developmental problem.

fetal alcohol syndrome   physical and mental abnormalities associated with infants born to mothers who consumed excessive amounts of alcohol during pregnancy.

frequency records   checklists for recording the presence or absence of, frequency of, or quality of selected behaviors.

functional assessment   focused observational method that links individual assessment to curricular intervention for one student.

gestational age   how long a baby had been developing in the uterus before birth.

grade-equivalent score   derived score giving a child's performance as that which is normal for a certain grade.

individualized academic tests   formal interviews of children on specific topics.

individualized family service plan   specific plan for the assessing of needs and for the services needed for a child with a developmental problem.

informal evaluation   task activities used to assess the instructional needs and levels of children.

interdisciplinary team   intervention team in which each team member performs his or her own assessment of a child but all team members including the parents meet together to discuss results and make program plans; each team member writes a report; one team member serves as the case manager.

interpolated score   derived score estimated from norm scores because no one with that particular score was actually part of the normative sample.

inter-rater reliability   *see* interscorer reliability.

interscorer reliability   ability of a test to produce same results regardless of who administers it.

intrinsically motivating   causing a child to do something or continue doing something because of the nature of the thing or activity itself.

inventory   test to assess overall ability in a given area.

learner outcomes   expectations for children's performances.

mean   the arithmetic average of a group of scores.

mediated learning experience   teaching approach in which the teacher uses questions, suggestions, and cues to prompt the child to think more consciously about the task and to expand learner expertise.

multidisciplinary staffing   group of professionals involved in the assessing of children with special needs, the teaching of these children, and the evaluation of their progress.

multidisciplinary team   intervention team in which each team member meets with the child and parents and develops his or her own plan independently of the other team members.

multiple intelligence theory   theory that children have seven areas of intellectual competence that are relatively independent of each other.

normal curve   bell-shaped curve representing the usual distribution of human attributes.

normal-curve equivalents   standard scores for group tests; scale has 100 equal parts, mean is usually 50, standard deviation is usually 21.06.

normative sample   subset of a population that is tested for a standardized test.

norm-based instruments   tests that compare children to others of similar age, grade level, or other important characteristics.

norm-referenced test   *see* standardized test.

norms   scores obtained from the testing of a normative sample for a standardized test.

observation records   written records of the observations of a child including anecdotes, daily logs, and in-depth running records.

observations   systematic means of gathering information about children by watching them.

parental interview   an interview of a child-care professional with a parent for determining how well a child is doing.

parental questionnaires   questionnaires given by child-care professionals to parents for obtaining information about a child.

parental reports   information from a parent concerning a child.

parent perspective   a parent's perception of a child's development, learning, and education.

percentile ranks   derived scores indicating the percentage of individuals in the normative group whose test scores fall at or below a given raw score.

performance assessment   determining developmental progress of children through a variety of means, including observations and special problems or situations.

P.L. 99–457   Education of the Handicapped Act Amendments, 1986.

population   group of individuals on which a standardized test is normed.

portfolios   places, such as folders, boxes, baskets, for keeping all the information known about the children in a class.

predictive validity   how accurately a test score can be used to estimate performance on some variable or criterion in the future.

prenatal testing   testing done prior to the birth of a baby.

presentation mode   way a task or learning situation is presented to a child as part of instruction.

primary responsibility   the person expected to perform a certain task.

psychological evaluation   assessment that incorporates developmental psychological and educational tasks.

range   the spread of the scores or the difference between the top score and the bottom score on a test.

rating scales   methods of recording whether or not children possess certain skills or attributes and to what extent.

raw score   the number of items that a child answered correctly on a test.

referral questions   questions posed in a child study to aid in the determination of the specific problems and needs of a child and the assessing of the developmental progress of the child.

reliability   consistency, dependability, or stability of test results.

report card   formal, written documents that form a legal academic history for a child.

response mode   how a child responds to a direction or instruction.

rubrics   scoring criteria for performance tasks.

running records   notes made of routine functioning of an individual child or a small group of children.

screening test   test used to identify children who may be in need of special services, as a first step in identifying children in need of further diagnosis; focuses on the child's ability to acquire skills.

sensitivity   percentage of children with developmental problems who are correctly identified by a developmental screening test.

specificity   percentage of children without developmental problems who are correctly identified by a developmental screening test.

stakeholders   people important in the lives of children, especially regarding the assessment of children.

standard deviation   the distance scores depart from the mean.

standard error of measurement (Sem)   estimate of the amount of variation that can be expected in test scores as a result of reliability correlations.

standardized test   test which interprets a child's performance in comparison to the performance of other children with similar characteristics.

stanines   standard scores with nine unequal bands; bands four, five, and six represent average performance.

task analysis   process in which large goals are broken down into smaller objectives or parts and sequenced for instruction.

technical issues   variables of task, learner, and context that can cause problems with performance assessment.

techniques   methods, whether formal or informal, for gathering assessment information.

test   instrument for measuring skills, knowledge, development, aptitudes, etc.

test-retest reliability   ability to get same results from a test taken twice within two weeks.

textbook tests   assessment materials published by textbook publishers to accompany their instructional materials.

time sampling   checklist for determining what is happening at a particular time with one or more children.

transdisciplinary play-based assessment   team of professionals observe a child at play to assess the need for intervention; *see* transdisciplinary team.

transdisciplinary team   intervention team in which all team members assess the child at the same time; all team members review the child's strengths and needs and develop a program plan together.

typical development   the usual or expected developmental pattern of children.

ultrasound   a prenatal test in which sound waves are used to determine a fetus's development.

validity   the extent to which a test measures what it is supposed to measure.

Index